LEARNING
STRATEGIES

THE EDUCATIONAL TECHNOLOGY SERIES

Edited by

Harold F. O'Neil, Jr.

Army Research Institute for
the Behavioral and Social Sciences
Alexandria, Virginia

Harold F. O'Neil, Jr. (Ed.) Learning Strategies

LEARNING STRATEGIES

Edited by

HAROLD F. O'NEIL, JR.

Defense Advanced Research Projects Agency
Arlington, Virginia

ACADEMIC PRESS   1978

A Subsidiary of Harcourt Brace Jovanovich, Publishers

New York   London   Toronto   Sydney   San Francisco

This publication is based on a program supported by the Defense Advanced Research Projects Agency (DARPA). Any opinions, findings, conclusions, or recommendations expressed herein are those of the authors and do not necessarily reflect the view of DARPA or the U.S. Government.

ACADEMIC PRESS, INC.
111 Fifth Avenue, New York, New York 10003

United Kingdom Edition published by
ACADEMIC PRESS, INC. (LONDON) LTD.
24/28 Oval Road, London NW1 7DX

Library of Congress Cataloging in Publication Data

Main entry under title:

Learning strategies.
    (Educational technology series)

    Includes bibliographies.
    1. Learning, Psychology of. I. O'Neil,
Harold F., Date
BF318.L4   153.1'5   77–92243
ISBN 0–12–526650–2

Contents

v

List of Contributors

Numbers in parentheses indicate the pages on which the authors' contributions begin.

JOHN SEELY BROWN (107), Bolt Beranek and Newman, Inc., 50 Moulton Street, Cambridge, Massachusetts 02138

ALLAN COLLINS (107), Bolt Beranek and Newman, Inc., 50 Moulton Street, Cambridge, Massachusetts 02138

DONALD DANSEREAU (1), Department of Psychology, Texas Christian University, Fort Worth, Texas 76129

GREGORY HARRIS (107), Bolt Beranek and Newman, Inc., 50 Moulton Street, Cambridge, Massachusetts 02138

ROBERT S. LOGAN (141), Telemedia, Inc., 310 South Michigan Avenue, Chicago, Illinois 60604

FRANK RICHARDSON (57), Department of Educational Psychology, University of Texas at Austin, Austin, Texas 78712

JOSEPH W. RIGNEY (165), Behavior Technology Laboratory, University of Southern California, Los Angeles, California 90007

ROBERT J. SEIDEL (207), Human Resources Research Organization, 300 North Washington Street, Alexandria, Virginia 22314

ROBERT N. SINGER (79), Motor Behavior Resource Center, The Florida State University, Tallahassee, Florida 32306

HAROLD WAGNER (207), Human Resources Research Organization, 300 North Washington Street, Alexandria, Virginia 22314

CLAIRE E. WEINSTEIN (31), Department of Educational Psychology, University of Texas at Austin, Austin, Texas 78712

Preface[1]

A program of research in learning strategies was initiated by the Defense Advanced Research Projects Agency (DARPA) in 1976. The goal of the program is to improve learning, decrease training time, and reduce training costs by developing and evaluating instructional materials designed to teach basic intellectual and affective skills. This book records the program's progress to date and suggests further avenues for research.

Learning strategies are potentially useful in a number of learning situations. The potential will be realized when a person acquires facility in their use and familiarity with their application. This is not to say that learning strategies will replace specific job skills or knowledge of specific content domains; they are simply a necessary condition for more efficient learning.

One example of learning strategy is the method of loci. Using this strategy, an individual is taught to associate isolated facts with particular locations (i.e., loci). When one wishes to recall the memorized facts, one simply revisualizes the place, bringing to mind the associated facts. Improved recall generally results from use of this strategy. The strategy can be used in other situations to make subsequent learning more efficient and effective.

A program of this type is based on the belief that effective education and training occur when high-quality instruction is presented under conditions conducive to learning to students who possess effective learning strategies. Recent studies indicate that many students lack effective learning strategies. Since the late 1960s, both aptitude and achievement scores of college-bound high school students have dropped (National Institute of Education, *Declining Test Scores: A Conference*

---

[1]The views and conclusions contained in this preface and the rest of the volume are those of the respective authors and should not be interpreted as necessarily representing the official policies, either expressed or implied, at the Defense Advanced Research Projects Agency or the U.S. Government.

Report, February 1976). At the same time, the sophistication of our technological society has increased. These factors indicate that this education and training problem will intensify.

DARPA has invested resources in the learning strategies program because it seemed to offer a promising means for improving our success at meeting training requirements within ever tighter fiscal constraints. The potential of success in this particular approach is analogous to improving reading skills as a known method for improving subsequent performance in a myriad of learning situations. In addition, teaching learning strategies directly should reduce the need and thus the cost for extensive instructional support in each and every course. For example, if a student's memory ability was increased, then one might expect a decreased requirement for remedial loops and extensive practice in all subsequent courses. Furthermore, as documented in this book (e.g., Chapters 1 and 2), prospects for the development and evaluation of such learning strategies look very favorable. The final evaluation criteria will focus on whether students trained to use learning strategies would learn more quickly or to a higher mastery level in subsequent courses. In the latter case, evaluation criteria will include existing course performance measures, amount of time, and costs. Each project was designed to follow this development and evaluation process.

In order to provide an intellectual foundation for the learning strategies program, several fields were surveyed for potential learning strategies. The fields were cognitive psychology (Chapters 1, 2, and 7), artificial intelligence (Chapter 5), behavioral modification (Chapter 3), and motor learning (Chapter 4). Furthermore, a technology base to support the ideas following from the intellectual disciplines must exist. We envision this technology base as consisting of instructional systems development (Chapter 6) and evaluation (Chapter 8).

This book summarizes our research to date in these fields and presents our collective ideas of where learning strategies research should be directed. It is both a preliminary progress report on the approaches we have developed for learning strategies and a means of sharing our ideas concerning ways of accomplishing our goals. We feel that our intellectual community consists of advanced students and researchers in the fields represented by the chapters.

This book could not have come into existence without the help and encouragement of many people. In particular, the intellectual and administrative support of Robert Young, Craig Fields, and Dawn Parnell of DARPA, and Robert Seidel, Harold Wagner, and Marilyn Knetsch of HumRRO was invaluable. Finally, I acknowledge my appreciation for the help and moral support I have received from the staff of Academic Press.

Harold F. O'Neil, Jr.[2]

[2]Present address: Army Research Institute, 5001 Eisenhower Avenue, Alexandria, Virginia 22333.

LEARNING STRATEGIES

The Development of a Learning
Strategies Curriculum[1]

DONALD DANSEREAU

INTRODUCTION

Educational research and development efforts have been directed almost exclusively at the improvement of **teaching**. The relative neglect of the **learning** aspect of education is probably unwarranted, especially when one considers the importance of ameliorating the transfer of classroom knowledge and skills to the job situation.

Studies on the improvement of teaching have dealt with a variety of aspects of the educational environment: the effects of manipulating mode of presentation (lecture, discussion, movie, reading, computer, etc.), activity level of the student (responses required), pacing (rate of presentation), and sequence of instruction (ordering of concepts). The major criticism of this approach stems from the general ineffectiveness of teaching manipulations. Dubin and Taveggia (1968), in an extensive review of the educational literature, conclude that there appears to be no difference among truly distinctive methods of college instruction when evaluated by student performance on final examinations.

To point up this apparent ineffectiveness at a more specific level, in our own research (Dansereau, Evans, Actkinson, & Long, 1974b; Dansereau, Evans, Wright, Long, & Actkinson, 1974c) we reviewed the literature and conducted a series of experiments on the effect of instructional sequencing on comprehension and retention. The literature review indicated that previous results on sequencing had not been very encouraging. Experiments comparing random versus logical

[1]This research was supported by the Department of Defense, U. S. Air Force Contract AF41609-75-C-0013, Defense Advanced Projects Agency (DARPA) Contract MDA 903-76-C-0218, and Texas Christian University Research Foundation Grant PS 7451. Views and conclusions contained in this document are those of the author and should not be interpreted as necessarily representing the official policies, either expressed or implied, of the above-named groups of the United States Government.

1

sequences of programmed learning material have resulted in marginal or null effects on performance variables. The Dansereau *et al.* experiments corrected a number of difficulties observed in previous studies but still found sequencing to produce only marginal effects. In these experiments as well as in previous ones, individuals receiving the same treatment performed substantially differently. These findings would lead to the hypothesis that individual aptitudes or strategies or both may be the primary causes of performance differences.

Besides being only marginally effective, an exclusive focus on improving teaching methods may lead to inadvertent reinforcement of inappropriate and nontransferable learning strategies. For example, many teaching and testing methods implicitly encourage rote memorization by specifying exactly what must be learned, rewarding verbatim answers on tests, and putting little emphasis on the development of relationships between incoming and stored information. Rote memorization usually involves multiple readings of the material with little or no effort devoted to assimilating the information. Therefore, the material learned through this method usually is not meaningfully related to other stored information, which limits the facility with which such information can be retrieved at a later date. Such a strategy, although perhaps useful in our present educational environments, is very maladaptive in many job situations, where understanding is far more important than mere storage. Although the limitations of rote memorization have been emphasized, the same arguments probably apply to a large number of other strategies developed by students to cope with a teaching-oriented education.

By not stressing learning strategies, educators, in essence, discourage students from developing and exploring new strategies, and, in so doing, limit students' awareness of their cognitive capabilities. For example, the results of the administration of an extensive learning strategy inventory (Dansereau, Long, McDonald, & Actkinson, 1975a) indicate that even good college students have very little knowledge of alternative learning techniques. This lack of awareness obviously limits an individual's ability in a situation requiring new learning strategies. In addition, if the strategies that individuals have spontaneously adopted do not match their cognitive capabilities, the emotional toll may be very large. Most of us know individuals who spend inordinate amounts of time memorizing college or high school materials and are still barely "getting by." Such an individual's personal, intellectual, and social development must certainly suffer from the pressures created by this use of a relatively inefficient learning strategy.

In summary, exclusive emphasis on teaching methods may lead to ineffective instructional manipulations, force students to develop nontransferable and inefficient strategies, limit a student's cognitive awareness, and, consequently, extract a large emotional toll. The answer to this situation is clear: Educators and researchers should be redirecting at least some of their efforts to the development and training of appropriate learning strategy skills. In order to provide a basis for such redirection it is informative to examine briefly the theoretical underpinnings of the teaching and learning approaches to the improvement of education.

The focus on teaching, in particular attempts to improve the presentation of materials, stems directly from the behavioristic (stimulus–response) influences that pervaded psychology until the mid-1950s. One salient example of this influence has been the efforts directed toward the development of teaching machines and pro-grammed texts (Fry, 1963). Advocates of behaviorism have traditionally ignored the organism and have concentrated on establishing relationships between stimuli presented (inputs) and subsequent responses observed (outputs). To most be-haviorists, the organism is an inscrutable "black box," which is not amenable to scientific investigation. In the 1950s there was an increasing emphasis on more complex behaviors, such as problem-solving and language processing. The failures of behaviorism to deal adequately with these "higher-order" activities stimulated the growth of a new school of thought: cognitive psychology. The cognitive psy-chologists, unlike the behaviorist, emphasized the role of the organism's "covert" manipulations of the incoming stimuli in predicting responses. Bruner, Goodnow, and Austin (1956) developed procedures to identify strategies used by students, and demonstrated that different strategies were differentially effective for concept learn-ing tasks. Newell, Simon, and Shaw (1958) effectively simulated problem-solving strategies via computer. Finally, Miller, Galanter, and Pribram (1960) analyzed and categorized strategies used in a wide range of tasks.

Since these early efforts, the cognitive approach has replaced behaviorism as the dominant school of thought in experimental psychology. As is usually the case, application lags behind basic research. Only since the early 1970s have cognitive findings had a substantial impact on education—and this impact has been relatively small compared to the possibilities. Much of the untapped potential lies in the area of learning strategy improvement. The research program to be described in this chapter is directed toward using this information to develop a systematic learning-strategy training program. The goal of such a program is to provide the student with synergic strategies for accomplishing the tasks required in learning text material. These strategies will be presented as prototypes that students can assimilate and modify in order to change or replace the strategies they have developed spontane-ously. In a sense, the goal is to give students the power to reprogram their own biocomputers.

LEARNING STRATEGIES:
A BRIEF REVIEW AND SYNTHESIS

In this section I will present a review of the basic and applied literature that has dealt with learning strategy manipulations (for a more detailed review, see Dan-sereau, Actkinson, Long, & McDonald, 1974a).

Before proceeding, it will be useful to delineate the domain of learning strategies with which I will be concerned. I distinguished between two classes of strategies: those used to operate directly on the materials and those used to operate on the

individual in order to maintain a suitable internal psychological climate. The first class of techniques will be termed *primary* strategies. Persons required to learn material must be able to identify the important, difficult and unfamiliar portions of the material, apply techniques to comprehend and retain this material, and sub-sequently recall and use the acquired information under appropriate circumstances. For example, in studying a manual on oscilloscope operation students must be able to identify the important aspects of operation that are unknown to them (identifica-tion). Once the unfamiliar material has been selected (e.g., operation of the vertical-hols knob) students must be able to decode the author's words and pictures into a meaningful system of propositions and images (comprehension). Using the vertical-hold knob example, the student may, to facilitate comprehension, convert the statement "Rotate the vertical-hold dial counterclockwise" into "Turn the knob in the upper right-hand corner to the left." After comprehending the informa-tion the student must act on the material in order to commit it to memory (retention). Finally, when faced with a test or task, the student must be able to recall the appropriate information and act accordingly (retrieval and utilization).

The second category of strategies, which I have labeled *support* strategies, con-sists of strategies to allow the primary strategies to flow efficiently and effectively. These would include techniques for establishing an appropriate learning attitude, and methods for coping with loss of concentration due to the presence of dis-tractions, fatigue, frustration, or the like. Additional procedures included under this category are techniques for monitoring (checking) and correcting the ongoing *pri-mary* strategies. Responses to a learning strategy inventory (see Dansereau *et al.*, 1975a) and anecdotal reports indicate that students could benefit from more effec-tive strategies in both categories: primary and support.

The prior research on learning strategies consists of those studies dealing exclu-sively with specific components (primarily via instructions to the student) and those designed to assess more generalized training, such as would be provided in a learning skills course. These two approaches will be reviewed separately.

MANIPULATION OF SPECIFIC
STRATEGY COMPONENTS

Most of the prior research on learning strategies has focused on assessing the effects on performance that result from isolated manipulations of component strategies. These studies have dealt with four *primary* strategy areas: identification, comprehension, retention, and retrieval; and one *support* strategy area: concentra-tion. A brief overview of prior attempts to study each of these components follows.

Accurate identification of important, difficult, and unfamiliar material is neces-sary for appropriate allocation of students' time and energy. If such allocations are not accurate, then the resulting learning will be inefficient. In the past, the general approach to research in this area has been to manipulate the identification and selection of stimulus material by varying anticipated recall requirements (Butterfield, Belmont, & Peltzman, 1971; Cermak, 1972; Jacoby, 1973) or monetary payoff conditions (McConkie, Rayner, & Mayer, 1971; McConkie, Rayner, & Wilson, 1973). These studies do show that students can be flexible in their processing of incoming information, but the manipulations are so task-specific that they appear to have little applicability to strategy enhancement in general.

In the area of comprehension and retention, most of the attempts at improving students' skills have been indirect, and have entailed stimulating the students to change their comprehension and retention activities with experimenter-generated, pre-, post-, and interspersed questions (e.g., Frase, 1968; Mayer, 1975; Richards and DiVesta, 1974; Rothkopf and Bisbicos, 1967),pre- and postsupplementary organizing materials (e.g., Allen, 1970; Ausubel & Youssef, 1966; Bauman & Glass, 1969; Frase, 1969; Gay, 1971; Scandura & Wells, 1967), and varying payoff conditions (McConkie & Meyer, 1974; McConkie & Rayner, 1974; McConkie *et al.*, 1973). The findings of these studies generally indicate that the procedures had positively influences on the students' comprehension and retention strategies (see Dansereau *et al.*, 1974a, for a more thorough discussion of these studies). However, since these approaches require experimenter or teacher manipulations, they are not directly transferable to less controlled situations.

More direct manipulations of comprehension and retention strategies have been based on simply instructing (generally without training) the student on a particular technique. Positive effects on performance have resulted from instructions to form mental images (pictures) of verbal materials (R. C. Anderson, 1970; R. C. Anderson & Hidde, 1971; Levine & Divine-Hawkins, 1974; Rasco, Tennyson, & Boutwell, 1975), instructions to state the material in the student's own words (DelGiorno, Jenkins, & Bausell, 1974), and instructions to reorganize the incoming material (DiVesta, Schultz, & Dangel, 1973; Frase, 1973). These instructional manipulations, although somewhat effective as they were first tried, could probably be enhanced by actual training and by integration with training on other aspects of the learning process.

There has been a dramatic upsurge of interest in mnemonic elaboration as a specific means for enhancing retention. Generally, mnemonic techniques involve embellishing the incoming material by creatively interrelating the items to be learned or by associating the items to a previously learned set of peg words or images (mental pictures). The following are some examples of mnemonic techniques:

First letter—in order to remember the ordering of the 12 cranial nerves (olfactory, optic, oculomotor, trochlear, etc.) many of us have learned the phrase "On old Olympus, towering top, a fat, agile German vaults and hops." The first letter of each word is also the first letter of each of the major cranial nerves.

Peg word—a person first learns a rhymed peg word list such as "one–bun, two–shoe, three–tree," and then learns to associate imaginatively each of these words with the members of a list to be learned. For example, in learning the items on a grocery list (e.g., steaks and potatoes) the student might first image bun and steak together as a sandwich, then potato and shoe as an Idaho potato in tennis shoes, etc. When asked to recall the second item on the list he locates the second pegword, shoe and then recalls the image of the potato in tennis shoes.

Method of loci—a learner mentally places items in distinct locations along a very familiar route (e.g., the route from the person's front door to the back bedroom). In order to recall the information, the student imagines traveling back through the route, picking up the items as they occur.

Many studies using lists of unrelated words and word pairs have shown that brief instructions on mnemonic techniques dramatically improve retention (Bower & Reitman, 1972; Danner & Taylor, 1973; Groninger, 1971; Lowry, 1974; Nelson & Archer, 1972; Santa, Ruskin, & Yio, 1973; Wanshura & Borkowski, 1974; Weinstein, 1975; Yuille & Catchpole, 1974). Although these mnemonic techniques have been successful with relatively artificial materials (nonsense syllables and unrelated words), very little effort has been made to apply these techniques to the more general problem of retaining connected discourse. (An exception to this is the work of Weinstein presented in Chapter 2 of this volume.)

Although the previously discussed approaches to strategy manipulation improve a student's ability to recall information, they do so indirectly, by operating on the student's storage processes. More direct approaches are possible, involving **retrieval** plans for accessing stored materials that are not immediately available. These plans would most likely take the form of coherent search strategies similar to those used in solving problems that have well-defined solutions (e.g., chess problems often require the search for an optimal next move). The problem-solving strategies explored by Newell *et al.* (1958) provide a good starting place for the development of such techniques.

Unfortunately, very little work has been done in training students to use search strategies as aids to memory retrieval. The one exception is a study by Ritter, Kaprove, Fitch, and Flavell (1973), which attempted to improve children's recall performance by instructing them in what the researchers called "planful retrievals" (e.g., systematic search strategies). The results of this study indicated that the retrieval instructions helped, but the stimuli employed were so artificial (unrelated word pairs) that it is difficult to generalize the results to more meaningful tasks.

The last component to be considered in this section is *concentration*. Generally, attempts to improve concentration have been oriented toward teaching students to talk to themselves in a constructive, positive fashion as a means of coping with distractions and anxiety (Meichenbaum & Goodman, 1971; Meichenbaum & Turk, 1975; Patterson & Mischel, 1975) or they have been oriented directly toward manipulating the student's attention through behavior modification techniques (Alabiso, 1975). Both these directions have been successfully increased the quantity of task-related behavior, but, unfortunately, they have not been coupled with strategies designed to increase the quality of such behavior (e.g., students may be trained to spend more time looking at a textbook, but additional training is probably needed to increase the quality and intensity of what they are doing while reading). Clearly this combination should be the ultimate target for a program designed to enhance learning skills. The strategy-training program that will be described later in this chapter is designed to achieve this goal.

In summary, the studies that have been reviewed to this point have suffered from at least two problems. First, the materials and tasks used to examine the manipulations have generally been highly artificial (e.g., serial and paired-associate lists of unrelated information). This artificiality limits the generality of these findings to educationally relevant situations. Second, specific components have been studied in isolation (i.e., they have not been integrated with training on other components of the learning process). This lack of integration is extremely troublesome in light of the obvious interrelationships between some of the components (e.g., enhancing comprehension–retention skills will clearly have an impact on retrieval, and vice versa). These interrelationships should enable a well-conceived, integrated program to have an impact greater than the sum of its individual parts. In the next section we will briefly examine some of the prior attempts that have been made at developing such integrated training.

PREVIOUSLY DEVELOPED PROGRAMS FOR ENHANCING LEARNING STRATEGIES

With the exception of our program, which will be discussed separately in the next section, virtually all of the reported learning-strategies programs have nonempirical foundations, provide relatively superficial strategy training (usually only a subset of the essential learning concepts), are evaluated against nonspecific criteria (such as grade point average), and, consequently, lack specific evidence on which to base modifications.

The majority of these learning skills programs are based on the SQ3R approach proposed by Robinson (1946), or some slight modification of this approach. The five steps in the SQ3R technique require students first to **survey** the text chapter by reading headings, boldface type, etc. On the basis of the survey students are encouraged to develop **questions.** Then they **read** the material with an eye toward answering these questions. After reading, students are encouraged to close the book and **recall** what has been read. Finally, they open the book and **review** the material. Generally, SQ3R training is nonspecific; very little detailed information is provided on how to carry out the operations. It is assumed that the individual student is able to arrive at these more specific procedures without guidance. In light of the results with the learning strategy inventory (Dansereau *et al.,* 1975a), this assumption is probably unwarranted; students appear to have little knowledge of alternative learning procedures, especially at a detailed level.

In any case, a number of programs of this type have been developed and shown to lead to improvement on measures of grade point average (Briggs, Tosi, & Morley, 1971; Whitehill, 1972) and on self-report study-habit surveys (Bodden, Osterhouse, & Gelso, 1972; W. F. Brown, Webe, Zunker, & Haslam, 1971; Haslam & Brown,

1968; Van Zoost & Jackson, 1974). Although these programs probably benefit the student in a general way, the locus of the effects has not been determined. In addition to general measures of academic success specific evaluations of learning performance should be made. Furthermore, these evaluations should be related to specific components of the programs to provide a basis for modification. However, even if the previously cited programs are successful, they could probably be improved by incorporating some of the more detailed strategies discussed in the previous section and by adding other strategies derived from the basic cognitive research literature on memory, comprehension, problem-solving, etc. The learning-strategy training program to be discussed in the next section was designed to overcome some of these criticisms.

PRELIMINARY WORK ON AN EMPIRICALLY BASED
LEARNING-STRATEGY TRAINING PROGRAM

The development of our initial learning strategy training program (Dansereau, Long, McDonald, Actkinson, Ellis, Collins, Williams, & Evans, 1975b) involved three basic steps: the identification of potentially effective and trainable learning strategies, the development of methods for teaching these and the assessment of the effectiveness of the strategies and training in the context of academic-like tasks.

The identification of effective strategies was accomplished by using information gathered from a review of the educational and psychological research literature dealing with strategies, and from an analysis of responses to the specially developed learning strategy inventory (Dansereau *et al.*, 1975a). As mentioned earlier, the results of research with the inventory indicated that students could be profitably trained in both primary and support strategies. For the initial study we chose three primary-strategy areas (identification, comprehension–retention, and retrieval) and one support-strategy area (concentration). Within this framework, it was assumed that effective learning required identification of important, unfamiliar, and difficult material, the application of techniques for the comprehension and retention of this identified material, the efficient retrieval of this information under appropriate circumstances, and the effective coping with internal and external distractions while these other processes are being employed.

After the four areas were selected, specific strategies relating to each were extrapolated from the educational and psychological literature. The process of applying techniques for enhanced comprehension and retention was believed to be most critical, and consequently, was given the greatest amount of attention.

Two main points were considered in the development of the Dansereau *et al.* (1975b) comprehension and retention strategies. First, according to the learning strategy inventory results (Dansereau *et al.*, 1975a) it appeared that many students tend to receive information passively, and, consequently, do not actively integrate it into their existing cognitive structures. (This integration process is surely a prerequisite for "true" understanding.) Second, many students apparently do not attempt to produce multiple memory representations (encodings) of the same material in order to enhance retrieval (especially in contexts that differ from the original learning situation). In view of these suppositions, it seemed reasonable to train students to encode information actively after it has been heard or read (that is, put it in a form compatible with their memory systems).

This active integration of information into an individual's cognitive structure has been considered in the basic educational and psychological research literature under the rubric of *mathemagenic behavior*. The mathemagenic concept was created by Rothkopf (1966), and is literally interpreted as behaviors that give birth to learning. The research that had been done in this area provided the basis for developing the comprehension and retention techniques used in our program. Also contributing to the development of these techniques was research resulting from the recent emphasis in cognitive psychology on memory encoding (see Melton & Martin, 1972, for a sampling of this work). The most direct contributions of this encoding construct came from research on mnemonics (e.g., Bower, 1973) and visual imagery (e.g., Paivio, 1971). Both these bodies of research support the notion that multiple encodings are more effective for subsequent retrieval than single encodings.

On the basis of these ideas, three techniques or strategies were developed: paraphrasing, questioning–answering (training students to ask and answer intelligent questions about the material), and the use of visual imagery. Methods of training the strategies related to the four aspects of the learning process were developed and combined in an integrated training program.

Method

Design Overview

The training program was assessed in a study that used four participant groupings. Three groups of students were given the strategy training program; the only difference between these groups was in the type of comprehension and retention techniques provided (paraphrase, question–answer, or imagery). A fourth group did not receive training, but was asked to respond to the dependent measures: an immediate multiple-choice and short answer test concerning four 1000-word prose passages and a delayed essay test concerning the same material.

Participants

One hundred undergraduates at Texas Christian University were recruited from general psychology classes and the School of Nursing to serve as participants. The students were given experimental participation credit and paid a fixed fee of $8 each. These participants were randomly assigned to the four groups (25 participants per group). Three members of the control group did not complete all of the required dependent measures; thus, three members of each of the three treatment groups were dropped randomly to maintain a balanced design.

Procedure

The three treatment groups were trained and tested in four sessions (each session on a different day). The first session lasted approximately 2.5 hours. The second session 2.16 hours, the third session 2 hours, and the fourth session 50 minutes (a total of approximately 7.5 hours). The control group participation was limited to three sessions lasting 35 minutes, 2 hours, and 40 minutes, respectively (a total of approximately 3.25 hours).

The content and sequence of steps involved in administering the training and testing components of the program are illustrated in Figure 1.1. Although the figure is essentially self-explanatory, a few clarifying comments are needed. First, the Delta Vocabulary Test in Box 2 is a 45-item multiple-choice test developed by Deignan (1973). Second, the training method related to the Understanding Judgments (Box 3), Retrieval (Box 4), and the three comprehension/retention techniques (Box 5) were all based on the same framework: The students were instructed in the technique, and then asked to apply it, and were subsequently provided with experimenter-generated feedback. These steps were repeated a number of times, the goal being to shape the student's technique application in accord with the a priori concepts. Third, the Internal–External scale material in Box 8 was developed by Rotter (1966) and the Imagery Self-Report Scale also mentioned in Box 8 was developed by Dansereau (1969). Finally, the tests in Box 9 were conducted 20 minutes after the studying of the passages in Box 7, whereas the delayed test (Box 10) was given 5 days later. For a more complete discussion of these procedures see Dansereau *et al*. (1975b).

Results

The results of this study (see Table 1.1) indicated that the training groups (paraphrase, imagery, and question–answer) did not perform significantly better than the "no-treatment" control group on the immediate training assessment test (administered 20 minutes after reading the passages). However, on the delayed test the effect of groups was significant [$F = 3.6$ (3,84 *df*), $p < .025$]. A Tukey's multiple comparison test indicated that the control group differed significantly from the imagery and paraphrase groups at the .05 level, whereas all other comparisons between means were nonsignificant. As can be seen in the right far column of Table 1.1, the paraphrase and imagery groups (and, to a somewhat lesser extent, the question–answer group) had substantially higher levels of mean performance than did the control group (over 55% greater performance in the case of the paraphrase group).

It should be noted that the immediate assessment and delayed assessment measures differed in two ways. The immediate measure consisted of true–false, multiple choice, fill-in-the-blank, and short answer questions, and was administered approximately 20 minutes after the reading of the four passages. On the other hand, the delayed measure was composed of essay questions and was administered 5 days

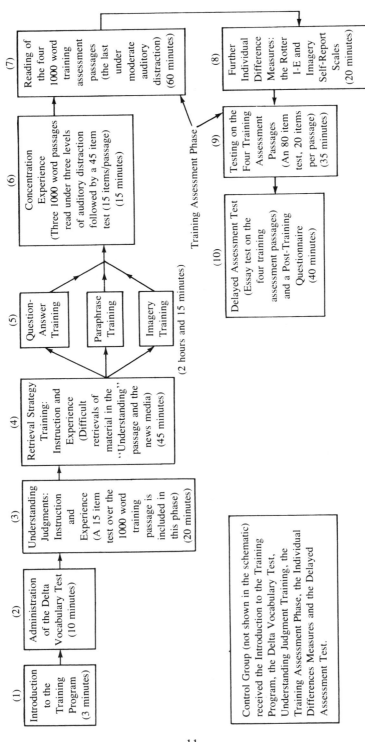

(1)
Introduction
to the
Training
Program
(3 minutes)

(2)
Administration
of the Delta
Vocabulary Test
(10 minutes)

(3)
Understanding
Judgments:
Instruction
and
Experience
(A 15 item
test over the
1000 word
training
passage is
included in
this phase)
(20 minutes)

(4)
Retrieval Strategy
Training:
Instruction and
Experience
(Difficult
retrievals of
material in the
"Understanding"
passage and the
news media)
(45 minutes)

(5)
Question-
Answer
Training

Paraphrase
Training

Imagery
Training

(6)
Concentration
Experience
(Three 1000 word passages
read under three levels
of auditory distraction
followed by a 45 item
test (15 items/passage)
(15 minutes)

(7)
Reading of
the four
1000 word
training
assessment
passages
(the last
under
moderate
auditory
distraction)
(60 minutes)

(8)
Further
Individual
Difference
Measures:
the Rotter
1-E and
Imagery
Self-Report
Scales
(20 minutes)

(9)
Testing on the
Four Training
Assessment
Passages
(An 80 item
test, 20 items
per passage)
(35 minutes)

(10)
Delayed Assessment Test
(Essay test on the
four training
assessment passages)
and a Post-Training
Questionnaire
(40 minutes)

(2 hours and 15 minutes)

Training Assessment Phase

Control Group (not shown in the schematic)
received the Introduction to the Training
Program, the Delta Vocabulary Test,
Understanding Judgment Training, the
Training Assessment Phase, the Individual
Differences Measures and the Delayed
Assessment Test.

Figure 1.1 Formal assesment study: Schematic of the training program treatments.

TABLE 1.1
Mean Assessment Scores

Groups	Immediate Test (Maximum Score = 80)	Delayed Test (Maximum Score = 60)
Paraphrase	45.1	28.4
Imagery	43.5	27.2
Question-Answer	42.7	25.6
Control	38.9	18.3

after the passages had been read. Obviously, this confounding of the factors of time and question type prevents us from drawing a definite conclusion about the locus of the training effect. Are the results due to improved long-term retention by the training groups or improved retrieval capabilities when faced with general questions (essay type), or a combination of both? In the experiments we are now conducting, we are counterbalancing test questions and delay of testing in order to determine which capability or combination of capabilities is being improved by training.

Although this study generated some promising results, it was really conceived as only a minor first step in the development of a learning-strategy training program. First, we looked at only a portion of the tasks required of an effective learner (e.g., we did not include a self-checking or monitoring strategy). The strategies we developed were not designed to support one another explicitly in a synergic fashion. Furthermore, we did not specify the strategies in very great detail and, consequently, we relied on the inductive powers of the students. We felt that more detailed strategies and training would allow us to have an impact on a broader range of students. Finally, the feedback received from students pointed out a number of directions for improving both the strategies and the training procedures.

Directions for Improving The Strategy Training Program

Ideas for improving the Dansereau *et al.* (1975b) program were identified through experimenter observation and through posttraining interviews with the students. These potential areas of improvement will be categorized according to the component of the program to which they most directly apply.

General Directions for Program Improvement

The ideas to be described here have applicability to most, if not all, of the four program components: identification (understanding ratings), comprehension–retention, retrieval, and concentration.

First, the pace of the training in this study was extremely rapid, and the techniques required a great deal of overt responding (e.g., drawing images, writing paraphrases). We feel that this situation led to frustration and fatigue in many of the students. In addition, owing to the rapid pace, a number of students felt they had not sufficiently learned their strategies. Apparently they felt that the application of the techniques was not automatic enough, and thus required too much time.

These problems can probably be reduced by decreasing the pace of training and extending training time. In addition, the knowledge of the techniques could be enhanced by using descriptions of the strategies and strategy-related background information as the actual training (practice) materials. In other words, the student can be given guided practice on applying each strategy to learning the conceptual and instructional level materials associated with subsequent strategies. In effect, as they progress through the training program students will be gradually increasing their strategy repertoire and will be using this repertoire to learn new strategy information. This approach has the advantage of giving the student extensive exposure to strategy information, both conceptual and instructional. The approach should also help to make the training program more generalizable and more autonomous.

Second, the dependent measures used in the initial study were not sufficient to reveal to the students their strategy weaknesses, nor were they adequate to evaluate the effectiveness of the program, especially the transferability of the strategies to more realistic situations. Most of the measures were at the associational–fact level of inquiry; in retrospect, it seems clear that more emphasis should be placed on conceptual (interrelating facts), inferential (going beyond the information given), and performance-oriented (application) questioning. This reemphasis would presumably aid in stimulating the student to acquire the strategies, and would provide a more valid assessment of the student's learning ability. In addition to these changes it is important to develop procedures for assessing the long-term effects of the program. Subjective reports, performance on regular class work, and/or job performance ratings should be monitored for graduates of the program. Relationships between these long-term measures and performance in the training program per se could be identified in order to provide a basis for program modification.

Third, the feedback given to students in the initial program was mainly in the form of idealized products resulting from strategy application by the experimenters. For example, in the imagery training section of the program, the student was asked to draw or describe a mental picture of the presented material and then was provided with an experimenter-generated drawing as feedback. The main problem that arises from this type of feedback is that students are not given information about the processes that led to the final formulation. In some cases, the feedback that was given may not have provided sufficient data for students to revise their behavior intelligently. There appear to be three approaches to overcoming this problem: individualized feedback on student constructions, experimenter-generated protocols of the process leading to acceptable products (i.e., transcripts of the thoughts involved in the construction of feedback), and dyadic or group discussions on application. The second of these is probably the most economical, whereas the third, if feasible in a given situation, would probably have the added benefit of increasing student motivation and interest.

In summary, we feel that the overall program could be improved by decreasing the pace of training, using written descriptions of the strategies as training materials, expanding the dependent measures to make them more diagnostic, and improving the feedback given to students on their strategy application. In addition, the initial study provided a number of ideas for improving the individual strategy components, which will be discussed separately in the next four sections.

Improvement and Extension of the Identification Strategy Component

This portion of the initial program was designed to instruct students on procedures for identifying important, difficult, and unfamiliar portions of the material so that they could eventually decide when to apply the comprehension–retention strategies. In our initial, study students may have been required to utilize their techniques too frequently for maximum efficiency. If strategy application is too frequent, the student may spend too much time processing relatively unimportant aspects of the information. A study explicitly varying the amount of material covered before technique application could provide information on the optimal frequency of application for any particular individual.

In addition to this refinement, it would seem useful to extend the identification component to include other forms of monitoring, such as degree of concentration, rate of learning, amount of physical tension, and when to attempt retrieval. These skills may be trainable by allowing the student to imitate ''good learners'' or by training the student on methods of self-inquiry.

Enhancing the Comprehension–Retention Techniques

The initial study suggested a number of steps that might lead to the improvement of the three comprehension–retention techniques (paraphrasing, question–answer, and imagery).

Some students reported on the post training questionnaire that the comprehension–retention technique seemed incompatible with their normal modes of information processing. This perceived incompatibility, which was most pronounced in the imagery group, seemed to make acquisition and use of the techniques difficult for some individuals. In future studies, students should probably be given exposure to all the techniques and then choose the one they feel most comfortable with for future training. In addition to facilitating the choice of compatible strategies, this approach would probably enhance motivation by allowing some personal choice.

Perhaps an even more fruitful extension of this approach would consist of training students on all the comprehension–retention techniques to criterion and then allowing them to use the techniques at their discretion. Since the techniques may be differentially applicable to different types of material (e.g., the imagery technique may be particularly useful with concrete materials) and since alternation of the techniques may allow for use of both the visual and verbal memory systems, it seems reasonable to train students to shift techniques intermittently, based on content and memory conditions.

A slightly different alternative to the preceding suggestions would involve the creation of an overall comprehension–retention strategy that would incorporate the best aspects of all three techniques. This strategy would be designed to increase conceptual connectivity (memory links between stored concepts to enhance retention and concentration) by utilizing **reorganization** (asking questions that require shifts in perspective), **integration** (linking incoming material with previously stored material), and **elaboration** (making the links interesting and unusual through imagery, analogies, and humor). Training could then be given on applying aspects of this technique flexibly, depending on the nature of the material, the state of the organism, and the existing learning objectives.

As was described previously, our posttraining questionnaire data indicated individual differences in receptivity to the techniques. An additional indication of the importance of individual differences can be seen in Table 1.2. Although the interaction between Delta Vocabulary Test subgroupings and the training groups failed to reach significance, the data reported in this table are suggestive. Even though the imagery group generally performed at a slightly lower level (nonsignificant) than the paraphrase group on the delayed assessment measure (a mean of 27.2 versus a mean of 28.4.), persons scoring poorly on the Delta Vocabulary Test apparently benefited more from the imaging strategy than from the paraphrase technique.

The importance of considering individual differences probably extends even to the detailed manipulations involved in carrying out the comprehension–retention strategies. Knowledge of an individual's cognitive style (pervasive, idiosyncratic ways of processing information) could profitably be used as a basis for making fine-grained alterations in an omnibus strategy in order to amplify processing strengths and to attenuate processing weaknesses. In fact, with some guidance, the students could probably be taught to make such modifications on their own.

TABLE 1.2
Mean Performance on the Delayed Assessment Measure

Groups	Delta Vocabulary Test Subgroups	
	High Scorers	Low Scorers
Paraphrase	37.4	18.9
Imagery	32.4	23.0
Question-Answer	30.27	18.64
Control	22.84	13.73

Possibilities for Improving the Retrieval Aspect
of the Program

The retrieval portion of the program was not objectively assessed, but was well received by the students. Experimenter-generated protocols related to the processes involved in conducting difficult retrievals were utilized as feedback. We feel this practice continue in future program development. In addition, it seemed reasonable to place greater emphasis on exposing the student to the relationships between conscious retrieval and heuristic problem-solving. Toward this end, the student would be given knowledge about problem-solving derived from the work of Simon and Newell (1971) as a prerequisite to retrieval training.

Potential Directions for Improving the
Concentration Aspects of the Program

Concentration training consisted of exposing the students to increasing amounts of external distraction (lectures and plays presented auditorily) during reading. Suggestions for coping were provided, but most of this training was left to the student. It was anticipated that giving students practice in coping with graded external distractions would allow them to develop generalizable coping skills. In particular, it was hoped that these skills would generalize to other external distractions and to internal distractions, such as task-unrelated thoughts and emotions.

However, the concentration experience did not lead to better performance by the training groups on the fourth training assessment passage. (This passage was read under a moderate level of retrieval distraction.) The lack of effect is far from conclusive evidence that the concentration experience failed to aid overall performance, but it does at least lead to the conclusion that this "experience" should be subjected to a more thorough evaluation in future studies. Students' reactions to the experience were mixed, as were perhaps the benefits received.

If concentration is conceived of as a shift in monitoring levels from task-unrelated information (time and future and past engagements) to task- or strategy-related information, then perhaps relaxation, behavior modification, and positive self-talk training could serve to facilitate this shift.

EFFORTS TO EXPAND AND IMPROVE THE
LEARNING-STRATEGY TRAINING PROGRAM

The ideas presented in the previous section have stimulated us to expand and modify our concept of the strategy training program. Before discussing our thinking on the specific strategy components I will briefly describe our current approach to strategy training.

In general, training on each strategy component will involve six different types of activities.

1. *Stimulation*. Prior to instruction on each component students will be given a brief experience to illustrate the importance and potential impact of what is to come. This experience (e.g., simple peg-word mnemonic instructions as stimulation for the comprehension–retention component) will serve to enhance motivation, involvement, and cognitive awareness.

2. *Conceptual level information*. This information will provide psychological and educational background for the actual strategy instruction. At this time the interrelationships between the components will be presented in order to increase the students' cognitive awareness and their perception of the validity of the program. Taken together, materials at this level will form a short cognitive psychology course, which should give the student the intellectual foundations for the strategies that will follow.

3. *Strategy instruction*. Material at this level will describe prodecures for applying the strategy. Preliminary exercises will be provided with this instruction.

4. *Strategy application*. The student will be given guided practice on applying each strategy to learning the conceptual and instructional (2 and 3) level materials associated with subsequent strategies. In effect, a students progress through the training program, they will gradually increase their strategy repertoire and will be using this increasing repertoire to learn new strategy infromation.

5. *Feedback on strategy application*. To give students a basis for modifying their strategy they will be provided with instructor-generated protocols that illustrate correct strategy usage and point out potential pitfalls. This feedback will be supplemented by student discussion of strategy application, thereby making use of their pooled knowledge as well as the beneficial effects of social reinforcement and feedback.

6. *Assessment and Diagnosis*. Activities at this level will include tests of comprehension and retention that make use of questions at the factual, conceptual, and inferential levels of understanding. These will be supplemented by subjective reports of effectiveness, understanding, retention, concentration, etc. These measures will provide a basis for additional feedback (via self-scoring, instructor intervention, group discussion, or all three) and a basis for evaluating the effects of the training program components.

As presently conceptualized, the training program will also have following additional features:

1. The information will be presented primarily in a written format (other media are being considered).
2. The program will be adaptable to either individual or group pacing.
3. There will be multiple entry points to accommodate those students with prior strategy skills.
4. The program will be designed to accommodate instructor, written, or group feedback.

5. The time for program completion will be minimized (12–18 hours appears to be a reasonable target range).
6. Training material complexity will be varied in order to provide a broad spectrum of strategy experience.

The next section will provide information on the characteristics of the individual strategy components.

The Component Strategies

As stated earlier, we have divided the prose-learning system into primary strategies (i.e., techniques used to operate on the material) and support strategies (i.e., techniques used to operate on the learner). The primary strategies we are currently working with are comprehension–retention and retrieval–utilization. The support strategies consist of developing positive attitudes, coping with internal and external distractions (concentration), and monitoring. We will discuss these strategy classes separately in the following section.

The Primary Strategies

Although they are highly interrelated, I will discuss the comprehension and retention strategies separately from the retrieval and utilization strategies in order to make the presentation as clear as possible.

Comprehension and Retention Strategies. As stated earlier, the results of our initial study indicated that, with respect to mean performance, the paraphrase and imagery techniques facilitated delayed retention of academic materials in comparison to a no-treatment control group. Although these results are promising, the techniques are only first steps toward development of more inclusive comprehension and retention strategies.

Our goal has been to develop strategies that will assist students in creatively reorganizing, integrating, and elaborating on incoming material in order to increase conceptual connectivity in a manner compatible with long-term memory structures. The premise is that the more connections or relationships between concepts, objects, ideas, or actions that individuals discover or create, the deeper will be their understanding, the greater their retention, and the better the retrievability of the material under a variety of circumstances.

In our current work, we have been exploring three alternative comprehension–retention strategies: paraphrase–imagery, networking, and analysis of key ideas. We will describe each of these techniques separately.

1. Paraphrase–Imagery. This technique is a simple combination of the paraphrase and imagery strategies developed in our initial program (see pages 8–9). The student is trained on both techniques and is then instructed to vary use of the techniques depending on the material being studied.

2. Networking. Unlike the paraphrase–imagery technique, which requires the student to transform text material into natural language or pictures, the networking strategy requires material to be transformed into node-link maps or networks. Before giving more information on the technique per se we will present some general background information on the concept of node-link networks.

Quillian (1968) suggested that human memory may in fact be organized as a network composed of ideas or concepts (nodes) and named relationships between these concepts (links). For example, the relationships (links) between the concepts (nodes) bird, parrot, and colorful can be expressed as, "A parrot is a *type* of bird " and "A parrot can be *described* as colorful." These node-link relationships can be represented spatially as follows

Since Quillan's early work, a number of network models of memory have been proposed and tested (e.g., J. R. Anderson, 1972; J. R. Anderson & Bower, 1973; Rumelhart, Lindsay, & Norman, 1972). The results of these efforts indicate that at least some aspects of human memory can be represented as networks. (See Chapters 5 and 7 of this volume for more detail.) For this and a number of other reasons we will discuss shortly, the node-link network was chosen as the basis for one of our comprehension–retention techniques.

The networking strategy requires the student to identify important concepts or ideas (nodes) in the material and to represent their interrelationships (links) in the form of a network map. Students are taught a set of named links that can be used to code the relationships between ideas. To date, we have used two sets of links, derived from examining the relationships expressed in a wide range of text material. The simpler set is composed of four relationships: *type* (e.g., "A dog is a **type** of animal"), *part* (e.g., "The hand is a **part** of the body"), *leads to* (e.g., "Reinforcement **leads to** repetition of the reinforced behavior "), and *description* (e.g., "The male peacock can be **described** as colorful"). Figure 1.2 shows the symbology associated with these relationships, and Figure 1.3 illustrates a network derived from a paragraph using this four-link system.

The details of the more complicated link system we have been using will not be discussed. Suffice it to say that this system is composed of 13 types of links, which expand on the four classes of links just described (e.g., *leads to* links are replaced by *cause, influence,* and *solve* links). In all other respects this system is used in the same way as the four-link system.

We believe that the transformation of prose into a network will assist the student in seeing the overall concept being presented by an author. In addition, having coded the material in terms of named links gives the student the option of using these links to gain access to the material during retrieval. (This possibility will be discussed further in the section on retrieval–utilization.) Besides these direct bene-

Link Name	Symbolic Representation	Example

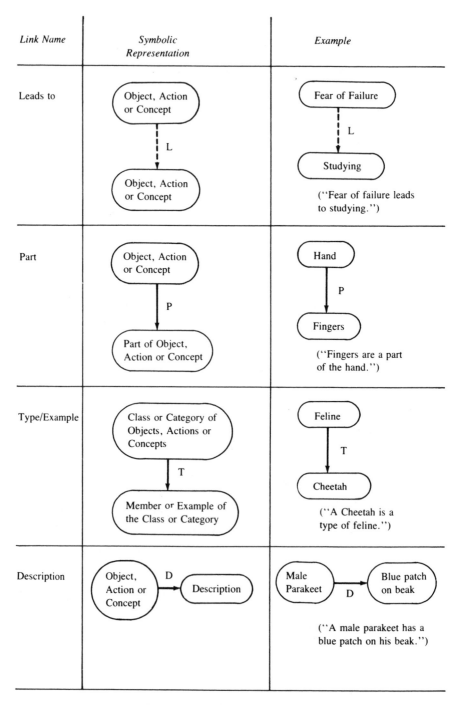

Figure 1.2 The four link system.

Most people don't know whether their present learning strategies are good or bad or whether there are other techniques that would work better for them. This is mainly because they haven't been given the chance to explore alternative techniques.

In fact many people who think of themselves as being only average intellectually may have capabilities that are being stifled or suppressed because they have not learned good techniques for dealing with information.

In some ways this would be like having a powerful, highly tuned sports car without ever having learned to drive it properly.

I think most of us are in this situation and that with some training we could substantially increase our intellectual ability.

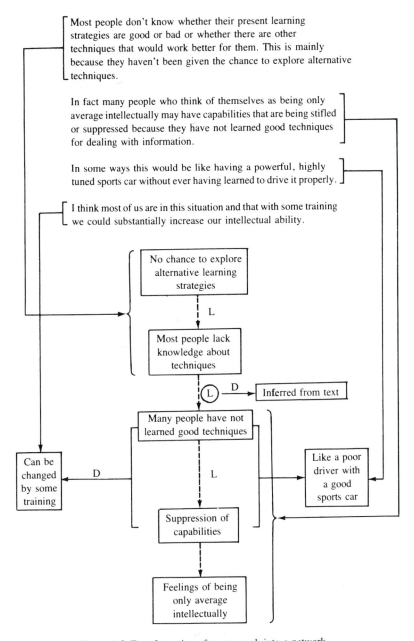

Figure 1.3 Transformation of a paragraph into a network.

fits, an expanded network approach appears to be applicable to a number of other domains.

From the teacher's perspective, networking can be used as an alternative to outlining in the preparation of lectures. Also, teacher-prepared networks can be presented as advance and postorganizers. Additional benefits may be derived from using networks teaching students who are employing networking as a learning strategy.

Networking can be used to facilitate individual and group problem-solving by providing a mechanism for systematically organizing and manipulating the problem space. This approach has been used in a graduate psychology seminar at Texas Christian University. Subjective reactions to it indicate that the approach has substantial promise as a problem-solving tool.

Conceptually it seems reasonable to expect that ability to devise networks (i.e., discover and organize meaningful relationships between ideas, objects, and actions) should be related to general reading comprehension ability. If this expectation is borne out, networking may serve as an alternative assessment and diagnostic device. In fact, the noun phrases in a body of text can be replaced by nonmeaningful symbols. A student's ability to network this material would seem to reflect a type of comprehension skill that is separable from vocabulary and prior knowledge.

The ease, accuracy, or both with which a text can be networked may provide a more valid index of comprehensibility (readability) than is presently available.

3. Analysis of Key Ideas. The final comprehension–retention strategy is also derived from network models of memory (Diekhoff, 1977). In this structured alternative to networking, the student identifies key ideas or concepts in a body of text, develops systematic definitions and elaborations of the concepts, and interrelates important pairs of concepts. The student is aided in these activities by worksheets which specify categories of definition and comparison. These categories are isomorphic to the four links described earlier (e.g., in defining operant conditioning one might say that it is a *type* of learning paradigm, a *part* of many behavior modification programs, *leads to* increases in the target behavior, etc.)

To date we have not conducted formal studies to assess these three strategies, but have taught them to a number of undergraduate students. Their subjective reactions have been generally favorable and have provided us with ideas for further modification. Eventually we hope to have students either use these three strategies in concert (i.e., have them learn and all three when applicable) or to use a particular strategy depending on their aptitude, style, and preference.

Retrieval and Utilization. Subjective reports from students and studies demonstrating "tip of the tongue" behavior (R. Brown & McNeil, 1966), and "feeling of knowing" (Hart, 1965) indicate that stored items are frequently available but, at least temporarily, not accessible. Individuals encountering such a situation may give up, randomly search, or attempt to execute a systematic retrieval strategy. It appears that students often opt for the first two alternatives rather than the third. This practice is unfortunate in that systematic attempts at retrieval often lead to success.

Lindsay and Norman (1972) give a brief example of how the systematic approach works. In response to the query: "What were you doing on Monday afternoon in the third week of September two years ago?" Lindsay and Norman's imaginary subject gradually homes in on the answer by breaking the query down into a rational sequence of subquestions that prove answerable by various mixtures of actual memories and logical reconstructions of what must have been ("Third week in September—that's just after summer—that would be the fall term . . . . I think I had chemistry lab on Mondays . . . . I remember he started off with the atomic table . . . ," etc.).

We feel that students can benefit from instruction on how to undertake a systematic retrieval. In particular, the named relationships (links) used in the network technique can form the basis of such a plan for retrieving stored information. On the basis of the question or the context, students will decide on the main structure (i.e., theme) that their answer or production should take. It is expected that these will often be either hierarchies (*type* or *part*) or chains of actions or arguments. The student can then lay these structures out in a network and elaborate them by a memory-searching process, looking for material related to the nodes in the "theme" structures. The nodes in the resulting compound network can then be numbered to provide a sequence for writing, acting, or speaking. This approach should provide a more systematic alternative to traditional outlining, in that it divides the process into two stages: First, the student establishes the conceptual relationships between portions of the material, and then determines a sequence for moving through the material. In typical outlining the individual must perform both functions simultaneously. Analogous approaches are being developed for those students trained on paraphrase–imagery or analysis of key ideas.

Substrategies are also being developed to supplement the flow of this systematic retrieval process. These include instructing students to relax and image the situations in which they may have acquired the target information. This involves using incidental and organizational cues to recapture the learning context. In addition, the student will be made aware of the ties between retrieval strategies and the processes involved in problem-solving. (both require a search through a problem space). In particular, the student will be instructed on means–ends analysis (setting and meeting subgoals) and planning (abstracting the problem to a more general level), two key components of the General Problem Solver created by Newell et al. (1958). The idea is to examine the difference between your present state of knowledge and your goal state in order to set up reasonable subgoals. Acquisition of these subgoals presumably leads you increasingly closer to your target state of knowledge. For example, if one were trying to remember who was the vice president of the United States in 1877, a reasonable first subgoal might be to determine who was the president during that time period. If that information were not immediately retrievable, the next step might be to set up the subgoal of trying to remember which major events took place during the latter 1870s. The process would continue until an achievable subgoal was reached. The information retrieved would then be used to access the previous subgoal, and so on. In this way one would work back up the chain of subgoals to the target.

In using the "planning" heuristic a student would first generalize the retrieval task to a simpler one, solve the simple retrieval via means–end analysis, and then use the solution to guide the more specific retrieval. For example, if a student were trying to recall the location and function of a particular part of a cat's brain (e.g., the hypothalamus), the first attempt might be to remember the location and function of the hypothalamus in mammals in general and then use these retrieval steps to guide the more specific inquiry.

Additional training will also be provided on interpreting the retrieval context (question, problem, etc.) to aid the student in deciding what should be retrieved in a particular situation. This will generally fall under the rubric of problem definition and will require further training on effective questioning (inquiry).

The Support Strategies

No matter how effective the primary strategies are, their impact on learning and utilization will be less than optimal if the student's internal psychological environment is nonoptimal. Consequently, the support strategies are designed to help the student develop and maintain a good internal state. These support strategies include techniques for developing a positive attitude toward learning, coping with internal and external distractions, and monitoring and diagnosing the dynamics of the learning system. These three classes of strategies will be discussed separately.

Strategies for Cultivating a Positive Learning Attitude. Interviews and discussions with students indicate that many have conflicting attitudes about learning. They view learning as something that is necessary and desirable, but when faced with an impending learning task they often experience a variety of negative emotions: anxiety, anger, guilt, fear, and frustration. These feelings and the self-talk and images that accompany them serve to decrease a student's motivation to study and act as distractors during the learning process and during evaluation periods.

The strategy we are developing help the student overcome attitude problems consists of a combination of elements from systematic desensitization (Jacobsen, 1938; Wolpe, 1969), rational behavior therapy (Ellis, 1963; Maultsby, 1971), and therapies based on positive self-talk (Meichenbaum & Goodman, 1971; Meichenbaum & Turks, 1975). Students are first given experiences and strategies designed to make them aware of the negative and positive emotions, self-talk, and images they generate in facing a learning task. They are then asked to follow these feelings and thoughts to their logical conclusions (e.g., "Just what will happen if I fail this exam?"). Very often the individual has not thought beyond the fact that a particular outcome will be "awful" or that such and such an outcome is "critical" (Maultsby, 1971). Stopping at this stage can be very illusory and may lead to emotions being blown out of proportion. In addition, the accompanying self-talk and imagery may be extremely destructive when viewed in relationship to the student's long term goals. In order to help them match self-talk with objectives, students are asked to evaluate the constructiveness of their internal dialogue and are given heuristics for making appropriate modifications.

In preparing for an impending study session students report that they usually spend very little conscious effort in establishing a positive learning state. It seems likely that thoughts and feelings associated with their immediately previous situation will mix with negative cognitions about learning, and will be carried over as distractors during task performance. To alleviate this situation the student is trained on a technique that forms the basis of systematic desensitization: imagination of the anxiety-evoking situation during relaxation. In effect, students are instructed to relax and "clear their minds" by counting breaths. Each individual is then instructed to imagine a period of successful studying, becoming distracted and successfully coping with the distraction. The student is also encouraged to replace the negative talk and images with more constructive thoughts.

Our experience with this strategy to date is that college freshmen and sophomores find the techniques relatively easy to grasp and apply. Subjective reactions to this approach have been positive.

Concentration: Coping with Internal and External Distractions.   The most common student complaints revolve around their inability to concentrate during a study or testing session. Interviews with students indicate that acts of will and fear-arousing self-talk are the most common methods of coping with distractions, frustration and fatigue. Apparently these methods are, at best, only partially effective and tend to put the student under considerable tension. This tension probably contributes to subsequent negative feelings about future learning episodes.

We have been developing concentration-enhancing strategies to supplement or substitute for those typically used. Again, the first step involves awareness training: Students are given experiences and techniques help them determine when, how, and why they get distracted; the duration of their distraction periods; and their typical reactions to distraction. They are then trained to cope with distractions by using the "attitude" strategies of relaxation, and positive self-talk and imagery to reestablish an appropriate learning state.

Monitoring.   To be effective learners, students must be able to detect when their behavior is insufficient to meet task demands, so that they can make appropriate adjustments. In the monitoring strategy, students are encouraged to skim the material and mark places in the text where they plan to check their progress and take "action". They then set a specific learning state by recalling previous experiences with related materials. They read to the first "action" point, rate their understanding and capability for retention, take action if necessary (in the form of implementing a comprehension and retention strategy), and evaluate the results. If their acquisition of information is less than satisfactory they attempt to diagnose the locus of the problem by checking concentration, need for background material, reading rate, etc. On the basis of this diagnosis they then make appropriate corrections and cognitively reinforce themselves for successful troubleshooting.

This strategy component acts as the executive routine in the learning strategy system in that it controls the onset of the other components.

CONCLUDING COMMENTS

In developing this program we have become very sensitive to the range of individual differences in reactions to the techniques and training. We plan to use a variety of cognitive style and aptitude measures to determine which types of individuals benefit most from the training. Also, an attempt will be made to provide feedback that will assist students in tailoring the techniques to their own needs.

Up to this point in our work, we have focused primarily on program development. We are satisfied with the results of this effort and in the near future will be placing more emphasis on evaluation of the program components. We would like to point out that although one of our purposes is to develop and assess a particular learning strategy system, another more general and perhaps more important goal is to create a framework from which both applied and basic extensions can be made. What we are trying to do is to form a blueprint or sketch of the interactive tasks required for effective learning in anticipation that details can be filled in by more fine-grained empirical studies.

ACKNOWLEDGMENTS

The work reported in this chapter is the result of a team effort. The following individuals have made important contributions to this effort: Collins, K. W.; McDonald, B. A.; Diefhoff, G.; Evans, S. H.; Garland, J.; Holley, S. D.; Long, G.; Irons, D.; Hilton, T.; Lehman, L. D.; Walker, C.; Halemanu, M.; Ellis, A. M.; and Fenker, R. M.

REFERENCES

Alabiso, F. Operant control of attention behavior: A treatment for hyperactivity. *Behavior Therapy,* 1975, *6*, 39–42.

Allen, K. Some effects of advance organizers and levels of questions on the learning and retention of written social studies materials. *Journal of Educational Psychology,* 1970, *61* (5), 33–339.

Anderson, J. R. A simulation model of free recall. In G. H. Bower (Ed.), *The psychology of learning and motiviation* (Vol. 5), New York: Academic Press, 1972.

Anderson, J. R., & Bower, G. H. *Human associative memory.* Washington, D.C.: Winston, 1973.

Anderson, R. C. Control of student mediating processes during verbal learning and instruction. *Review of Educational Research,* 1970, *40* (3), 349–369.

Anderson, R. C., & Hidde, J. L. Imagery and sentence learning. *Journal of Educational Psychology,* 1971, *62*, 526–530.

Ausubel, D. P. & Youssef, M. The effect of consolidation on sequentially related, sequentially independent meaningful learning. *Journal of General Psychology,* 1966, *74* (2), 335–360.

Bauman, D. J., & Glass, G. V. *The effect on learning of the position of an organizer.* Paper presented at the meeting of the American Educational Research Association, Los Angeles, February 1969.

Bodden, J. L., Osterhouse, R., & Geloso, C. The value of a study skills inventory for feedback and criterion purposes in an educational skills course. *Journal of Educational Research,* 1972, *65*(7), 309–311.

Bower, G. H. How to... uh... remember! *Psychology Today,* October 1973, pp. 63–70.

Bower, G. H., & Reitman, J. S. Mnemonic elaboration in multilist learning. *Journal of Verbal Learning and Verbal Behavior,* 1972, *11*, 478–485.

Briggs, R. D., Tosi, D. J., & Morley, R. M. Study habit modification and its effect on academic performances: A behavioral approach. *Journal of Educational Research,* 1971, *64*(8), 347–350.

Brown, R., & McNeil, D. The "tip of the tongue" phenomenon. *Journal of Verbal Learning and Verbal Behavior,* 1966, *5*, 325–337.

Brown, W. F., Webe, N. D., Zunker, V. G., & Haslam, W. L. Effectiveness of student to student counseling on the academic adjustment of potential college dropouts. *Journal of Educational Psychology,* 1971, *62*, 285–289.

Bruner, J. S., Goodnow, J. J., & Austin, G. A. *A study of thinking.* New York: Wiley, 1956.

Butterfield, E. C., Belmont, J. M., & Peltzman, D. J. Effects of recall requirement on acquisition strategy. *Journal of Experimental Psychology,* 1971, *90*(2), 347–348.

Cermak, L. S. Rehearsal strategy as a function of recall expectation. *Quarterly Journal of Experimental Psychology,* 1972, *24*, 378–385.

Danner, F. W., & Taylor, A. M. Integrated pictures and relational imagery training in children's learning. *Journal of Experimental Child Psychology,* 1973, *16*, 47–54.

Dansereau, D. F. *Self-Report Mental Imagery Test.* Unpublished manuscript, Institute for the Study of Cognitive Systems, Psychology Department, Texas Christian University, 1969.

Dansereau, D. F., Actkinson, T. R., Long, G. L., & McDonald, B. *Learning strategies: A review and synthesis of the current literature* (AFHRL-TR-74-70, Contract F41609-74-C-0013). Lowry Air Force Base, Colo.: Air Force Human Resources Laboratory. 1974. (AD-07722) (a)

Dansereau, D. F., Evans, S. H., Actkinson, T. A., & Long, G. L. *Factors relating to the development of optimal instructional information sequences* (AFHRL-TR-73-51 (II), Contract F41609-73-C-0023). Lowry Air Force Base, Colo.: Air Force Human Resources Laboratory, 1974. (AD-783843) (b)

Dansereau, D. F., Evans, S. H., Wright, A. D., Long, G. L., & Actkinson, T. A. *Factors related to developing instructional information sequences: Phase I* (AFHRL-TR-73-51 (I), Contract F41609-73-C-0023). Lowry Air Force Base, Colo.: Air Force Human Resources Laboratory, 1974. (AD-777832) (c)

Dansereau, D. F., Long, G. L., McDonald, B. A., & Actkinson, T. R. *Learning strategy inventory development and assessment* (AFHRL-TR-75-40, Contract F41609-74-C-0013). Lowry Air Force Base, Colo.: Air Force Human Resources Laboratory, 1975. (AD-A01472) (a)

Dansereau, D. F., Long, G. L., McDonald, B. A., Actkinson, T. R., Ellis, A. M., Collins, K., Williams, S., & Evans, S. H. *Effective learning strategy training program: Development and assessment* (AFHRL-TR-75-41, Contract F41609-74-0013). Lowry Air Force Base, Colo.: Air Force Human Resources Laboratory, 1975. (AD-A014722) (b)

Deignan, G. D., Delta Vocabulary Test. Personal communication, 1973.

DelGiorno, W., Jenkins, J. R., & Bausell, R. B. Effects of recitation in the acquisition of prose. *Journal of Educational Research,* 1974, *67*, 293–294.

Diekhoff, G. M., *The node acquisition and integration technique: A node-link based teaching/learning strategy.* Paper presented at the meeting of the American Educational Research Association, New York, April 1977.

DiVesta, F. J., Schultz, C. B., & Dangel, I. R., Passage organization and imposed learning strategies in comprehension and recall of connected discourse. *Memory & Cognition,* 1973, *1*, 471–476.

Dubin, R., & Taveggia, T. C., *The teaching-learning paradox.* Eugene: University of Oregon Press, 1968.

Ellis, A. *Reason and emotion in psychotherapy.* New York: Lyle Stuart, 1963.

Frase, L. T. Effect of question location, pacing, and made upon retention of prose material. *Journal of Educational Psychology,* 1968, *59*; 224–248.

Frase, L. T. Paragraph organization of written materials: The influence of conceptual clustering upon level and organization of recall. *Journal of Educational Psychology,* 1969, *60*, 394–401.

Frase, L. T. Integration of written text. *Journal of Educational Psychology,* 1973, 65, 252–261.

Fry, E. B. *Teaching machines and programmed instructions.* New York: McGraw-Hill, 1963.

Gay, L. R. *Temporal position of reviews and its effect on the retention of mathematical rules.* Tallahassee: Florida State University Computer-Assisted Instruction Center (Contract N00014-68-A-1494), Personnel and Training Research Program, Office of Naval Research, April 1971. (AD 279-055)

Groninger, L. D. Mnemonic imagery and forgetting. *Psychonomic Science,* 1971, *23*(2), 161–163.

Hart, T. J. Memory and the feeling of knowing experience. *Journal of Educational Psychology,* 1965, *56,* 208–216.

Haslam, W. L., & Brown, W. G. Effectiveness of study skills instruction for high school sophomores. *Journal of Educational Psychology,* 1968, *59,* 223–226.

Jacobsen, E. *Progressive relaxation.* Chicago: University of Chicago Press, 1938.

Jacoby, L. L. Test appropriate strategies in retention of catagorized lists. *Journal of Verbal Learning and Verbal Behavior,* 1973, *12,* 675–685.

Levine, J. R., & Divine-Hawkins, P. Visual imagery as a prose learning process. *Journal of Reading Behavior,* 1974, *6,* 23–30.

Lindsay, P. H., & Norman, D. A. *Human informal processing: An introduction to psychology.* New York: Adademic Press, 1972.

Lowry, D. H. The effects of mnemonic learning strategies on transfer, interference, and 48-hour retention. *Journal of Experimental Psychology,* 1974, *103*(1), 16–20.

Maultsby, M. *Handbook of rational self-counseling.* Madison, Wis.: Association for Rational Thinking, 1971.

Mayer, R. E. Forward transfer of different reading strategies evoked by testlike events in mathematics text. *Journal of Educational Psychology,* 1975, *67*(2), 165–169.

McConkie, G. W., & Meyer, B. J. Investigation of reading strategies: II. A replication of pay-off condition effects. *Journal of Reading Behavior,* 1974, *6,* 151–158.

McConkie, G. W., & Rayner, K. Investigation of reading strategies: I Manipulating strategies through pay-off conditions. *Journal of Reading Behavior,* 1974, *6,* 9–18.

McConkie, G. W., Rayner, K., & Mayer, B. J. *Manipulating reading strategies through pay-off conditions.* Unpublished manuscript, Cornell University, 1971.

McConkie, G. W., Rayner, K., & Wilson, J. S. Experimental Manipulation of reading strategies. *Journal of Educational Psychology,* 1973, *65*(1), 1–8.

Meichenbaum, D. H., & Goodman, J. Training impulsive children to talk to themselves: A means of self-control. *Journal of Abnormal Psychology,* 1971, *77,* 115–126.

Meichenbaum, D. H., & Turk, D. *The cognitive-behavioral management of anxiety, anger, and pain.* Paper presented at the Seventh Banff International Conference on Behavior Modification, Canada, May 1975.

Melton, A., & Martin, E. (Eds). *Coding process in human memory.* New York: Wiley, 1972.

Miller, G. A., Galanter, E., & Pribram, K. H. *Plans and the structure of behaviors.* New York: Holt, 1960.

Nelson, D. L., & Archer, C. S. The first letter Mnemonic. *Journal of Educational Psychology,* 1972, *63*(5), 482–486.

Newell, A., Simon, H. A., & Shaw, J. D. Elements of a theory of human problem solving. *Psychological Review,* 1958, *65,* 151–166.

Paivio, A. *Imagery and verbal processes.* New York: Holt, 1971.

Patterson, C. J., & Mischel, W. Plans to resist distraction. *Developmental Psychology,* 1975, *11*(3), 369–378.

Quillian, M. R. Semantic meaning. In M. Minsky (Ed.), *Semantic information processing.* Cambridge, Mass.: M.I.T. Press, 1968.

Rasco, R. W. Tennyson, R. P., & Boutwell, R. C. Imagery instructions and drawings in learning prose. *Journal of Educational Research,* 1975, *67*(2), 188–192.

Richards, J. P., & DiVesta F. J. Type and frequency of questions in processing textual material. *Journal of Educational Psychology,* 1974, *68,* 354–362.

Ritter, K., Kaprove, B. H., Fitch, J. P., & Flavell, J. H. The development of retrieval strategies in young children. *Cognitive Psychology,* 1973, *5*, 310–321.

Robinson, F. P. *Effective study.* New York: Harper, 1946.

Rothkopf, E. A. Learning from written instructive materials: An exploration of the control of inspection behavior by test-like events. *American Educational Research Journal,* 1966, *3*, 241–249.

Rothkopf, E. Z., & Bisbicos, E. E. Selective facilitative effects of interspersed questions in learning from written materials. *Journal of Educational Psychology,* 1967, *58*, 56–61.

Rotter, J. B. Generalized expectancies for internal versus external control of reinforcement. *Psychological Monographs,* 1966, *80*(1), (00, Whole No. 609).

Rumelhart, D. E., Lindsay, P. H., & Norman, D. A. A process model for long-term memory. In E. Tulving & W. Donaldson (Eds.), *Organization of memory.* New York: Academic Press, 1972.

Santa, J. C., Ruskin, A. B., & Yio, J. H. Mnemonic systems in free recall. *Psychological Reports,* 1973, *32*, 1163–1170.

Scandura, J., & Wells, J. Advance organizers in learning abstract mathematics. *American Educational Research Journal,* 1967, *4*, 295–301.

Simon, H. A., & Newell, A. Human problem solving. *American Psychologist,* 1971, *26*, 145–159.

VanZoost, F. L., & Jackson, B. T. Effects of self-monitoring and self-administered reinforcement on study behaviors. *Journal of Educational Research,* 1974, *67*(5), 216–218.

Wanshura, P. B. & Borkowski, J. G. Development and transfer of mediational strategies by retarded children in pair-associate learning. *American Journal of Mental Deficiency,* 1974, *78*, 631–639.

Weinstein, C. E. *Learning of elaboration strategies.* Unpublished doctoral dissertation, University of Texas at Austin, 1975.

Whitehill, R. P. The development of effective learning skills programs. *Journal of Educational Research,* 1972, *65*(6), 281–285.

Wolpe, J. *The practice of behavior therapy.* New York: Pergamon, 1969.

Yuille, J., & Catchpole, M. Effects of delay and imagery training on the recall and recognition of object pairs. *Journal of Experimental Child Psychology,* 1974, *17*, 474–481.

2

Elaboration Skills as a Learning Strategy[1]

CLAIRE E. WEINSTEIN

The purpose of this chapter is to explore the possibility that students can be taught to be more effective learners, independent of specific subject matter, and to relate this concept to current research results in several related areas of cognitive psychology. First, the appropriate literature will be reviewed because the integration of the information from these sources was influential in the thinking and development necessary to produce a prototype of a cognitive learning-strategies training program. Then, an initial study by Weinstein (1975) will be described. This project was our first attempt to develop a diversified elaboration learning-strategies training program. Finally, a description of our ongoing research and development efforts will be presented.

Today all sectors of our society are calling for some sort of educational reform. One common criticism of current educational practices involves the lack of effective instructional procedures to facilitate student learning. Fundamental to this problem is the almost universal assumption that students will learn simply because they are asked, or told, to learn, or because we supply them with one of the increasing number of technological devices or supports available. Educational research has contributed little to our knowledge of how to facilitate a learner's ability to develop and utilize effective and efficient learning strategies or intellectual skills.

Even at the earliest levels of our educational system one can repeatedly find teachers directing their students to a certain lesson or reading with nothing more

[1]Some of the initial conceptualizations and research reported in this chapter derive from my doctoral dissertation. Our current research effort is supported in part by Contract No. DAHC19-76-C-0026 with the Defense Advanced Research Projects Agency and monitored by the Army Research Institute for the Behavioral and Social Sciences. Views and conclusions contained in this document are those of the author and should not be interpreted as necessarily representing the official policies, either expressed or implied, of the Defense Advanced Research Projects Agency, the Army Research Institute, or of the United States Government.

than the instruction to learn the information, concepts, or skills contained. We tell our students **what** to learn but we say nothing about **how** to go about learning. The assumption that the abilities involved in learning are either innate or naturally acquired by every child is probably fallacious. Although it is true that many children and adults do acquire effective intellectual skills as a function of their individual experience, the schools do little to systematize or universalize these experiences.

An accumulated body of evidence indicates that we use strategies to store and retrieve information; we do not function as simple and passive receptacles in which associative bonds are imprinted and then remain available for later activation when the proper stimulus is presented (Melton & Martin, 1972; Rigney, 1976; Tulving & Donaldson, 1972). Gagné and Briggs (1974), state that learning acts require the presence of several internal states in the learner. Among these are information storage and retrieval capabilities, intellectual skills, and cognitive strategies. In addition to possessing certain information necessary to understand new content, the learner needs a variety of intellectual skills, such as problem-solving skills, concept acquisition skills, and discrimination learning skills. Cognitive or intellectual learning strategies are needed for the individual to select and govern his or her behavior in attending to the learning situation, managing the information storage and retrieval, and organizing the learning or problem solution.

Educational researchers and practitioners have begun to place greater emphasis on creating techniques to foster a learner's development of these cognitive skills and strategies. The conceptual bases and methodological procedures used to study cognitive elaboration skills and strategies derive from an extension of classical verbal-learning research traditions. During attempts to elucidate the mechanisms of human learning and retention, a variety of mnemonic, or memory facilitation, techniques have recently been investigated.

VERBAL LEARNING TRADITION

The Learner as a Variable

For many years, verbal learning had been studied in the tradition of the British associationists. For them, the basic learning unit was an association of ideas. Conceptually, the notion of association also drew upon nineteenth-century ideas concerning the reflex arc. In this scheme, associations were assigned the character of simple bonds that do not alter the discrete elements they connect. These connections were perceived as simple mechanical connections. Research generated by this paradigm and its underlying assumptions involved such things as looking at various stimulus characteristics or task demands across all learners. The individual learner was not an important variable.

Beginning in the late 1950s there emerged a significant shift in the methodologies and concepts used to study verbal learning. One such paradigm shift involved new conceptions of the stimulus. For example, it was noticed that when a particular verbal unit was presented as a stimulus in a paired-associate task, the learner might use the first letter or the first syllable as a cue. In order to differentiate more clearly the presented stimulus from its encoded counterpart, the terms *nominal* and *functional stimulus* were introduced. The nominal stimulus is the stimulus as defined by the experimenter, whereas the functional or effective stimulus is that part of the stimulus used by the individual as a cue for a response (Underwood, 1963). The process whereby a student selects only a part of the stimulus provided by the experimenter was defined as *stimulus selection.*

It was also recognized that the verbal response provided by the experimenter might undergo some transformation by the student during the learning process. Thus, given the trigam VIP to learn as a response, the learner might code it as "very important person" with the mental note, "first letter of each word only." Finally, it was hypothesized that even the association between the stimulus and the response may be neither as simple nor as direct as was previously assumed.

These ideas about the learner's active role in transforming or organizing to-be-learned material were extended by subsequent research. Organizational procedures utilized by learners occupy a prominent position in many contemporary theories of learning and memory. Miller, Galanter, and Pribram (1960) discuss the concept of *the plan,* which they consider to be a hierarchical process that controls the order in which a sequence of operations is performed. Thus, memory techniques involve the construction and execution of an organizing strategy that governs performance. Miller (1956) investigated the role of one type of organization in the learning of verbal material. He found that people seem to be able to store in short-term memory no more than seven (plus or minus two) units at any one time, but that each of these units can be made richer in meaning and structure by *chunking.* Chunking involves recoding the material to be learned into larger, internally connected chunks. Bousfield (1953) also investigated the storage and retrieval mechanisms in memory. In a single trial, free-recall learning experiment, learners were presented with a randomized list of 60 items made up of four 15-item categories: animals, names, professions, and vegetables. Immediately after the item presentation, learners were given 10 minutes to list all of the words they could recall. Results indicated that students showed a definite tendency to place items in groups that contained members of the same general category. From experiments like these, Bousfield inferred an organizing tendency on the part of human learners which he termed *clustering.*

Further evidence for the role students play in organizing a learning event can be found in the studies conducted by Tulving (1962, 1967, 1968) on cued recall. In the recall of categorized lists, supplying the names of categories at the time of testing enhances recall. In addition, the work of Paivio (1971), Posner (1969), and Underwood (1969) indicates that various codes for attributes of learning materials are used by learners to organize information to be learned and retained for later use.

Classical Mnemonic Systems

These and other new conceptions of the encoding and decoding processes in learning and recall, contributed to a renewed interest in the classical mnemonic systems. Mnemonics are techniques for improving the efficiency of one's memory.

In general, these memory skills can be used by learners to recode, transform, or encode presented materials either by reducing the content, as in stimulus selection, or by elaborating the content, as in making a sentence or integrated mental picture out of a noun pair. Therefore, there is a common conceptual base underlying research in mnemonics, elaboration, encoding, and mediation.

The development of mnemonic systems is not recent; it has been traced to a Greek poet named Simonides (ca. 500 B.C.). The inspiration for this discovery supposedly resulted from a disaster that occurred at a banquet Simonides was attending. Immediately after he was called out to receive a message, the roof of the banquet hall collapsed, crushing all of the remaining guests. By recalling the seating arrangement of the guests, Simonides was able to assist the families in reclaiming their dead (Yates, 1966).

Simonides' system utilized vivid mental imagery and stressed the importance of orderly arrangement as an aid to memory. Familiar places, or loci, must be selected, and then mental images of the things or words which were to be remembered could be "stored," or associated, with these locations. The natural order of the familiar places would provide cues for the sequenced retrieval of the things or words to be remembered.

Cicero and Quintilian elaborated on this system of places and images. The most detailed description of the method of loci and the rules governing it were given in the *Ad Herennium* (Yates, 1966). These rules were taught to ancient orators as a strategy for memorizing the major points of a speech.

With the passage of time, many variations of this basic technique were developed. For example, in the early nineteenth century, Gregor von Feinaigle, a famous European mnemonist, developed a system that combined the method of places and images with a number–alphabet–word code (Paivio, 1971). Essentially, the practitioner was to image a room and to divide the walls, floor, and ceiling into an hierarchically ordered set of numbered, square sections. In addition to its numerical designation, each room segment also contained the image of an object. When some unit of information was to be remembered, it was stored by forming an association with one of the images in the room. Item recall was supposed to involve mentally "returning" to the appropriate square, whereas larger units of related discourse could be recalled by using the ordered arrangement of the room's segments to connect the images.

Metrical mnemonics have also arisen (Norman, 1969). These allow the user to connect seemingly unrelated items into rhythmic patterns. Rhymes can be used to aid remembering ordered relations or patterns because forgetting any step in the sequence destroys the rhyme. The rhyming pattern provides a contextual constraint on recall. For example, it would be difficult for someone to recite a young child's "ABC song" without including all the letters in sequence.

A technique designed for remembering sequences of numbers or dates involves changing numbers into sounds or letters, sounds or letters into words, and words into phrases or sentences (Norman, 1969). Consonants are used to represent the numerals 1, 2, 3, 4, 5, 6, 7, 8, 9 and 0 in some consistent way. Vowels have no numerical value but are used to help create meaningful words. For example, in the Lorayne Link Methods (Lorayne & Lucas, 1974) 3 is represented by m, whereas 2 is represented by n, and 1 by t, th, or d. Thus the number "321" could be represented by the word "month" or "mint".

Processes Underlying the Classical Mnemonic Systems

The classical mnemonic systems were founded on several basic assumptions that are relevant to current theoretical positions concerning mechanisms of memory, associative thinking, and human learning in general. The classical mnemonic theories assume that perception, imagination, and thought are continuous modes of experience rather than disjointed components of human functioning. This can easily be related to the current emphasis being placed on the commonlity of perceptual and symbolic modalities discussed by Paivio (1971). The ancient systems also stressed visual processes in thought and memory, the importance of which is currently reflected in the tremendous revival in imagery research. In addition, a sequence of symbolic transformations from words to images and back to words was implicit in some of the classical systems. The mechanisms of mediation in verbal behavior are still being investigated today in the context of the experimental study of imagery in associative learning and memory (Bower, 1970).

Certain principles of memory are also suggested or implied by the techniques of the classical practitioners. The importance of organization was stressed by Simonides when he emphasized orderly arrangement. The images of places used for recall must form a series and they must be remembered in a specific order.

Although interference was not a primary concept in the memory systems of the ancients, we can note some points that relate to this contemporary construct. First, students were warned not to select places that were very similar when they created their mental images. Furthermore, it was suggested that they select unusual or distinctive images so that they would be easier to recall. Thus, it is apparent that many of our current assumptions about learning have their basis in these classical mnemonic systems.

EMPIRICAL MNEMONIC RESEARCH

Effectiveness Studies

Although we can show that a number of well-established principles relating to human learning and memory processes are incorporated in many mnemonics, it is only in recent years that the anecdotal evidence attesting to the utility of mnemonic systems and techniques has begun to be supplemented and amplified by controlled laboratory experiments. Typically, these studies compare the recall of students instructed to learn a list of items by using a mnemonic method, such as the method of loci, to the recall of students who are told to learn the items, but are not given any special instructions. The items may be related or unrelated; they may be objects, events, persons, words, or concepts. For example, college students were asked to study a group of 40-item lists for one trial, using as loci 40 locations spread around the college campus (J. Ross & Lawrence, 1968). Each list of 40 nouns was presented once at the rate of 13 seconds per item. The students were tested for their recall immediately after studying the list, and 24 hours later, just prior to learning a new list. Immediate recall averaged 38 out of 40 from each list, whereas delayed recall averaged 34 out of 40. These results are quite significant when compared to the scores usually obtained in rote-learning experiments (Bower, 1970).

In a classic study, Wood (1967) attempted to investigate several dimensions of mnemonic systems. Five separate experiments were designed to investigate three questions:

1. Under what circumstances, if any, do mnemonic systems facilitate learning?
2. What are the elements of the mnemonic device responsible for this facilitation?
3. What are the relationships between mnemonic devices and several variables that have been demonstrated to affect learning, such as transfer paradigm, type of list, and list abstractness in free recall?

In the first experiment, the recall of a list of 40 words was compared for seven groups, four of which received mnemonic peg lists (word to be used to form associations with the experimental word lists). The four groups that received peg lists were differentiated by the kind of association they were asked to make when connecting each peg and response word. Bizarre imagery was used by two of the groups, common imagery by the third group, and a form of verbal mediation by the fourth group. Of the two groups told to use bizarre imagery one group was told not to use rehearsal. For the three groups not given peg words, one group was told to make an image of each response word. The second received instructions to link each successive response word with a bizarre image. The last group was a control, which received standard free-recall instructions.

Experiment II compared a 2-second and a 5-second presentation rate to determine if there was an optimal presentation rate for learners using mnemonics. The last three experiments compared a bizarre imagery group and a verbal mediation group to ascertain whether these groups would perform differently on a negative transfer paradigm, a high interference or a mediation list, and word tests of varying degrees of abstractness.

The results of all five experiments yield several main findings. The groups receiving peg words and the group instructed to link successive items of the list with a bizarre image performed better than the control group given standard free-recall instructions. However, both rehearsal and instructions to use bizarre images had no additional effect on performance when compared to unrehearsed common images. When groups receiving instructions to link the peg and response words by either verbal mediation or by bizarre imagery were compared, no differences in recall scores were found for any of the experimental conditions described for Experiments III–V. A significant interaction was obtained between instructions and presentation rate

(Experiment II). The group told to use peg words and bizarre imagery performed significantly better than the standard free-recall control group at a 5-second presentation rate than at a 2-second presentation rate. In addition, although most of the experimental conditions involved only one trial, for those studies involving more than one trial, students given peg words tended to show an improvement with practice whereas those who were not given peg words did not.

Rohwer (1966) investigated verbal context as an aid to paired-associate learning in sixth grade students. The variables of meaningfulness, syntactic structure, and the semantic constraint imposed by a specific verbal context on the response member of a word pair were examined. Four sets of eight paired-associates each were constructed, two for pretraining and two for the learning task. The design included 14 different conditions. Of the 14 groups, 12 received pretraining in which the three variables of interest were manipulated and the last 2 groups served as controls. Results indicated that sentence pretraining groups that saw the words embedded in verbal strings learned the materials significantly faster than the control group.

Rohwer and his colleagues have used the paired-associate paradigm to expand on studies of elaboration in children (Rohwer, 1966, 1970; Rohwer & Levin, 1968; Rohwer & Lynch, 1967; Rohwer, Lynch, Levin, & Suzuki, 1967a: Rohwer, Lynch, Suzuki, & Levin, 1967b; Rohwer, Shuell, & Levin, 1967c). Typically, in these experiments, a series of noun pairs is presented to grade school children in either written, pictorial, or aural form. Whereas the control groups are only exposed to the word pairs, the experimental groups receive an elaborated form of the pairs with either a sentence or an integrated image (picture). In general, the groups receiving elaboration aids have significantly higher posttest scores than their respective control group.

For example, in one experiment Rohwer et al. (1967b) investigated the use of verbal and pictorial elaborators in facilitating paired-associate learning in grade school children. All students were asked to learn a list of 24 pictures of pairs of objects by a pairing-test method. There were three types of pictorial representations: coincidental, locational, or actional; and four types of verbalization: naming control, conjunction string, preposition string, and verb string. The results indicated that both visual and verbal elaborators facilitated performance equally well when compared to a naming-only control group.

The results of these studies lend support to the contention that learning efficiency is increased when students are instructed in the use of an elaborational skill. In addition, experimenters began to investigate other variables that might also affect a student's ability to learn.

Training and Transfer Studies

Many modern information-processing theorists believe that the interactions of an individual's cognitive structures and processes with incoming information result in the acquisition, retention, and retrieval of the information (Craik & Lockhart, 1972;

Craik & Tulving, 1975; Melton & Martin, 1972; Montague, 1972; Moscovitz & Craik, 1976; Rigney, 1976). Starting with the assumption that students do play an active role in controlling what and how they learn, procedures have been developed to examine the effects of mediational skills on learning and retention by instructing students in the use of such skills, presenting encodings along with the to-be-learned materials, and training. The findings of the previously discussed research on the classical mnemonic systems and their modern adaptations and derivations demonstrate that substantial increments in learning efficiency, particularly for paired-associate learning, can be produced when the learner is either instructed in the use of an elaborative mediational skill or is provided with an encoding by the experimenter. However, thus far, there is a very limited body of literature reporting results of experiments designed to investigate training and transfer effects of mediational skills. Most of the studies reported involve using normal or mildly retarded children and adolescents.

Several researchers investigating children's learning have been interested in identifying the processes or manipulations that characterize the learning act in a successful child. A few studies have been conducted to train young learners in the use of a specified mediational skill. Elaboration training to facilitate paired-associate learning was investigated by Rohwer and Ammon (1971). They divided 60 high-socioeconomic status (SES) and 60 low-SES second graders into three treatment conditions. Students in the training condition received instructions in the use of self-repetition of presented pairs, verbal labeling of pictorially presented stimuli, visualization for verbally presented stimuli, and the generation of sentence elaborators. Students in the practice condition received instruction only in the use of self-repetition of the pairs, and students in the control condition participated only in the posttesting sessions. Training and practice sessions were administered for 20–30 minutes on 5 successive school days. Posttesting sessions were conducted during the following school week. All students were required to learn a list of 25 noun pairs presented aurally and a mixed list of 25 noun pairs presented both aurally and visually.

Elaboration training was found to be differentially effective for the two SES groups: High-SES students in the training condition performed significantly better than students in the practice or control conditions on the aural list, whereas low-SES students in the training conditions performed significantly better than students in the practice or control conditions on the mixed list. The authors suggested that future elaboration training research should utilize a variety of posttest tasks in an attempt to control for the possibility that training may have different effects for different subgroups.

Yuille and Catchpole (1973) developed a training technique designed to encourage children to create and utilize relational images during paired-associate learning. The students were 38 children from two kindergarten classes. Children in Group I (no training) received one study trial with pairs of objects shown side by side. Group II (interaction–no training) saw the same pairs of objects but with the pair members interacting in some way, such as a hat on a duck's head instead of merely a hat next to a duck. Group III (training) received training in the formation of interactive images before the study trial. Training consisted of showing the pairs of objects twice: first side by side and then in interactions. Instructions were then given to the children to try to think of interactions for the pairs to be presented during the study trial. Both the interaction–no-training and the training group were significantly superior to the no-training group on the immediate response recognition test, but not different from each other.

A more recent study by Yuille and Catchpole (1974) extended this research paradigm. Students participating in the same training procedures displayed significantly higher performance than nontrained students on tests of immediate, delayed, and second-learning-set memory. These results were obtained on tests of recall as well as of response recognition.

Another study of relational imagery training for paired-associate learning was conducted by Danner and Taylor (1973). The children who participated in this study were from grades one, three, and six. One group (the control group) received pictures that incorporated sets of noun triplets into an integrated scene, whereas the second group received training in creating imaginary relations between separated pictures of the noun objects (relational imagery training). Training consisted of the experimenter showing the pictures of the three objects and asking the children to incorporate them into one active or spatially contiguous scene, which was then drawn on paper. The children were then asked to describe the relations between the objects in their drawings, and their recall of two of the objects of the triplet was tested by using the third object as a recall cue. A total of three practice sets was given. A third group received a combination of the relational imagery training and the sets of noun triplets depicted in an interacting scene. Children in this group were trained to focus on the relations between the depicted objects. They were required to describe the activity portrayed in the integrated pictures provided by the experimenter. On the last two sets of triplets they were also asked to make a quick sketch of the scene from memory and to describe the relations portrayed. Once again, testing consisted of recalling two items from the triplet when cued with a picture of the remaining item.

All the children then viewed 15 experimental sets of noun triplets either separately or in an interacting picture. Recall was again prompted by showing one member of each triplet. Both training groups performed significantly better than the control group. A superiority of self-generated interacting images over experimenter-provided images was found for the sixth grades but not for the earlier grades, suggesting a possible developmental trend.

In addition to the research on normal children, a number of investigators have attempted to identify the sources of information-processing deficits in retarded youngsters. Several of these studies have also developed training methods to reduce or eliminate these deficits. Typically, studies investigating the acquisition, retention, and use of mediational skills by educable mentally retarded (EMR) children have tested recall of previously learned items (Jensen & Rohwer, 1963a) or have compared groups receiving mediational training to no-training control groups on a new but highly similar list of words (Jensen & Rohwer, 1963b; Milgram, 1967). Jensen and Rohwer (1963a) measured retention as a function of the relearning of paired-associate items to a criterion of one errorless trial. Their experimental groups did not, however, seem to benefit from the use of an elaboration strategy in which the noun pairs to be learned were embedded in sentences. In a second study (Jensen & Rohwer, 1963b), the same authors reported little or no transfer of newly acquired mediational skills to the learning of new paired-associate lists 10 days after the training session. Milgram (1967) also found no mediational transfer 1 week after his EMR students received training in the use of elaborative sentences to facilitate paired-associate learning.

Contrary to the negative results of these early studies, most recent investigations do suggest that retarded individuals can learn to use mediational skills to learn. Borkowski and Kamfonik (1972) used a three-stage chaining paradigm (A–B, B–C, A–C) to determine if students who became aware of the associative strategy during the initial learning session could transfer its use to a second learning task 2 weeks later. Postman (1968) had reported significant positive transfer when this paradigm was used with college students. Borkowski and Kamfonik divided 40 retarded adolescents into two groups: a mediational group and a control group. The mediational group was exposed to the chaining paradigm whereas the control group saw A–B, D–C, A–C lists. For both groups, the initial study materials consisted of highly associated common nouns (A and B terms) or names of colors (C words). The D words for the control condition were nouns that were commonly linked to the C words but not the A words. Three lists were used, each consisting of six word-pairs. For the second session, the authors wanted to increase the difficulty of list learning. The A terms were made adjective modifers of the B nouns, and the C terms were numbers. The control group saw D nouns associated with the C numbers. Students in the experimental group were able to employ the experimenter-provided mediation chains successfully, and the superiority of the experimental group increased from Session 1 to Session 2. However, it should be noted that these were experimenter-provided, not student-generated, mediators.

Sentence mediation training within the context of a 6-week special music program was tried by D. M. Ross (1971). Retarded students ranging in age from 6 to 10 years were divided by classroom into experimental and control groups. Early in the training, mediators were provided for the experimental group and then in later sessions the children were encouraged to create their own aids. The control group participated in a program encouraging rote learning of the materials. In both conditions, students were required to learn associations between pictorial, verbal, or motor stimuli, and between various combinations of the three types. On a series of posttests the experimental-group students performed significantly better than the control-group students. In addition, this superiority transferred to an unrelated paired-associate task. Because of the use of both experimenter-provided and student-generated, mediators in this study, it is impossible to separate the effects of these two training approaches. The confounding of these two training components in this study and much of the subsequent research makes it difficult to derive specific guidelines for a mediational skill training program.

A more recent study by Ross, Ross, and Downing (1973) extended this paradigm to determine if EMR children could acquire skill in formulating elaborative mediational links through observational learning rather than direct instruction. One group was given explicit training in the formation and use of mediational links, whereas a second group observed models formulating mediators. A control group received no mediational instructions. In this experiment, all students participated in a story and table game program during three 20-minute sessions each of 5 consecutive weeks. The paired-associate test materials were colored pictures of familiar objects. Students in the intentional training condition heard stories in which a child used conjunction, rhyming, or sentence mnemonics to remember pairs of objects or events. Each story was followed by experimenter-provided questions and a game designed to teach whatever strategy had been demonstrated in the story. In addition, these students sometimes played unrelated card or word games that provided additional practice in creating mediational links. Students in the observational learning group saw two experimenters playing the games or reading modified versions of the stories. An experimenter provided the mediational aids as the activities progressed. Later, these students were given an opportunity to play the games or hear the stories. Students in the control group heard analogous stories and played pairing games but received no direct or indirect mediational training. The paired-associate posttest task consisted of pictures of common objects. The intentional learning and observation groups performed equally well when compared to each other and significantly better than the control group.

MacMillan (1970) attempted to replicate and extend the Jensen and Rohwer (1963a) and Milgram (1967) studies using noninstitutionalized participants and thereby eliminating the possible confounding effects of personality correlates due to institutionalization that may have been included in the earlier studies. Two groups received pretraining with experimenter-provided sentences to connect the pairs of common objects presented to them. One of these groups was also provided with sentences to connect the pairs on the test list, whereas the other group received no elaborators during testing. The control group saw the same object pairs but never received any pretraining or mediators. The results indicated that the group receiving experimenter-provided elaborators during training and testing outperformed the control group and the group receiving mediators during the training phase only. However, the training-only group did perform significantly better than the control group. The difference between the two experimental groups could depend upon the small number of pairs used during pretraining. It is doubtful that pretraining on just two word-pairs was sufficient practice to bring the pretraining-only participants' performance to the same level as that of the participants in the experimenter-provided mediational group, which received elaborators during pretraining and testing.

In another study designed to promote transfer of verbal elaborative training, Turnure and Thurlow (1973) exposed 42 EMR children to one, two, or no elaboration experiences and then presented them with a standard paired-associate task. The stimuli were always pairs of colored pictures of common objects. Two-sentence elaborators were constructed for each pair; half the pairs were elaborated with a semantic paragraph (both stimulus and response items occurred in the first sentence) and half with a syntactic paragraph (stimulus items occurred in the first sentence and the response items in the second). The children receiving one elaboration training experience did not perform significantly differently than those receiving no elaboration experience. But children receiving two training sessions did display significant positive transfer on test lists with experimenter-provided mediators. These data suggest that additional practice in using mediational skills is an important component of an effective training program.

Wanschura and Borkowski (1974) also investigated the development and transfer of elaboration skills in EMR children using experimenter-provided mediational aids. All the children studied three paired-associate lists. Those in the 100% aid group were supplied with prepositional mediators (presented visually, verbally, or in combination) for all pairs, whereas those in the 50% aid group received mediators for half the pairs. The children in the control group received no mediational aids. A posttesting session was administered to all groups participants 2 weeks after the training session. A new paired-associate list was used and no mediators were supplied to any of the groups. Results indicated that although the 50% aid group did not perform significantly better than the control group the 100% aid group was superior. It was hypothesized that the inconsistent presentation of pairs in the 50% aid group may have contributed to the poor utilization of the mediation strategy by students in that group.

The results of these training studies suggest the need for research concerning the training of cognitive processes that govern the selection or creation of appropriate strategies to be used with a variety of learning needs. In addition, the failure of studies that supply the training on the same day or 1 day prior to testing (Jensen & Rohwer, 1963b; Milgram, 1967) suggest that the training interval may also be an important variable. Stoff and Engle (1971) suggest that learning skills require training over time—not simple exposure. Like any skill, it seems reasonable to conclude that mediational skill training requires practice in a variety of task situations to refine its utility. This provides the learner with a repertoire of skills that can be applied in an heuristic fashion to adapt to the requirements of any specific learning need.

ELABORATION SKILLS TRAINING

The use of elaboration as a cognitive strategy or skill implies that the learners use a symbolic construction to add meaning to information they must learn (Rohwer, 1970). For example, in a paired-associate task, this might involve forming an integrating mental image or sentence to associate the two members. When studying one or more paragraphs, elaboration could involve the drawing of inferences or implications. Alternatively, the learner could relate the material to previous knowledge either directly or by analogy. A common goal for each of these procedures is to make the new information more meaningful by forming a relationship between the new and unfamiliar material and the old, already-learned information.

If the use of elaboration is truly a cognitive skill, then it is reasonable to speculate that a learner acquiring or refining such skills would require practice and feedback spread over time and involving a variety of cognitive skills as well as a variety of stimulus and task dimensions.

A study performed by Weinstein (1975) was designed to investigate the effects of a diversified elaboration-skill training program upon the learning and retention efficiency of ninth graders. A variety of cognitive skills, learning task typologies, and stimulus materials were selected to provide the learners with guided practice in the use of elaborative mediational skills. Unlike previous studies, a variety of cognitive strategies, including sentence elaboration, imaginal elaboration, analogies, drawing implications, creating relationships, and paraphrasing were included in the training. In addition, learning tasks ranged from simple paired-associates and free recall to reading comprehension. Stimulus materials were drawn from various curriculum areas.

A total of 75 students were selected from the ninth grade population of the Austin Independent School District in Austin, Texas. These students were selected by the school personnel with the only restriction being that they were at or above the midrange of ninth grade reading ability as defined by the Nelson–Denny Reading Test (Brown, Nelson, & Denny, 1973). In addition approximately half were male and half female.

Overview of the Research Design

The study was conducted over a 10-week interval. Participants were randomly assigned to one of three conditions: (a) the experimental (training) group, (b) the control group, or (c) the posttest-only group. The students in the experimental group attended five training sessions followed by two testing sessions. Students in the control group also attended the first five training sessions but were only exposed to the training materials. They received no instructions or directions as to how the information they were studying could be learned. During Weeks 6 and 10 these students were also administered the posttests. The posttest-only group did not meet at all during the first 5 weeks of the study, and thus were not exposed to the training materials or the training directions. They did, however, complete the posttests during Weeks 6 and 10.

Task Materials

Nineteen readings were selected or created after consultation with the staff of the Textbook Library Collection and of the school library at the University of Texas at Austin. Several considerations guided selection of the materials: First, it was necessary that they be appropriate for the target population and use a simple vocabulary and sentence structure so that readability would not become a serious problem. Second, in an attempt to foster generalization of the use of an elaboration learning-strategy, a variety of subject matter contents and task typographies was needed. However, an emphasis was placed on materials and tasks requiring memorization. The content areas represented included astronomy, biology, English, history, and vocational education. The elaboration tasks selected included such diverse activities as the serial memorization of a list of nine planets, distinguishing the arteries from the veins, learning the meaning of road signs, recalling phone numbers, and relating a passage about Sam Houston to their own value system. Each of the 19 learning tasks was typed on a separate sheet of paper. A packet containing the task sheets, scrap paper, and penicils was created for each student.

Task Administration

A series of seven 45-minute sessions was scheduled for administration of the experiment. Students met in groups of three to seven for each session. For the experimental group, the first session consisted of a 10-minute orientation and the presentation of the first three elaboration tasks, which required about 10 minutes each. The second through the fifth sessions were for the administration of the remaining tasks, at a rate of four per session.

The students in the experimental (training) condition were required to create a series of elaborators or mediational aids for each of the 19 learning tasks. Experimenter-provided directions for the early tasks emphasized the properties of effective elaborators. Once all the students indicated that they understood the task, they were asked to work on their own and told to begin. The experimenter met with each student to discuss the individual's "aids" and provide supportive and directive feedback. For example, if a student was having difficulty creating an aid the experimenter would agree that the task was difficult and provide a simple example for the student to work on. Or, if a student was engaging in an inappropriate activity, such as rewriting the material instead of creating elaborators, the experimenter would paraphrase the original instructions and provide additional examples. Successful students were complimented on their work and encouraged to produce additional aids.

As the sessions progressed, the experimenter provided less direction and fewer examples or suggestions. During the final training session no directions or guidance were provided.

The control group was exposed to the same stimulus materials as the training group, but they were told to simply learn the information. They were not given any additional directions or strategy prompts. A series of immediate posttests was administered to both the experimental and control groups, as well as the posttest-only group, during the sixth session. The seventh session, a delayed posttest, occurred approximately 1 month after the sixth session.

Samples of Training Materials

The following three samples were selected from the training materials to demonstrate the types of tasks used as well as the experimenter-provided directions emphasizing the properties of effective elaborators. In these particular examples the students were asked to use imagery, comparisons, analogies, phrase and sentence mediation, as well as stories or themes, to make the new information more meaningful or memorable.

READING 1

How Do the Arteries Differ from the Veins?

Arteries and veins are both hollow tubes through which the blood flows. The two differ, however, in three important respects. The work of an artery, first of all, is to carry blood rich in oxygen from the heart to the various organs of the body. The work of a vein, on the other hand, is to return to the heart blood laden with carbon dioxide. In structure, too, veins and arteries differ markedly. Although the walls of both are composed of three coats of tissue, the veins are thinner than the arteries and less elastic. A third point of difference is the way the blood moves within the two types of vessels. Propelled by the force of the heartbeat, the blood rushes through the arteries, which expand and contract to push it forward in spurts. In the veins, however, the blood flows slowly and smoothly. [Source: Tressler and Christ (1960).]

Directions. I want you to learn the information contined in this paragraph and, most important, I want you to develop learning aids to study this information. You must learn to distinguish between the veins and the arteries. For example, the veins are thinner than the arteries. To help you remember this fact you might try to form a picture in your mind of a thin hollow tube when you think of a vein. Or you might make up a sentence or story which would associate a vein with a thin tube such as the vain woman was thin as a rubber tube. Although the word vain in this sentence is not the same as the word vein meaning a structure in the body it could still help you to learn this property of veins.

Concentrating on pictures or images we form in our minds can be a powerful aid to our memory; so can forming sentences or little stories which help us to remember information we must learn. These are both different ways of trying to make new or unfamiliar material more meaningful to us so that it will be easier to learn.

You can also try to relate the information contained in the reading to something else you already know. Then try to figure out as many ways as you can that the two are related or similar. For example, a vein is like a thin rubber water pipe. Both are thin tubes, relatively rigid and have fluid going through them.

I would like each of you to read this passage carefully and try to create some learning aids that you think will help you to learn the different properties of arteries and veins.

Any questions?

Please write your ideas down so I will be able to look at them with you.

READING 2

Home Economics Shopping List

Crackers
Tomatoes
Chicken
Pickles
Soup
Lettuce
Tea
Mustard
Ice
Bread
Salt

Directions. *This is a shopping list for a home economics class. Imagine you are in the class and you must remember this list when you get to the grocery store. Assuming you cannot take the list with you, how could you remember it? The order is not important but you must remember all of the items.*

In learning a list of items it is helpful for a student to have some way of associating all of the items in the list. One way to do this is to create a little scene or story that would include each of the items. For example, to remember a list of school supplies such as pencil, paper, and textbook, you might imagine a student reading a textbook and using her pencil to take notes. Remembering the image or story would help you to remember the acticles on the list. Making up a story is one way to help someone learn this list. See how many different learning aids you can create that would help you. Remember, you do not have to remember the items in order, but you must remember all of them.

Also notice that for different materials some types of aids are better than others. Try to come up with stories or images that would help you to connect all the words so that if you forget one of them the logic or theme of the story could help you to remember it.

Any questions?

Pleast write your ideas down so that I will be able to look at them with you.

READING 3

Know These Signs by Their Shapes So That
You Will Know What to Do at a Distance

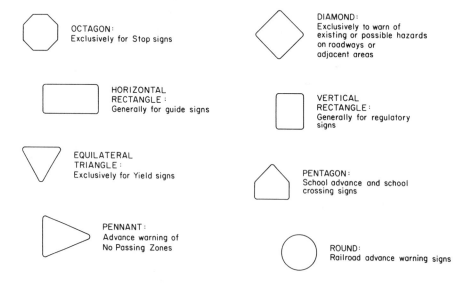

OCTAGON:
Exclusively for Stop signs

DIAMOND:
Exclusively to warn of existing or possible hazards on roadways or adjacent areas

HORIZONTAL RECTANGLE:
Generally for guide signs

VERTICAL RECTANGLE:
Generally for regulatory signs

EQUILATERAL TRIANGLE:
Exclusively for Yield signs

PENTAGON:
School advance and school crossing signs

PENNANT:
Advance warning of No Passing Zones

ROUND:
Railroad advance warning signs

Directions. *All driver education students must learn the meanings of the different shapes used for road signs. I would like each of you to try to create learning aids that would assist a student in relating the sign shapes to their meanings. For example, a sign with a round shape warns the driver that there are railroad tracks up ahead. A student trying to learn this might concentrate on associating the round sign with the round wheels of a train. He could make up a sentence like "the wheels of a train go round and round" or he could concentrate on an image of round train wheels when he looks at the sign shape.*

To help you learn the meanings of the different shapes, I would like each of you to try to devise ways of relating these sign shapes to their meanings. Remember the examples we have discussed before, using images, phrases, sentences, and stories.

Any questions?

Please write your ideas down so I will be able to look at them with you.

Test Materials

Although the training materials were selected from common classroom and everyday tasks, the testing materials were selected from laboratory-type tasks. The greater degree of control provided by these methodologies allowed for a clearer comparison of the learning proficiency among the three groups on the transfer tasks.

All students were tested on paired-associate, free recall, serial learning, and reading comprehension tasks. To construct the word lists needed for the test, a total of 154 words were selected from the norms published by Paivio, Yuille, and Madigan (1968). These norms provide the concreteness, imagery and meaningfulness values for 925 nouns, as well as the corresponding Thorndike–Lorge frequencies. The items chosen for this study were moderately concrete and meaningful with average concreteness ratings in the range 3.00–5.50 on a 7-point scale and meaningfulness values in the range 4.75–6.75. The meaningfulness values are the average number of associates given in a 1-minute period. Words were selected randomly from this pool to construct the paired-associate, free recall, and serial recall lists.

The reading comprehension passages and questions were selected from the California Reading Test, Form AA (Tiegs & Clark, 1950a) and Form BB (Tiegs & Clark, 1950b).

Test Procedures

Students were tested in groups of 8–14, and each student performed the tasks in the following sequence: (*a*) free recall, (*b*) serial recall, (*c*) paired-associate learning, and (*d*) reading comprehension. Every student was required to perform each of these tasks during both the immediate and the delayed posttests.

Free Recall

A list of 20 words was presented one at a time on a Da-Lite screen. The presentation rate was 6 seconds per word. Following this learners had 2 minutes in which to write down as many of the items as they could recall without regard to order.

Serial Recall

A list of 16 words was presented one at a time on a Da-Lite screen. The presentation rate was 6 seconds per word. Following this were two test-trials during which the words were presented again in the same order. The learners were asked to write each word on the blank side of an IBM card before it appeared on the screen. Again, the presentation rate was 6 seconds per word.

Paired-Associate Learning

A list of 21 word pairs was presented one at a time on a Da-Lite screen. The study–test method was used with 8-second exposures of each pair for the study portion and 8-second exposures of each stimulus for the test portion. Two complete trials were given to each learner.

Reading Comprehension

Each student was given a typewritten copy of a reading selection, and had 3 minutes to study the passage. Following this, a sheet of questions was distributed The students then had 3 minutes in which to answer six questions about the reading. The process was then repeated with a second reading assignment and an 8-question test.

Results

The data from the immediate posttest revealed no significant differences between the means of the experimental, control, and posttest-only groups on the reading comprehension or serial recall measures. The results of the data analyses for the free-recall measure did reveal a significant performance difference in favor of the training group when compared to a combination of the control and posttest-only groups. The paired-associate learning data analyses also revealed a significant performance difference favoring the experimental group but only for the Trial 2 data.

The delayed posttest data analyses revealed significant performance differences on the reading comprehension and Trial 1 of the serial learning tasks. Again, these differences favored the experimental group over a combination of the control and posttest-only groups. All other comparisons failed to reach significance, but it should be noted that in all comparisons involving the experimental group, on both the immediate and the delayed posttests, the direction of the differences between the means favored the experimental group. The consistency of this finding is encouraging, although the fact that many comparisons did not reach significance is disappointing.

Previous research had indicated that cognitive mediational skills could be taught to naive learners. However, the narrow definition of these skills imposed by the restricted task and stimulus dimensions used in these studies limited their usefulness in developing generalizable elaboration skills.

The study by Weinstein (1975) provided evidence that a generalizable learning strategy program could be developed and implemented in an educational or training environment. The successful development of a program to teach organizational cognitive strategies will provide the individual learner with a set of heuristic procedures that can be used to maximize the acquisition, retention, and retrieval out-comes of any learning act.

If the systematic learning of cognitive skills is to become an integral part of classroom instruction, further research in this area is needed. First, it will have to be demonstrated that positive transfer can definitely result from a generalized skill-training program. From the experience gained in conducting the dissertation study, it appears that several variables must be investigated, such as the types of training materials and tasks to be used, sequencing of tasks by difficulty and complexity, length of training, individual differences in mediation skill acquisition, and appro-priate postexperimental evaluation techniques.

THE COGNITIVE LEARNING STRATEGIES PROJECT

A number of these variables are being investigated as part of the Cognitive Learning Strategies Project at the University of Texas at Austin. This research and development effort involves a series of interdependent projects designed to define further the covert processes involved in utilizing cognitive elaboration skills as well as the procedures necessary to train an individual in their use. The ultimate goal is to design and field test a program to teach cognitive strategies to one or more of the following target populations: high school students, college freshmen entering a university on a probationary status due to poor prior academic performance, or trainees in an armed services technical training setting. The final product will be a function of both the previous research by Weinstein (1975) and the data gathered during the course of the research effort discussed here, which is still in its early stages.

Although many educators and psychologists agree that successful learners use a variety of effective elaboration strategies to organize and execute any particular learning act, the types and essential components of these strategies have not been systematically identified or classified. Previous research on the training of cognitive strategies has been based on the experimenter's conjecture about what constitutes an effective cognitive strategy rather than on broad-based evidence gathered from a large number of successful learners. Dansereau, Long, McDonald, Actkinson, Ellis, Collins, Williams, and Evans (1975) did develop an assessment instrument to determine a learner's use of certain study skills and some specific cognitive strategies, but the emphasis was not on elabora-tion strategies. (For a more detailed description, see Chapter 1 of this volume.) The initial stage of this project involves conducting several exploratory studies to ascer-tain the types of elaboration learning strategies utilized by learners in an academic or training environment.

Interview Study

The first portion of this study utilized the semistructured interview as a research vehicle. The sessions were conducted around a core of structured questions from which the interviewer could diverge to probe for underlying factors or relationships, developmental history, or more specific factual information.

The participants were 72 undergraduate students in a teacher education course at the University of Texas at Austin. The students were given five learning tasks to perform and then asked to identify and explain the kinds of methods, strategies, processes, or "mental tricks" they used to learn the materials. They were also asked to suggest any other strategies they thought might be useful. The learning tasks included paired-associates, free recall, and reading comprehension.

All students were randomly assigned to one of three groups. In order to gather data about a wide range of learning materials, each group received two different paired-associate lists, two different free-recall lists, and one reading. The paired-associate lists included a list of names paired with phone numbers, a list of dates paired with events, a list of high-imagery words, a list of low-imagery words, a list of high-meaningfulness words, and a list of low-meaningfulness words. The free-recall lists included a highly structured grocery list, a list of random words, a list of words from several different categories, a list of things around the home, a hierarchical list of animal names and categories, and a high-meaningful list of words. The readings included a first-aid guide to poisons, a discussion of conformity, and an old Eskimo tale about a war between ghosts.

As the students studied the task materials, they were asked to write down any of their learning methods or strategies. The interviewer then discussed, in as much detail as possible, the specific use or application of each method identified.

For example, if a student identified a strategy that could be called mental imagery by saying something like "I see it in my head" or "I just picture it or think about it," the interviewer would follow up on the statement by requesting a concrete description of the image and of the process by which it was formed. Detailed descriptions were requested whenever sufficient information was not spontaneously provided.

A careful examination of the student's protocols indicated that they used about seven different learning methods. One method involved using study skills, practicing, or production. This involved either rereading the material several times or rewriting it as well as taking notes, underlining key ideas, and periodic reviews. Another method, physical word similarities and differences, included looking at common patterns in the spelling of two or more words or counting the number of syllables. Several methods, such as the use of abbreviations or acronyms, or abstracting the main ideas involved selecting a part of the words or reading to study. Using mental images to relate the words or make ideas more salient was another method. A major technique of particular interest to us was creating some meaningful elaboration of the material. This included such methods as relating the words or ideas to the students' previous experience, knowledge, or attitudes, and attempting to think about the logical relations in the stimulus materials. Creating a phrase or sentence relating the words or paraphrasing the major ideas was another popular strategy. On the free-recall lists, categorization was frequently cited.

Questionnaire

A second study involves creating and administering a questionnaire about the use of learning strategies. This research questionnaire is designed to provide more specific information from a large number of individuals concerning their knowledge about learning strategies and how they use them.

This instrument, the Learning Activities Questionnaire, has three major sections. In Part I the participants study seven different materials to be learned: three paired-associate tasks, two free-recall tasks, and two readings. These materials were selected from the tasks used in the interview study. The specific activities selected were the ones that elicited the greatest range of different learning methods in the interview study.

After studying each set of materials the learners answer a series of questions about the ways, methods, or "mental tricks" they would use to help them learn, or remember, the materials. For each method identified, the individual is asked:

How did you learn to use this method?
How old were you when you first learned to use this method?
In what way, or ways, do you think it helps you to learn?
Do you use this method for other learning activities?
If yes, what kinds of activities?
How often do you use this method?
Any additional comments?

In Part II the respondents are asked to look again at the seven learning materials but are asked simply to check the examples of methods they would use to learn the materials. The methods and examples provided were derived from the data of the interview study. For example, after studying materials six and seven, the reading tasks, the learners must select methods and examples from the following list:

Method 1.   Using Study Skills, Practice or Production
_____ A. Read the material over several times.
_____ B. Underline key ideas or words.
_____ C. Take notes.
_____ D. Summarize the material.
_____ E. Summarize by paragraph or section
_____ F. List major words or ideas.
_____ G. Rewrite it.
_____ H. Paraphrase; that is, write the information in your own words.
_____ I. Review to check your understanding.
_____ J. Ask yourself questions.
_____ K. Draw pictures or cartoons relating to the material.
_____ L. Create an outline.

Method 2.   Selecting Parts of the Reading
_____ A. Select out the main ideas.
_____ B. Select out the key words or terms.
_____ C. Select out the action phrases.
_____ D. Select out the characters.

Method 3. Using "Pictures" in your Mind or Mental Images
_____ A. Picture the main ideas or information.
_____ B. Picture examples.
_____ C. Picture a story.
_____ D. "See" and "hear" the events in your mind.

Method 4. Meaningful Elaboration of the Material
NOTE: Please try to think of an example of how you would use this method. If you can't, it's OK.
Check the Method anyway.
_____ A. Think about the purpose or need for the material.
Example:

_____ B. Relate it to your experience or characteristics.
Example:

_____ C. Relate it to your beliefs or attitudes.
Example:

_____ D. Think about your emotional reactions to the content.
Example:

_____ E. Relate it to people in general.
Example:

_____ F. Think about the ideas that you have as you read it.
Example:

_____ G. Think about other people's reactions to the content or ideas.
Example:

_____ H. Relate it to what you already know.
Example:

_____ I. "Free associate" to the topic or ideas, that is, just think about the topic or ideas and
see what comes to your mind.
Example:

_____ J. Think about the implications, or effect, of what the material is saying.
Example:

_____ K. Look for common sense or logical relationships in the material.
Example:

_____ L. Relate the content to the theme.
Example:

_____ M. Relate key words or concepts to ideas.
Example:

_____ N. Discussion with other people.
Example:

Other
Please write down any other methods or comments you have. Also write down any combinations you
make of two or more methods. (Feel free to use the back of this page if you need more room.)

Part III is an attempt to identify any additional methods the learners might use. They are again asked a series of questions about any other methods they might use to learn or remember information in textbooks, novels, newspapers, magazines, work materials, or any other activities.

The Learning Activities Questionnaire has been extensively field tested and revised. It has already been administered to groups of community college, undergraduate and graduate students, several categories of Army recruits, junior college students in a vocational training program, and several other populations. The data derived from using this questionnaire are being used to identify promising variables for further research as well as to provide frequency of usage data for identified strategies across different learner populations.

Results thus far indicate that more successful learners, and those with more years of schooling, use meaningful elaboration strategies in preference to the more rote, or superficial, strategies. For example, Army recruits with no high school experience, or a GED equivalency diploma, report using rote repetition as their major learning strategy, whereas second- and third-year undergraduate college students report meaningful elaboration and other more active processing strategies. Ongoing efforts at the University of Texas at Austin are focused on the development and evaluation of elaboration strategies instructional materials based on our previous findings.

THE FUTURE

Research efforts like the ones reported in this volume are creating new and challenging assumptions about learners. We are moving toward—via what Dember (1974) calls the "cognitive revolution" in psychology—a model of the learner as an active, self-determining individual who processes information in complex, often idiosyncratic ways that can rarely be predicted entirely in advance, represented in simple formulas, or wholly captured in conventional laboratory learning experiments, and who learns through active use of complex learning or cognitive strategies that must be well in hand **before** he or she confronts a new learning task. Learners are seen as always and essentially **active** interpreters, processors, synthesizers of a continual barrage of information from the outside environment and from their own thinking processes. Thus, it becomes possible to focus analysis and research on the learner's ability to develop and utilize effective intellectual skills.

These new concepts of learning activities reduce the hope of finding or inventing scientifically based teaching methods, materials, or curricula that will routinely and automatically produce effective learning in students or trainees. But it opens the possibility of developing means to teach learners active cognitive strategies which, if adopted, may enable them to learn well and perform adequately in most learning or training situations.

Such means would move the learning of cognitive skills out of the realm of chance and place them under the systematic control of the individual learner.

REFERENCES

Borkowski, J. G., & Kamfonik, A. Verbal mediation in moderately retarded children: Effects of successive mediational experiences. *American Journal of Mental Deficiency,* 1972, *77,* 157–162.

Bousfield, W. A. The occurrence of clustering in the recall of randomly arranged associates. *Journal of General Psychology,* 1953, *49,* 229–240.

Bower, G. H. Analysis of a mnemonic device. *American Psychologist,* 1970, *58,* 496–510.

Brown, J. I., Nelson, M. J., & Denny, E. C. *Nelson Denny Reading Test.* Boston: Houghton, 1973.

Craik, F. I. M., & Lockhart, R. S. Levels of processing: A framework for memory research. *Journal of Verbal Learning and Verbal Behavior,* 1972, *11,* 671–684.

Craik, F. I. M., & Tulving, E. Depth of processing and the retention of words in episodic memory. *Journal of Experimental Psychology: General,* 1975, *104,* 268–294.

Danner, F. W., & Taylor, A. M. Integrated pictures and relational imagery training in children's learning. *Journal of Experimental Child Psychology,* 1973, *16,* 47–54.

Dansereau, D. F., Long, G. L., McDonald, B. A., Actkinson, T. R., Ellis, A. M., Collins, K., Williams, S., & Evans, S. H. *Effective learning strategy training program: Development and assessment* (Tech. Rep. AFHRL-TR-75-41). Brooks Air Force Base, Tex. Air Force Human Resources Laboratory, June 1975.

Dember, W. N. Motivation and the cognitive revolution. *American Psychologist,* 1974, *29,* 161–168.

Gagné, R. M., & Briggs, L. J. *Principles of instructional design.* New York: Holt, 1974.

Jensen, A. R., & Rohwer, W. D., Jr. The effect of verbal mediation learning and retention of paired-associates by retarded adults. *American Journal of Mental Deficiency,* 1963, *68,* 80–84. (a)

Jensen, A. R., & Rohwer, W. D., Jr. Verbal mediation in paired-associate and serial learning. *Journal of Verbal Learning and Verbal Behavior,* 1963, *1,* 346–352. (b)

Lorayne, H. & Lucas, J. *The memory book,* New York: Stein & Day, 1974.

MacMillan, D. L. Facilitative effect of verbal mediation on paired-associate learning by EMR children. *American Journal of Mental Deficiency,* 1970, *74,* 611–615.

Melton, A. W., & Martin, E. (Eds.). *Coding processes in human memory.* Washington, D.C.: Winston, 1972.

Milgram, N. A. Verbal context versus visual compound in paired-associate learning by children. *Journal of Experimental Child Psychology,* 1967, *5,* 597–603.

Miller, G. A. Magical number 7, plus or minus two: Some limits on our capacity for processing information. *Psychological Review,* 1956, *63,* 81–97.

Miller, G. A., Galanter, E., & Pribram, K. *Plans and the structure of behavior.* New York: Holt, 1960.

Montague, W. E. Elaborative strategies in verbal learning and memory. In G. H. Bower (Ed)., *The psychology of learning and motivation: Advances in research and theory* (Vol. 6). New York: Academic Press, 1972.

Moscovitch, M., & Craik, F. I. M. Depth of processing, retrieval cues, and uniqueness of encoding as factors in recall. *Journal of Verbal Learning and Verbal Behavior,* 1976, *15,* 447–458.

Norman, D. A. *Memory and attention.* New York: Wiley, 1969.

Paivio, A. *Imagery and verbal processes.* New York: Holt, 1971.

Paivio, A., Yuille, J. C., & Madigan, S. Concreteness, imagery, and meaningfulness values for 925 nouns. *Journal of Experimental Psychology,* 1968, *79,* 509–514.

Posner, M. I. Abstraction and the process of recognition. In G. H. Bower & J. T. Spence (Eds.), *The psychology of learning and motivation: Advances in research and theory* (Vol. 3). New York: Academic Press, 1969.

Postman, L. Studies of learning to learn: VI. General transfer effects in three-stage mediation. *Journal of Verbal Learning and Verbal Behavior,* 1968, *7,* 659–664.

Rigney, J. W. *On cognitive strategies for facilitating acquisition, retention, and retrieval in training and education* (Tech. Rep. No. 78). Los Angeles: University of Southern California, Department of Psychology, May 1976.

Rohwer, W. D., Jr. Constraints, syntax and meaning in paired-associate learning. *Journal of Verbal Learning and Verbal Behavior,* 1966, *5,* 541–547.

Rohwer, W. D., Jr. Images and pictures in children's learning. *Psychological Bulletin*, 1970, *73*, 393–403.

Rohwer, W. D., Jr., & Ammon, M. S. Elaboration training and paired-associate learning efficiency in children. *Journal of Educational Psychology*, 1971, *62*, 376–383.

Rohwer, W. D., Jr., & Levin, J. R. Elaboration preferences and differences in learning proficiency. In J. Hellmuth (Ed.), *Cognitive studies: Deficits in cognition* (Vol. 2), New York: Brunner-Mazel, 1968.

Rohwer, W. D., Jr., & Lynch, S. Form class and intralist similarity in paired-associate learning. *Journal of Verbal Learning and Verbal Behavior* 1967, *6*, 551–554.

Rohwer, W. D., Jr., Lynch, S., Levin, J. R., & Suzuki, N. Grade level, school strata, and learning efficiency. *Journal of Educational Psychology*, 1967, *59*, 26–31. (a)

Rohwer, W. D., Jr., Lynch, S., Suzuki, N., & Levin, J. R. Verbal and pictorial facilitation of paired-associate learning. *Journal of Experimental Child Psychology*, 1967, *5*, 294–302. (b)

Rohwer, W. D., Jr., Shuell, T. J., & Levin, J. R. Context effects in the initial storage and retrieval of noun pairs. *Journal of Verbal Learning and Verbal Behavior*, 1967, *6*, 796–801. (c)

Ross, D. M. Retention and transfer of mediation set in paired-associate learning of educable retarded children. *Journal of Educational Psychology*, 1971, *62*, 323–327.

Ross, D. M., Ross, S. A., & Downing, M. L. Intentional training versus observational learning of mediational strategies in EMR children. *American Journal of Mental Deficiency*, 1973, *78*, 292–299.

Ross, J., & Lawrence, K. A. Some observations on memory artifice. *Psychonomic Science*, 1968, *13* 107–108.

Stoff, D. M., & Engle, M. N. The relationship among reported strategies, presentation rate, and verbal ability and their affects on free recall learning. *Journal of Experimental Psychology*, 1971, *87*, 423–428.

Tiegs, E. W., & Clark, W. W. *California Reading Test: Form AA*. Los Angeles: California Test Bureau, 1950. (a)

Tiegs, E. W. & Clark, W. W. *California Reading Test: Form BB*. Los Angeles: California Test Bureau, 1950. (b)

Tressler, J. C., & Christ, H. I. *Junior English in action*. Boston: Heath, 1960.

Tulving, E. Subject organization in free recall of "unrelated" words. *Psychological Review*, 1962, *69*, 344–354.

Tulving, E. The effects of presentation and recall of material in free recall learning. *Journal of Verbal Learning and Verbal Behavior*, 1967, *6*, 175–184.

Tulving, E. Theoretical issues in free recall. In T. R. Dixon & D. L. Horton (Eds.), *Verbal behavior and general behavior theory*. Englewood Cliffs, N.J.: Prentice-Hall, 1968.

Tulving, E. & Donaldson, W. (Eds.). *Organization of memory*. New York: Academic Press, 1972.

Turnure, J. E., & Thurlow, M. L. Verbal elaboration and the promotion of transfer of training in educable mentally retarded children. *Journal of Experimental Child Psychology*, 1973, *15*, 137–148.

Underwood, B. J. Stimulus selection in verbal learning. In C. N. Cofer & B. S. Musgrave (Eds.), *Verbal behavior and learning*. New York: McGraw-Hill, 1963.

Underwood, B. J. Attributes of memory. *Psychological Review*, 1969, *16*, 559–573.

Wanschura, P. B., & Borkowski, J. G. Development and transfer of mediational strategies by retarded children in paired-associate learning. *American Journal of Mental Deficiency*, 1974, *78*, 631–639.

Weinstein, C. E. *Learning of elaboration strategies*. Unpublished doctoral dissertation, University of Texas at Austin, 1975.

Wood, G. Mnemonic systems in recall. *Journal of Educational Psychology*, 1967, *58*(6), 1–27.

Yates, F. A. *The art of memory*. Chicago: University of Chicago Press, 1966.

Yuille, J. C., & Catchpole, M. J. Associative learning and imagery training in children. *Journal of Experimental Child Psychology*, 1973, *16*, 403–412.

Yuille, J. C. & Catchpole, M. J. The effects of delay and imagery training on the recall and recognition of object pairs. *Journal of Experimental Child Psychology*, 1974, *17*, 474–481.

3

Behavior Modification and Learning Strategies[1]

FRANK RICHARDSON

The thesis of this chapter is that there are ideas and methods in the fields of contemporary behavior modification and clinical behavior therapy that can contribute substantially to the development of learning strategies. The first part of this chapter presents some background concerning behavior modification and behavior therapy techniques and their rationalizations in theory. The second section explores behavior therapy approaches to teaching skills in managing anxiety, and discusses their potential for inclusion in a learning strategies curriculum. The final section examines behavioral techniques for self-assessment or self-monitoring in a similar manner.

From the type of cognitive social-learning theory perspective presented in this chapter, counseling and behavior-change activities of all sorts are viewed primarily as the teaching of active self-management strategies for coping with problems of living. Most of these strategies have a heavily cognitive component—they are executed mainly **between** the stimulus and the response. There appear to me to be profound similarities, and perhaps some identities, between what are beginning to be conceptualized as learning strategies and the coping strategies taught in clinical contexts. Both kinds of strategies have at their core the teaching of skills in the active self-management and self-direction of cognitive processes in order to produce a behavioral result. Some of these coping strategies may come usefully to form an essential part of a learning strategies curriculum. Examination of coping strategies and processes may illuminate the nature and workings of learning strategies. Consideration of how behavior therapists and modifiers conceptualize the behavior change process and how specifically they teach or train coping strategies may

[1]Preparation of this chapter was supported in part by the Defense Advanced Research Projects Agency. Views and conclusions contained in this document are those of the author and should not be interpreted as necessarily representing the official policies, either expressed or implied, of the Defense Advanced Research Projects Agency or of the United States Government.

suggest ways to teach or train learning strategies more effectively (and vice versa, of course). In these and other ways, ideas about coping and learning strategies may cross-fertilize each other.

BEHAVIOR MODIFICATION:
BACKGROUND AND PERSPECTIVE

The modern field of behavior modification, having its origins in the work of such individuals as Wolpe (1958), Eysenck and Rachman (1956), and Skinner (1953) began in a very ideological and reformist manner. It began, at least in theory, as an attempt to identify laboratory-based proven principles of learning and apply them to clinical problems in a rigorous and replicable manner. Behavior modification was presumably grounded in learning theory, and extended its applications into new areas, providing additional empirical support for the theory. The fact that there were available different and often contradictory "laws" of learning to draw upon was either ignored or left to future research to resolve.

Most classical behavior modification techniques were suggested and rationalized by principles of classical conditioning or operant or instrumental learning. According to such principles, most human behavior is under the control of external environmental stimuli that impinge upon the organism from the outside. Behavior, normal or pathological, is a function of past conditioning and reinforcement influences and present reinforcement contingencies. The way to change problem behavior (or improve some performance) is to rearrange evoking stimuli or reward contingencies to produce a different desired behavioral result directly and automatically. From this perspective it may be allowed, as does Skinner, that inner experiences and cognitions exist. But such "mental way-stations" are not regarded as playing a causal role in behavior. They are epiphenomenal. Information about them does not improve predictions of behavior, nor are they of any practical significance in behavior change efforts.

Whatever its inadequacies (and they are legion), I would argue that behavior therapy has supplied a much needed corrective to the counseling and psychotherapy field by providing what might be called a *focus on behavior* as a subject matter in its own right. To quote Skinner (1953),

> The field of psychotherapy is rich in explanatory fictions. Behavior itself has not been accepted as a subject matter in its own right, but only as an indication of *something wrong somewhere else*. The task of therapy is said to be to remedy an inner illness of which the behavioral manisfestations are really "symptoms".... [This view] has encouraged the therapist to avoid specifying the behavior to be corrected or showing why it is disadvantageous or dangerous [p. 37] .

Skinner was wrong to deny the functional significance of cognition. But he was right to doubt the relevance of many abstract, static, mentalistic constructs that have made up most traditional theories of personality and behavior change—monolithic psycholigical traits and underlying personality forces that are remote from and only tenuously connected with, in either a scientific or practical sense, the everyday struggles of human beings. Skinner also steadfastly resisted physiological as well as mentalistic explanations of behavior, refusing to reduce behavior to anything other than itself, to any other kind of entity or process existing to any other level of analysis. Its laws were to be its own laws, not those of any other science.

The difficulties with Skinner's view, I believe, is not his philosophical commitment to a focus on behavior as a subject in its own right, but the fact that he focuses on only a small, in some ways quite unrepresentative part of human behavior. The bulk of human behavior, and the most characteristically human part of it, consists not of coordinating one's responses with the prevailing reinforcement contingencies in fixed environments, but of attempts to **change** current physical and social environments to make them more rewarding or to realize other kinds of goals in living. And the kind of behavior we most commonly engage in, in almost all situations, is "thinking behavior."

In order to implement a commitment to a focus on behavior we must focus largely on effective and ineffective thinking behavior. Active, purposive, more-or-less effective thinking, evaluating, fantasizing, problem-solving, worrying, etc. form a great part of manifest human behavior. It is just as real and observable as any other kind of behavior, and it can be described and modeled to the same extent as any other kind of behavior without resorting to explanatory fictions or behind-the-scenes causal entities that are not themselves part of behavior.

Behavior modification brought to the behavior change scene some new, modestly effective behavior-change techniques, a learning theory rationale that provided an aura of scientific respectability, and a sincere (not at all common) ethical commitment to careful evaluation of treatment effectiveness. No sooner had early behavior modification crystalized in this fashion, however, than new trends began to develop that have quickly revolutionized the field. The learning theory foundations of behavior modification techniques have been largely undermined and replaced by explanations that resort heavily to active cognitive and imaginal processes. Also, new, and often more effective techniques and change strategies have been developed that consist of teaching persons actively to self-direct and self-manage their own cognitive processes in order to produce desired changes in feelings and behavior.

Most behavior therapy techniques were inspired and rationalized in theory by what Mahoney (1974) calls "unmediated conditioning models" of human functioning. In such models, the "laws of behavior" relate environmental stimuli to subsequent overt responses, with little practical or theoretical interest taken in such intervening events as may occur in the black box. Such passive conditioning models have been widely discredited (Bowers, 1973), and today they are invoked in a very pragmatic spirit, with little of the ideological fervor of former times. Still, such models continue to exert a restrictive and deleterious influence on behavior modification research and programming. Partly because few clear theoretical options are available for description and explanation of behavior therapy techniques, unmediated conditioning models and language continue to hover in the background, and are often used in extended, metaphorical ways to rationalize techniques and results.

"Behavior modification" is as old as humanity, and virtually every known behavior influence technique or strategy has been employed for centuries (London, 1972). The practical effect of the contemporary fields of behavior modification and behavior therapy has been to identify these strategies clearly, separate them from ethical and religious considerations, refine and systematize them, and begin to evaluate their effectiveness scientifically. Some writers, such as London (1972) and Lazarus (1971), have announced an "end of ideology" in the behavior modification field, and have tried to inaugurate an era of "technical eclecticism," in which a practical science of behavior change would be built up by collecting and organizing techniques that work. This line of thought is naive and unworkable in attempting to dispense entirely with theory and espouse of a kind of radical pragmatism. Some theory of human functioning is implicit in all our efforts to devise and refine behavior-influence techniques, and some value commitment is implicit in our choice of the ends toward which we choose to influence our own or others' behavior. But technical eclecticism is constructive in its attempt to free the rich panoply of behavior modification techniques from outmoded forms of behavioristic theorizing.

Although their inadequacies have long been apparent and noted by many writers, scientists, and philosophers (e.g., Scriven, 1973), it appears that the back of passive models of human functioning may finally be broken once and for all by what Dember (1974) calls the "cognitive revolution" in psychology. The cognitive revolution holds that the individual is always and inherently active in interpretating, processing, and synthesizing a continual barrage of information from internal and external environments. Every input, every form of contact with the environment, is actively interpreted and managed by the person in some manner, more-or-less accurately, and actively utilized, more-or-less effectively, in the guidance of subsequent behavior.

The fields of behavior therapy and behavior modification have recently undergone their own cognitive revolution. In the following sections we shall see how the increasingly cognitive reconceptualization of behavior therapy techniques for reducing anxiety and the self-monitoring of behavior suggests perspectives and techniques of high potential relevance to a learning strategies curriculum.

ANXIETY MANAGEMENT SKILLS

Behavior therapy approaches to understanding and treating anxiety, especially performance anxiety of all types, seem pertinent to a learning strategies curriculum. There is extensive evidence that anxiety can interfere with the learning process and with performance in testing situations (Sarason, 1960; Spielberger, 1966). Suinn (1968) and Emery and Krumboltz (1967) describe the effects of test anxiety as including an inability to recall and organize material, difficulty comprehending simple sentences and instructions on exams, feelings of tension, disruption of eating and sleeping patterns prior to exams, and sometimes nausea. Test anxiety often leads to failure in the university environment (Alpert & Haber, 1960; Paul & Eriksen, 1964; Suinn, 1968). Eysenck and Rachman (1965) estimate that as many as 20% of students have high fear of examinations. There is evidence that highly test-anxious students receive lower grades and have higher attrition rates than do less anxious students of equivalent intellectual ability (Paul, 1968; Spielberger, 1962; Spielberger & Katzenmeyer, 1959).

Since about 1972, a number of college and university counseling centers have developed special treatment programs for test anxiety. Most of these programs involve the application of the behavior therapy procedure known as *systematic desensitization* (Wolpe & Lazarus, 1966) to test-anxious students, either individually or in groups. The experience of psychologists and counselors in these agencies supports the notion that test anxiety is a widespread problem among students and that it often interfers with successful academic performance. When students become aware of such programs, enrollment in them is high. Although clinical impressions indicate that some students who are highly test anxious are able to perform fairly well on tests despite intense fear and discomfort, high test-anxiety may engender negative attitudes toward academic work that causes students subject to it to curtail or restrict their intellectual or professional development. However, most students who request treatment indicate that test anxiety often substantially interferes with their performance on tests. A common pattern is the junior or senior student who has superior intellectual ability and is highly motivated to succeed, but because of severe test anxiety is barely able to stay in school and is about to have his plans to attend graduate or professional school ruined. Often, students who suffer from test anxiety (which, like any phobia, does not yield to conventional "will-power" methods or advice) blame themselves for the problem, thinking that they would not have it if only they tried harder or had more courage. Thus, the test-anxious student sometimes suffers from lowered self-esteem and general unhappiness as a result of the anxiety problem.

The literature concerned with the nature and remediation of test anxiety tends to fall into two broad traditions, the first dealing with test anxiety as a personality variable, the second focusing on behavior therapy treatment procedures for alleviating the problem. In very recent years, these two traditions have been drawn together, leading to enriched perspectives on the nature of test anxiety and improved techniques for dealing with it.

The first stream of literature was innagurated by Mandler and Sarason's (1952) original version of test anxiety theory, which assumed that two kinds of learned "drives" are evoked by the testing situation. These are (a) task drives that are reduced by response sequences that lead to the completion of the task, and (b) an anxiety drive that may elicit responses that interfere with task completion. These latter responses "may be manifested as feelings of inadequacy, helplessness, heightened somatic reaction, anticipations of punishment or loss of status and esteem, and implicit attempts at leaving the test situation [Mandler & Sarason, 1952, p. 166]." This quote illustrates the perceptive genius with which Mandler and Sarason identified early on the kind of self-oriented, self-critical worried thoughts that deflect test-anxious students' attention from the task at hand and amplify their senses of threat, leading to bodily symptoms of anxiety and disrupted performance. But these critical features of anxious students' behavior are characterized primarily as effects of hypothetical underlying "drives." Such a characterization discourages the development of a more refined description of the cognitive and attentional dynamics of the anxious person under the stress of tests. It directs attention to underlying causal entities (drives that are unobservable and the origins of which are so obscure as to discourage useful reflection about practical means to modify debilitating performance anxiety.

Wine (1971) summarizes the results of numerous studies that present a clear pattern of results concerning the differential performance of high- and low-test-anxious students under instructional conditions that are stressful or arouse achievement anxiety. Almost all these studies have used various types of verbal types of verbal learning laboratory tasks but although results indicate that high-test-anxious individuals perform more poorly following highly evaluative, "ego-involving" instructions than do low-test-anxious students, it had also been shown that high-test-anxious students perform as well or better following nonevaluative "anonymous" instructions than their low test-anxious counterparts. Other studies have provided greater detail about the manner in which high-anxious-individuals approach evaluative tasks. For example, such individuals show pronounced self-deprecatory, self-ruminative tendencies (Sarason & Ganzer, 1962, 1963; Sarason & Koenig, 1965) and not only engage in debilitating self-criticism in evaluative situations, but generally describe themselves in more negative terms than low-test-anxious students in any performance situation.

In a review of test anxiety research on its "twentieth anniversary," Sarason (1972) suggested a basic revision of test anxiety theory, recasting it in more simple and direct terms relating to the uses of attention and interpretation of stressful events. He stated that

> What distinguishes the high test-anxious individual are [sic] (1) the manner in which he attends to the events of his environment and (2) how he interprets and utilizes the information provided by these events. These characteristics may be viewed as habits or acquired attributes whose strength is influenced by specific types of person-environment encounters [p. 382].

In this review, Sarason stresses the need to turn attention to the development of therapeutic approaches to test anxiety that, it is hoped, combine "the best features of extant behavior influence methods [p. 399]." Curiously, his preview ignores the large volume of research dealing with the application of behavior therapy methods to test anxiety and similar problems. This omission may be due to the fact that until quite recently behavior therapists and researchers have treated test anxiety as a simple conditioned emotional response—essentially a reflex, something quite different from the rich notion of test anxiety as interfering cognitive "worry" and the maladaptive deployment of attention.

The second major stream of literature dealing with test anxiety focuses on behavior therapy methods for treating the problem. A vast amount of research (including many test-anxiety treatment studies) has indicated that systematic desensitization therapy (Wolpe, 1958, 1969) can reliably produce measurable benefits for clients with a wide range of emotional and behavioral problems in which anxiety plays a fundamental role (Paul, 1969).

Wolpe (1958) and other early behavior therapists characterized anxiety essentially as a reflex—a conditioned emotional response that is automatically and reflexively elicited by certain situations or stimuli. This viewpoint holds that the stimuli(like tests) that elicit anxiety are usually harmless, but because they have been paired or associated inthe past with aversive or punishing stimuli of some sort, they continue to evoke fear and avoidance behavior that can cripple effective functioning.

The classic behavior method for treating anxiety is systematic desensitization, in which a client, while relaxed or hypnotized, visualizes a series of scenes (usually 10–15) in which he or she comes into progressively closer or more intense contact with the feared situation or stimulus. The therapist guides the client gradually up the hierarchy of scenes, moving to a new scene only when the client can visualize the preceding one with complete comfort. Desensitization to imaginally presented stimuli often transfers to their real-life counterparts.

Desensitization was originally conceptualized as a process of ''counterconditioning.'' The view was that since anxiety had been conditioned to harmless external stimuli, this conditioning could be undone by counterconditioning, a relaxation response to these same stimuli. The relaxation response gradually outcompetes and replaces the undesired anxiety response. A response antagonistic to anxiety (relaxation) is made to occur in the presense of an imaginal representation of the anxiety-evoking stimuli. The responses of an essentially passive organism and the stimuli impinging upon it are altered and rearranged to produce a different behavioral result.

The growing criticism of unmediated conditioning models has raised serious questions about whether they can account for the effectiveness and generalization of systematic desensitization treatment. (Wilkins, 1971). In the face of this criticism many writers have reexamined the desensitization process and reconceptualized it as something like a very clever way to teach several self-management strategies for coping actively with anxiety. Thus, desensitization appears to involve actively learning to relax physically and emotionally—a skill that can be utilized subsequently in stress situations. It also seems to involve a kind of training in making attentional shifts (Wilkins, 1971), in shifting one's attention back and forth in a calm, deliberate manner between a stressful situation or stimulus and relaxation or pleasant imagery. The ability to make such shifts, rather than relentlessly obsess about real or imagined feared events, may be crucial to effective coping with stress. Desensitization also seems well designed to promote the realignment of some fearful perceptions (Lazarus, 1974) and the rational reevaluation of fear-producing beliefs about stressful situations (Goldfried & Goldfried, 1975). Repeated exposure to a situation under conditions that prevent panic and flight almost inevitably promotes such reevaluation (Lazarus, 1971).

Once it became clear that self-management processes and cognitive variables were heavily implicated in desensitization therapy, efforts were made to increase treatment effectiveness by exploiting those variables more fully. Two of the best examples of the congnitive "new look" in behavior therapy treatment are Wine's (1971) "attentional training" and Meichenbaum's (1972) "cognitive modification" programs for alleviating test anxiety.

Wine's (1971) attentional training program shows students how self-evaluative worry deflects attention from productive work on the test, exposes them to videotaped models working in an effective, businesslike manner on tests, and gives them intensive practice on a variety of testlike tasks with instructions and training on how to inhibit self-relevant thinking and focus attention on the task at hand. Results showed that the program was highly effective in reducing self-report of anxiety and improving performance on several testlike behavioral measures.

Meichenbaum's (1972) cognitive modification program for test anxiety resembles attentional training, but undertakes to modify more systematically some of the cognitive processes that are thought to mediate against effective test-taking behaviors. In the first phase of this program, students undergo an "insight" therapy procedure in which they are made aware of the specific self-oriented, task-irrelevant, worried thoughts they characteristically emit in testing situations. They then generate alternative "self-instructions" or "self-talk," which have effect of avoiding worry and directing attention to the task. In the second phase of treatment, students go through a brief, modified desensitization procedure in which they visualize themselves actively coping with test anxiety in a graded series of test-taking scenes. But instead of the conventional desensitization procedure of visualizing themselves as perfectly calm and relaxed in the fear situation, this part of the cognitive modification treatment employs what Meichenbaum calls "coping imagery" in which students visualize themselves as beginning to get a little anxious but then coping successfully with anxiety by means of slow deep breaths and appropriate self-instruction and self-talk. Results showed that the cognitive modification treatment program was significantly more successful in reducing test anxiety, as assessed by several self-report and performance measures, than a conventional systematic desensitization treatment procedure of the same length.

A SEMI-AUTOMATED TEST ANXIETY
REDUCTION PROGRAM

A few years ago at the University of Texas at Austin several colleagues and I contemplated the results of a number of studies (reviewed in O'Neil, Judd, & Hedl, 1977; O'Neil & Richardson, 1977) which indicated that high anxiety often interferes with performance on tests in a computer-based learning environment, but that available modifications in instructional design or manner of test presentation would not substantially reduce test anxiety. Thus, we developed a semi-automated, media-based program to teach anxiety management skills to interested, highly anxious students completing a series of computer-managed instructional modules that formed the major part of an undergraduate educational psychology course. The program was developed within the framework of a cognitive–attentional view of test anxiety and its effects on learning and performance. It was automated to a large degree in order to reduce the demand on relatively scarce professional time and energy and to make it potentially available to a very large number of anxious students. The apparent success of a number of semi-automated desensitization treatment programs utilizing audio or video tape (Richardson & Suinn, 1973; Suinn & Hall, 1970) and the large amount of literature demonstrating the vicarious desensitization of fear through observation of live or symbolic models (Bandura, 1969) encouraged belief in the possibility of an effective automated program.

The literature on test anxiety and its treatment was surveyed for techniques and approaches that might be incorporated into or modified for the automated format. In addition, some new approaches were developed. The program and three validation studies are described in detail by Richardson, O'Neil, and Grant (1977).

The four principal components of the program are as follows:

1. Reading and completing written exercises in a special manual, written for the program, on coping with test anxiety. The text of this 75-page manual is available in a separate technical report (Richardson, 1973), and is described in greater detail later in this chapter.

2. A symbolic modeling component consisting of half-hour video-tape of a female student modeling effective and ineffective management of anxiety (including verbalized self-talk) while completing intelligence test questions presented on the cathode-ray tube of a terminal in a computer-based learning situation.

3. A brief, modified desensitization procedure in which students are given half an hour of deep-muscle relaxation instructions by a therapist on videotape, and, at a later date, are instructed by videotape to visualize themselves, while relaxed, coping with anxiety in a graded series of test-taking scenes by means of slow deep breaths and the use of appropriate self-instructions to relax and pay attention to the test.

4. A practice test-taking component in which students respond for about 45 minutes to testlike questions at a computer terminal. Periodic reminders presented by the terminal instruct them to practice various anxiety-management techniques they have learned in the program.

In each of the three validation studies the treatment procedure was completed for each student during a 2-week period early in a given semester. All students (between 400 and 500 each semester) completed the 37-item Test Anxiety Scale (Sarason, 1972) at the outset of the course. Those with scores in the upper 20% of the scale were contacted and invited to participate in the program. Those choosing to do so (about four out of five, on the average) were given a copy of the manual and then completed a five-part treatment procedure consisting of (a) reading the first two parts of the manual over the weekend; (b) attending the first scheduled, individual session consisting of watching 1 hour videotape, the first half-hour being the modeling sequence, and the second half-hour being deep muscle and slow deep breathing relaxation instructions; (c) reading the third part of the manual and completing the written exercises it contained; (d) attending a second scheduled session, consisting of viewing a second 1 hour videotape presenting the modified desensitization component of the program; and (e) attending the last scheduled session of the program, the practice test-taking session at a computer terminal.

Three studeis were undertaken over a period of 2 years to investigate the effectiveness of the automated test-anxiety-reduction program. A preliminary study found very promising results in terms of reducing self-reported test anxiety, with some indications of improved performance on module tests for treated students. A second, larger-scale study found only very weak treatment effects for students who completed the program as compared with a control group that did not. However, it appeared that certain aspects of the procedure in this study may have led students to feel depersonalized and thus may have reduced the effectiveness of the program. Steps were taken in a third study to personalize the procedure of completing the program without altering the content of the automated program itself. The results of this study showed very substantial treatment effects, similar to the results of the first study.

The marginally significant improvement in module test scores obtained in the first and third studies might be improved by adding some training in study skills to the program. There is evidence (Allen, 1972) that adding such training is likely to improve academic performance. The program might also be modified to apply broadly to most types of academic testing situations. It is inexpensive and could be used to impart valuable knowledge and coping skills to an almost unlimited number of interested persons in a wide variety of academic and training settings.

The test-anxiety manual used in these studies may be an especially promising means of communicating useful information and skills to interested learners. A fuller description of the content of this manual may indicate some of the potential for this type of "bibliotherapy" in a learning strategies curriculum.

A number of prominent writers in the fields of psychotherapy and behavior modification have stressed that the straightforward provision of new information about behavior and the environment may be an overlooked but perhaps basic ingredient in most behavior change procedures (Lazarus, 1971; Murray & Jacobson, 1971; Sarason, 1972; Urban & Ford, 1971), one that could profitably be expanded and utilized in a more systematic manner (Sarason, 1972). Students who receive a test-anxiety treatment are usually **treated** in a manner based on some reasonably well-developed theory about test anxiety and its alleviation. However, they are not usually provided systematically with the full extent of available information about the behavioral and emotional dynamics of test anxiety and techniques for coping with it. Yet, in many cases, simply the provision of new and useful information about these matters and the increased awareness regarding their own functioning it triggers may enable students to modify their test-anxious behavior. Also, conveying this information in a permanent written form may be not only an economical means of communication, but an effective way of making this information available as a continuing resource to students. The manual developed for this program was an attempt to present comprehensive information about test anxiety and coping with it to anxious students in a manner most likely to assist them in implementing new behavioral strategies in the testing situation.

The manual is divided into three parts. The first part describes, in text and diagrams, the process whereby new information (e.g., that directing attention to the task instead of to oneself during tests lowers anxiety) may lead to new coping solutions for behavioral problems, and it stresses that intelligent adults are often able to utilize new, accurate information in this manner without the intervention of a professional helper. A brief section then presents some guidelines for the readers in the use of the manual. Students are encouraged to use imagination and fantasy in reading the material, to relate the material to their personal experiences, and to complete the written portions of the manual which will aid them in working the new information into their behavior functioning. This section simply restates in nontechnical terms the rationale and expectations for the manual as a treatment device. Several sample ''case histories'' of test anxiety in college students are recounted, giving an idea of the range of background events and symptoms commonly found in test-anxious students. Then readers complete a test-anxiety check list containing a comprehensive list of symptoms of test anxiety in order to acquaint themselves in detail with the manner in which high anxiety manifests itself in their behavior and thinking on tests.

This part of the manual concludes with a relatively lengthy discussion of some different sources of test anxiety. It is claimed that high and debilitating anxiety on tests may usually be ascribed to (a) lack of ability or preparation, (b) lack of motivation or interest, (c) a reflection of other emotional or behavioral concerns, or (d) test anxiety. Test anxiety is defined as *both* a kind of automatic, habitual reaction of anxiety to tests that is difficult to control, *and* something the student actively does to himself in terms of self-oriented panicky thinking and fantasizing that generates high anxiety. Detailed examples of lack of preparation, lack of motivation, and the intrusion of other concerns are given. For example, the case is cited of a student who is pursuing a major that chosen by parents, is resentful, has difficulty studying, and then gets anxious on tests. The solution given in this case is to become aware of one's own wishes and resolve the conflict with one's parents, not treatment for test anxiety.

The purpose of this section is to provide a self-screening procedure so that individuals for whom the program was not appropriate could drop out. The assumption is that in most cases students are capable of deciding for themselves whether the program is appropriate for them. They are asked to make some written notes on the extent to which these various factors play a role in their test anxiety, and to decide whether any of the factors besides test anxiety play the **predominant** part in their difficulties with tests. If so, they are told that they may wish to consult with a faculty member or professional counselor about their difficulty with tests.

The second part of the manual provides detailed information about the behavioral and emotional dynamics of test anxiety, and about a number of strategies for coping with it. First, a discussion of test anxiety makes the point that although there is good reason to be somewhat anxious about tests—especially in a society that places a great deal of pressure on its members to compete and succeed at school and work— there is **no** good reasons for the capable and prepared student to panic or "freeze up" on tests. The point is also made that the only real difficulty for such students is to cope adequately with the anxiety that is ubiquitous and quite normal on tests.

Techniques for coping with test anxiety are discussed under four headings: (*a*) emotional state; (*b*) the direction of attention away from the self and to the test; (*c*) eliminating anxiety-arousing self-talk; and (*d*) the overall management of preparation, time and pressures before and during tests. A relaxation technique of slow deep breathing and procedures for practicing it are outlined for dealing with physical tension and emotional arousal. The difference between self-oriented and task-oriented thinking on tests is discussed in detail, and parallels in other behavioral spheres (such as social anxiety) are described. A number of illustrations of the process of task-oriented thinking on tests are given, such as using task-relevant fantasy and a kind of free association to assist recall, and stopping the process of reflection when a "best answer" is first determined on a multiple-choice test, avoiding further fruitless rumination. The manner in which self-oriented thinking usually enters the process is illustrated for the reader.

In the section on self-talk, a number of examples of panicky self-instructions and self-talk (collected for this research from students' written records of their ruminations during tests) are provided for the reader, as well as a representative list of examples of appropriate self-talk that tends to focus attention on the test rather than oneself. In the section on overall management of time and preparation several general considerations regarding behaving in a manner that fosters a sense of control over the preparation and completion of tests are discussed. It is stressed that **behaving** as if one feels calm and confident about tests often brings anxious **feelings** into line.

The third and final part of the manual contains a series of written exercises in which the student outlines behavioral strategies for coping with test anxiety. For example, the student generates a personal list of instances of panicky self-talk, and then develops a list of alternative, incompatible self-statements that might be used to counter anxiety and foster task-relevant thinking and behaving. The student is also asked to follow certain guidelines (including review of previous written material) to help devise several realistic strategies for fostering a sense of control and maintaining attention to the test.

A manual of this type might be used to present and make permanently available to students information about effective strategies for learning or coping in a wide range of training settings. Another body of information and skills growing out of behavior modification theory and research that may prove relevant to learning strategies has to do with self-monitoring skills and pressures, to which we now turn.

SELF-MONITORING SKILLS

Frequently, a key ingredient in behavior modification programs, especially behavioral self-control programs in which a voluntary client plays an active role in implementing his or her own change program, is the client's self-monitoring of behavior in the area targeted for change. Self-monitoring typically involves the client keeping a permanent written record of the incidence, time of day, and circumstances of some discrete, countable behavior, which may vary widely from depressed thoughts to angry outbursts to eating between meals. There is reason to believe that self-assessment and self-monitoring activities, including training students in basic and generalizable skills of self-observation and self-assessment of progress or change, hold considerable promise for enhancing the quality and generalizability of learning in a wide variety of academic and skill-training programs.

Several case studies presented by Maletzky (1974) illustrate very well the technique of self-monitoring as an ingredient in a behavior-change program. Maletzky points out that a number of studies on self-monitoring have employed the practice of having the subjects count their own behaviors prior to, during, and after treatment, both as part of the change program itself and as a way of obtaining data about its effectiveness. Several of these studies, reviewed by Kanfer (1970), showed that having clients keep an accurate record of certain behaviors can significantly increase a positive behavior (like resisting an urge to smoke) or decrease a negative behavior (like smoking) without any other intervention. In each case, however, Maletzky notes, self-monitoring activities were confounded with positive expectations for change on the part of the subjects. In the several case studies he reported, Maletzky attempted to minimize such expectations by informing subjects that keeping a record of their problem behavior would assist the therapist in understanding their problems, but would not necessarily have any effect on their unwanted behaviors.

All of Maletzky's subjects wore wrist counters, counted each unwanted behavior by pushing a button on the counter, and recorded totals at the end of each day of graph paper, thereby providing a running record of progress over time. One subject was a 52-year old woman with a 30-year history of repetitive scratching leading to unsightly lesions on her arms and legs. After 8 weeks of recording scratches, their frequency had declined to zero. Recording was discontinued and a 12-month follow-up showed no recurrence of the problem. A 9-year-old boy who repeatedly raised and waved his hand inappropriately in class recorded his own inappropriate hand waving over an 8-week period. As verified by his teacher, the unwanted behaviors declined to zero frequency and, without further use of the counter, remained at zero during a 6-month follow-up period. Both these subjects underwent a reversal period after 4 weeks, during which recording was discontinued and the undesired behavior returned to about half its original frequency. Similar results were obtained with a 20-year-old woman with a life-long history of severe nail biting, facial tics of 12 years' duration in a 65-year-old woman, and constantly out-of-seat behavior in an 11-year-old school girl.

Numerous more-or-less adequately controlled group studies have investigated the effectiveness of self-monitoring both alone and in combination with other strategies. For example, Mahoney, Moura, and Wade (1973) compared the effectiveness of self-monitoring, no self-monitoring, self-reward, self-punishment, and both self-reward and self-punishment combined in reducing weight in obest subjects. In this study, self-monitoring formed an essential part of the self-reward and self-punishment strategies by providing information that set the occasion for their application, but did not, by itself, produce greater weight loss than the control condition.

An especially interesting group study by Mahoney, Moore, Wade, and Moura (1973) was conducted in an educational context that permitted an unusual degree of experimental control together with high relevance to real-life educational concerns. Students responded to newspaper advertisements offering a free program for preparation for the Graduate Record Examination. Volunteers responded to questions or problems in both the mathematics and verbal areas presented in a programmed-learning format by a machine that provided the student with feedback on the correctness of each response or answer. A continuous self-monitoring group that recorded or counted each correct response, an intermittent self-monitoring group that counted or recorded only every third correct response, a feedback-only group, and a control group that received neither correctness feedback nor self-monitored correct responses were included in the study. The two self-monitoring groups, as compared with the feedback-only and control groups spent more time at the task and had greater accuracy in mathematics, although not in the verbal problems. The continuous compared with intermittent self-monitoring procedure was superior only in terms of time spent on the task.

Reviews or critical discussions of self-monitoring as a research tool or ingredient in behavior-change programs may be found in Kazdin (1974), Thoreson and Mahoney (1974), and Kanfer (1971, 1975). The literature that is the subject of these reviews treats self-monitoring fairly narrowly as the self-observation and recording of some relevant, discrete, observable behavior that can be counted in such a way that variations in its frequency across time and circumstances may be charted or kept track of in some manner, usually in the form of a permanent record. However, "covert" behaviors, such as depressed thoughts or positive self-statements, may be the target of self-monitoring activities, and in some cases may be as reliably monitored as overt acts. In this sense, self-monitoring seems to involve (*a*) a conscious **discrimination** or discernment of the presence or absence of a particular response, and (*b*) some kind of **systematic recording** or charting of the observed response. These two steps are undertaken, of course, in order to proceed to (*c*) some **evaluation** or self-evaluation of the individual's performance in relation to certain standards or goals.

Some of the main empirical findings concerning self-monitoring and its contribution to behavior change may be summarized in the following manner.

1. Persons are generally poor or inaccurate observers of their own behavior, which may be speculated to have a number of deleterious effects as they attempt to apply specific learning or coping strategies in specific life situations.
2. Self-monitoring is used widely as part of contemporary behavior-change programs, either as a change strategy in its own right or as a source of crucial information for developing or applying other techniques or maneuvers.
3. Self-monitoring is not generally reliable enough to serve as an "objective" measure of change in a target behavior over time. However, well-motivated subjects generally use it in a fairly reliable manner, and in some studies, substantial change has been observed despite quite inaccurate self-monitoring records.
4. Self-monitoring has been shown to have dramatic positive effects on the behavior monitored, but such effects have often not been observed, depending on the problem and population studies. And self-monitoring by itself probably will not suffice for durable change in most instances.
5. No final or elaborate self-monitoring technology, with fixed rules for application to learning or behavior-change problems seems likely to emerge. Some rules of thumb are occasionally helpful, such as utilizing a self-monitoring response that maximally interrupts a maladaptive behavior sequence. But different responses, persons, and situations are likely to require somewhat different procedures and techniques. Still, application of **general** principles of self-monitoring under diverse circumstances should not prove difficult, and use of such principles holds considerable promise for enhancing learning and behavior change in many situations.

Many of the common explanations of self-monitoring and its effects leave the learner or client in a more-or-less passive role that fails to account for the phenomenon. Behavioral self-control explanations of self-monitoring (Kazdin, 1974; Thoreson & Mahoney, 1974) utilize concepts from operant psychology. Characteristically they divide the organism functionally into two persons or "selves," one active and one passive. The active self functions like an operant psychologist who monitors the behavior of the essentially passive organism and decides to administer rewards and punishments in order to direct or redirect behavior toward desired goals. The behavior of the passive self is appropriately *conditioned* in this manner. Thus a *behavioral self-control* model attempts to preserve laws of learning that require an essentially passive organism while incorporating genuinely active agency and self-direction into the account of behavior.

This explanation is unsatisfactory. If the choices and actions of the "active" self are themselves the passive products of prior conditioning, then they are not genuinely active and do not have initiating force in behavior. If they do have initiating force, then they are exceptions to the laws of learning invoked by the theory, and are wholly unaccounted for by it.

At a more practical level, operant explanations of self-monitoring (Ferster, Nurnberger, & Levitt, 1962; Kazdin, 1974) have emphasized that in most situations calling for increased self-control, maladaptive approach behaviors (e.g., overeating) have strong immediate reinforcing consequences and delayed aversive consequences. It is contended that self-monitoring, then (with or without additional interventions, such as self-reward for more adaptive responses), functions to make the individual more aware of the undesirable response and its connection with ultimate aversive consequences more salient, thus bridging the delay between response and negative outcome. There is, of course, considerable truth to this analysis. But the explanation is not satisfactory. If awareness or salience of cognitive connection is the key factor, then self-operant maneuvers are not necessary for the change and another sort of explanation is needed. Why was such awareness not developed previously? If the strength of the immediately reinforcing consequences are invoked to answer this question, then why would a subject so reinforced not simply discontinue self-monitoring? It is the individual's prior **decision** to change and endure at least some initial frustration in the process that calls for explanation? Such a decision may lead to or produce something like self-operant maneuvers, but it cannot itself be a consequence of rearranged stimuli or reinforcers without destroying the idea of genuine, active self-control or self-direction.

Kanfer (1975) has argued that such operant analyses of self-control or self-management behavior fail because they employ ''open loop'' input–output analyses of functioning that derive from outdated causal models inherent in traditional S–R theorizing in psychology. He suggests an alternative model of self-regulatory behavior based on a ''closed loop,'' information processing conceptualization of the organism's interaction with its environment. This simple model seems an excellent starting point for an adequate theoretical account of self-monitoring.

According to Kanfer's model, self-regulation has three main phases. The first of these is *self-monitoring,* as it has been previously described. The second is self-evaluation, wherein individuals compare the information feedback from the environment and their own behavior that they have monitored and recorded with relevant performance criteria or standards. They discriminate whether the performance does not meet, meets, or exceeds the standard set for it. The last phase is *self-reinforcement,* in which individuals positively or negatively reinforce themselves, depending upon the relationship of performance and standard.

There are some problems with this model. It is not clear whether ''self-reinforcement'' is meant in the sense of self-operant maneuvers as already described, with all their attendant conceptual problems, or as cognitive confirmatory feedback to the person concerning goal attainment, which would be more acceptable from an information-processing viewpoint. Also, there is the question of where ''standards'' for performance come from. Even if they are set by others, the individual must somehow acquiesce if self-regulation is to occur. Obviously the selection or creation of standards for one's performance, which must occur at some point, involves higher-order kinds of self-assessment and self-evaluation than are described by this model. In such processes the individual's own cognitive and evaluative activities and standards themselves become the objects of scrutiny and evaluation.

In the absence of any developed, systematic theory of self-regulation, including self-monitoring, but keeping in mind the kinds of higher-order self-determination of goals and standards for performance that must form part of any such theory, we may summarize the possible uses of functions of the self-monitoring or self-assessment of one's ongoing performances in the following manner.

1. Self-monitoring is often essential if individuals are to have accurate information about their interaction with the environment. Explicit, semiformalized self-monitoring seems desirable in many circumstances for the reason that most persons are relatively poor or inaccurate observers of their own behavior.

2. Self-monitoring may itself serve as an adaptive response that initiates a constructive problem-solving sequence, cued by an effective problem-solver's recognition (prompted by frustration or confusion) that the student has a problem in learning or living.

3. Self-observation of discrepancies between performances and standards can set the occasion for specific kinds of self-corrective behaviors, self-reward or punishment, seeking new information, consideration of alternative solutions or routes to goals, etc.

4. Self-observation of discrepancies can set the occasion for higher-order critical consideration of standards and goals that produce the discrepancies, leading to widely varying outcomes from minor adjustment of immediate performance standards to alteration in long-term goals in education or life.

5. Self-observation and the awareness of self–environment interactions it engenders may, by itself, have enormous positive effects on behavior. It may provide more accurate information about behavior enabling cognitive or behavioral skills already in the individual's repertoire to be successfully exercised. It may bring important, longer-term positive or negative consequences of behavior into the psychological present where, now cognitively present and emotionally more salient, they can exert much greater influence on deliberation and action. Thus it may operate to "decompartmentalize" thinking and undo rationalizations that interfere with effective learning or change. This may have profound effects on what is commonly called "motivation" to learn or change one's behavior. Making remote positive or negative consequences more salient in the present may supply needed arousal for effective actions, or compel hard decisions about one's behavior that, once made, will further energize the individual and promote positive action.

A TRAINING MODEL

Following is an outline of an ideal course of education or training built around the idea of using self-monitoring and self-assessment skills to maximize the active self-direction of the learner or trainee. The model consists of a sequence of nine overlapping types of activities. Some of these activities, such as contracting and goal-setting, have considerable empirical support as to their effectiveness in helpfully structuring facilitating learning situations. This literature is not reviewed here, but it is hoped that these activities and their potentially fruitful interaction with self-assessment procedures will be intuitively plausable.

1. Making Explicit the Decision to Learn

Students make explicit in discussions and writing the decision to learn or undergo training by specifying the short or long-term goals of an educational or professional sort they presently entertain. Some clarification of goals may take place as a result of this specification and examination of goals. It is verified that the course of training is an appropriate means to the ends specified, and that it is feasible for this particular learner at this particular point in time.

2. Setting Specific Goals for the Course of
Learning or Training

Students make explicit in discussion and writing goals for the immediate academic or training experience. Goals will specify the content to be mastered and the level of skill or mastery desired. They may also specify portions of a plan to reach these goals such as the time involved in completing the course, the pace of training, or its relationship with other concurrent professional or learning activities. Additional goals may involve the acquisition of increased self-discipline or self-confidence, or others. Goals must be specified in writing to permit explicit ongoing and terminal evaluation of success in attaining them at later points in time.

3. Contract

An informal contract is prepared and signed that specifies the reciprocal obligations and benefits of learner and training program. The program is committed to provide specified materials, lectures, counseling and consultation, etc., and to adhere to such standards of evaluation as can be specified in advance. The student or trainee agrees to work towards the goals set for performance in Phase 2, and to complete the various procedures for self-assessment and self-monitoring of progress built into the training program.

4. Initial Self-Assessment of Skills and Preparation

With instructor consultation the student briefly in writing, for each goal, specifies (a) strengths of skill and preparation, (b) deficits in background, skill, knowledge, (c) any other kinds of barriers to successful performance, such as anxiety about tests, memory problems, or study skills or habits, and (d) steps to be taken, if desired or feasible, to remedy these deficits and blocks to successful performance. Assessment may include psychometric instruments, such as a survey of study habits or test anxiety scale.

5. Supplementary Skill Training Programs

Certain deficits or barriers to successful performance in the training program, based on the initial self-assessment, can best be remedied through brief training in the content of the program. Thus training in study skills or habits, coping with test anxiety, or development of effective learning or cognitive strategies may be indicated. A brief training program in self-assessment skills may also be provided. Some of these programs may have potential to enhance learning or performance in many or most trainees, not just those who present serious deficits or problems in these areas.

6. Course Content or Training

Educational or training procedures, modified to include procedures for individuals' self-monitoring of progress, are completed by students.

7. Self-Monitoring of Progress and Performance

In some manner appropriate to the course of training students monitor and keep a permanent record of their performance and progress. Although specific examples could be developed, it is difficult to specify general rules for the development and application of self-monitoring techniques beyond indicating that monitoring and recording of units of progress towards goals should be prominent and fairly frequent, but not obtrusive or cumbersome.

8. Ongoing Self-Evaluation and Self-Correction

Self-monitoring of performance should be punctuated with periodic explicit self-evaluations of progress that may lead to various self-corrective responses, such as repeating a training sequence, correcting one's performance or approach, reevaluation of performance standards, and so forth.

9. Terminal Self-Assessment and Self-Evaluation

Some kind of terminal, explicit, relatively formalized assessment of progress and performance in relation to initial or modified goals should be completed. Progress in the relationship to long-term goals should be noted, including any changes in overall perspective or longer-term goals as a result of training.

Typically a useful procedure may be to provide all information and materials for goal-setting, self-monitoring, and self-evaluation in a single notebook or sourcebook for a course or training sequence. Everything that can be done should be done to emphasize and symbolize in word and procedure that undertaking the course of education or training is a self-directed activity on the part of the learner in relationship to self-chosen goals. It should be noted that the heart of this model, the active self-monitoring and self-evaluation of ongoing performance and progress, can be used with courses and training programs that are highly structured, traditional, and characterized by few learner options concerning content or procedure. Most of the other procedures described here could also be used in such a setting. Highly structured teacher or curriculum-centered training procedures are appropriate for some content and settings, and do not in any way preclude active choice and utilization of these procedures by students in order to implement their self-chosen, longer-term goals with instructors, learning settings, etc., represented as aids or consultants to the student's self-directed learning project. However, courses of education or training that are authoritarian in the sense that they actively discourage independent thinking or action will very likely prevent these procedures from being meaningfully utilized by students and/or enhancing learning.

Supplementary skill-training programs might focus on learning strategies, programs to reduce test and performance anxiety, training in very general anxiety or stress management skills (Richardson, 1976), or training in study skills.

The importance of self-assessment activities and skills and their central role in self-directed learning suggests the possibility of a general self-assessment skills training program. A manual similar to the test anxiety coping skills manual described earlier might be developed that explained the principles of self-monitoring and its role in a wide variety of learning and everyday life situations, with extended examples and "case studies" of its uses and benefits. It might also include materials and guidelines for practice in the self-monitoring of selected personal behaviors and recording and charting their change over time. Such projects should include behaviors from several different areas of functioning, not just training-related activities, in order to promote sharpened and generalizable skills. However, in most settings it would be highly desirable to include training in the monitoring of study behaviors, progress toward training goals, or fluctuations in levels of motivation or anxiety about performances that would mesh smoothly with and support self-monitoring activites embedded in the course proper.

In conclusion, it seems likely that improved skills in the management of stress and anxiety and in self-monitoring one's academic or training progress are learning strategies that hold considerable promise for increasing student efficiency and satisfaction in learning. There may be other skills (for example, effective study or time management skills) that might be adapted from counseling and clinical psychology and fruitfully made part of a learning strategies curriculum. In other cases, the kinds of procedures for restructuring maladaptive thinking processes and teaching new coping skills utilized by behavior modifiers may prove useful to educational psychologists in considering how to most effectively impart learning strategy skills such as cognitive elaboration or the use of mnemonics. The prospects for collaboration seem bright.

REFERENCES

Allen, G. J. The behavioral treatment of test anxiety. *Behavior Therapy,* 1972, *3*, 253–262.

Alpert, R., & Haber, R. N. Anxiety in academic achievement situations. *Journal of Abnormal and Social Psychology,* 1960, *61*, 207–215.

Bandura, A. *Principles of behavior modification.* New York: Holt, 1969.

Bowers, K. S. Situationism in psychology: An analysis and a critique. *Psychological Review,* 1973, *80*, 307–336.

Dember, W. N. Motivation and the cognitive revolution. *American Psychologist,* 1974, *29*, 161–168.

Emery, J. R., & Krumboltz, R. D. Standard versus individualized hierarchies in desensitization to reduce test anxiety. *Journal of Counseling Psychology,* 1967, *14*, 204–209.

Eysenck, J. J. & Rachman, S. *The causes and cures of neurosis.* London: Routledge & Kegan Paul, 1965.

Ferster, C. B., Nurnberger, J. I., & Levitt, E. B. The control of eating. *Journal of Mathematics,* 1962, *1*, 17–23.

Goldfried, M. R., & Goldfried, A. P. Cognitive change methods. In F. H. Kanfer & A. P. Goldstein (Eds.), *Helping people change.* New York: Pergamon, 1975.

Kanfer, F. H. Self-monitoring: Methodological limitations and clinical applications. *Journal of Consulting and Clinical Psychology,* 1970, *35*, 148–152.

Kanfer, F. H. The maintenance of behavior by self-generated stimuli and reinforcements. In A. Jacobs & L. B. Sachs (Eds.), *The psychology of private events: Perspectives on covert response systems.* New York: Academic Press, 1971.

Kanfer, F. H. Self-management methods. In F. H. Kanfer & A. P. Goldstein (Eds.), *Helping people change.* New York: Pergamon, 1975.

Kazdin, A. E., Self-monitoring and behavior change. In M. J. Mahoney & C. E. Thoreson (Eds.), *Self-control: Power to the person.* Monterey: Brooks/Cole, 1974.

Lazarus, A. A. *Behavior therapy and beyond.* New York: McGraw-Hill, 1971.

Lazarus, A. A. Desensitization and cognitive restructuring. *Psychotherapy: Theory, research, and practice.* 1974, *11*, 98–101.

London, P. The end of ideology in behavior modification. *American Psychologist,* 1972, *27*, 913–920.

Mahoney, M. J. *Behavior therapy: Some critical comments.* Paper presented at the meeting of the American Psychopathological Association, Boston, May 1974.

Mahoney, M. J., Moore, B. S., Wade, T. C., & Moura, N. G. M. The effects of continuous and intermittent self-monitoring on academic behavior. *Journal of Consulting and Clinical Psychology.* 1973, *41*, 65–69.

Maletzky, B. M. "Assisted" covert sensitization in the treatment of exhibitionism. *Journal of Consulting and Clinical Psychology,* 1974, *42*, 34–40.

Mandler, G., & Sarason, S. B. A study of anxiety and learning. *Journal of Abnormal and Social Psychology,* 1952, *47*, 228–229.

Meichenbaum, D. Cognitive modification of test anxious college students. *Journal of Consulting and Clinical Psychology,* 1972, *39*, 370–380.

Murray, E. J., & Jacobson, L. I. The nature of learning in traditional and behavioral psychotherapy. In A. Bergin & S. Garfield (Eds.), *Handbook of psychotherapy and behavior change.* New York: Wiley, 1971.

O'Neil, H. F., Jr., Judd, W. A., & Hedl, J. State anxiety and learning in computer-based education. In J. Sieber, H. F. O'Neil, Jr., & S. Tobias (Eds.), *Test anxiety, cognition, and instruction.* Hillsdale, N.J.: Lawrence Erlbaum Associates, 1977.

O'Neil, H. F., Jr., & Richardson, F. C. Anxiety and learning in computer-based learning environments: An overview. In J. Sieber, H. F. O'Neil, Jr., & S. Tobias (Eds.), *Test anxiety, cognition, and instruction.* Hillsdale, N.J.: Lawrence Erlbaum Associates, 1977.

Paul, G. L. A two year follow-up of systematic desensitization in therapy groups. *Journal of Abnormal Psychology,* 1968, **73,** 119–130.

Paul, G. L. Outcome of systematic desensitization II: Controlled investigations of individual treatment, technique variations, and current status. In C. Franks (Ed.), *Behvaior therapy: Appraisal and status.* New York: McGraw-Hill, 1969.

Paul, G. L., & Eriksen, C. W. Effects of test anxiety on "real-life" examinations. *Journal of Personality,* 1964, **32**, 480–494.

Richardson, F. C. *A self-study manual on coping with test anxiety* (Tech. Rep.) Austin: University of Texas, Computer-Assisted Instruction Laboratory, 1973.

Richardson, F. C. Anxiety management training. In A. A. Lazarus (Ed.), *Multimodal behavior therapy.* New York: Springer, 1976.

Richardson, F. C., O'Neil, H. F., Jr., & Grant, R. D. Development and evaluation of an automated test anxiety reduction program for a computer-based learning environment. In J. Sieber, H. F. O'Neil, Jr., & S. Tobias (Eds.), *Test anxiety, cognition and instruction.* Hillsdale, N.J.: Lawrence Erlbaum Associates, 1977.

Richardson, F. C., & Suinn, R. M. A comparison of traditional systematic desensitization, accelerated massed desensitization, and anxiety management training in the treatment of mathematics anxiety. *Behavior Therapy,* 1973, *4*, 212–218.

Sarason, I. G. Empirical findings and theoretical problems in the use of anxiety scales. *Psychological Bulletin,* 1960, *57*, 403–415.

Sarason, I. G. Experimental approaches to test anxiety: Attention and the uses of information. In C. D. Spielberger (Ed.), *Anxiety: Current trends in theory and research* (Vol. 2). New York: Academic Press, 1972.

Sarason, I. G., & Ganzer, V. J. Anxiety, reinforcement, and experimental instructions in a free verbalization situation. *Journal of Abnormal and Social Psychology,* 1962, *65*, 300–307.

Sarason, I. G., & Ganzer, V. J. Effects of test anxiety and reinforcement history on verbal behavior. *Journal of Abnormal and Social Psychology,* 1963, *67*, 513–519.

Sarason, I. G., & Koenig, K. P. The relationship of test anxiety and hostility to descriptions of self and parents. *Journal of Personality and Social Psychology,* 1965, *2*, 617–621.

Scriven, M. The philosophy of behavior modification. In C. E. Thoreson (Ed.), *Behavior modification in education.* Chicago: University of Chicago Press, 1973.

Skinner, B. F. *Science and human behavior.* New York: Macmillan, 1953.

Spielberger, C. D. The effects of manifest anxiety on the academic achievement of college students. *Mental Hygiene,* 1962, *66*, 420–426.

Spielberger, C. D. Theory and research on anxiety. In C. D. Spielberger (Ed.), *Anxiety and behavior.* New York: Academic Press, 1966.

Spielberger, C. D., & Katzenmeyer, W. G. Manifest anxiety, intelligence, and college grades. *Journal of Consulting Psychology,* 1959, *23*, 278.

Suinn, R. M. The desensitization of test anxiety by group and individual treatment. *Behavior Research and Therapy,* 1968, *6*, 385–387.

Suinn, R. M., & Hall, R. Marathon desensitization group. *Behaviour Research and Therapy,* 1970, *8*, 97–98.

Thoreson, C. E., & Mahoney, M. J. *Behavioral self-control.* New York: Holt, 1974.

Urban, H. B., & Ford, D. H. Some historical and conceptual perspectives on psychotherapy and behavior change. In A. E. Bergin & S. L. Garfield (Eds.), *Handbook of psychotherapy and behavior change.* New York: Wiley, 1971.

Wilkins, W. Desensitization: Social and cognitive factors underlying the effectiveness of Wolpe's procedure. *Psychological Bulletin,* 1971, *76*, 311–317.

Wine, J. *Investigations of an attentional interpretation of test anxiety.* Unpublished doctoral dissertation, University of Waterloo, 1971.

Wolpe, J. *Psychotherapy by reciprocal inhibition.* Stanford, Calif.: Stanford University Press, 1958.

Wolpe, J. *The practice of behavior therapy.* New York: Pergamon, 1969.

Wolpe, J., & Lazarus, A. A. *Behavior therapy techniques.* New York: Pergamon, 1966.

4

Motor Skills and Learning Strategies[1]

ROBERT N. SINGER

For many years, people have been relatively naive as to the nature of motor skills, more particularly, the process and mechanisms involved in learning and performing them. We have usually associated the term *motor skills* with the physical, and in an athletic or recreational context.

Yet, motor behaviors (also referred to as psychomotor or movement-oriented behaviors) permeate a wide variety of occupational and daily-living activities. Mere talking requires the synchronized movement of facial muscles if communication is to be effective. Movement-oriented behaviors are associated with industrial, technical, and vocational skills; military tasks; agricultural duties; secretarial and clerical functions; business operations; driving and piloting demands; music, art, and dance works; physical activity, sport, and recreation endeavors, as well as routine daily responses to situations. The various ways psychomotor behaviors are involved in so many of the things we do are often taken for granted.

We walk, jump, run, throw, catch, swim, manipulate, balance, demonstrate controlled performances, and execute skilled movement. Yet, we apparently do not concern ourselves with how these skills and the abilities that underlie them are acquired and developed. Whereas research attention has generally been focused on cognitive and affective behaviors, the psychomotor domain has been relatively neglected. And yet, cognitions and emotions are entwined with movement behaviors; indeed, all must be coordinated for skillful performance.

The focus in this chapter is on cognitive processes and learner strategies, and their involvement in the learning and performance of motor skills. In a sense, the purpose

[1]Preparation of this chapter was supported in part by the Defense Advanced Research Projects Agency under contract number MDA903-77-C-0200. Views and conclusions contained in this document are those of the author and should not be interpreted as necessarily representing the official policies, either expressed or implied, of the Defense Advanced Research Projects Agency or of the United States Government.

of this material is to provide an orientation and an overview. After a brief description of the nature of learner strategies (other sections of this book contain more detailed work), conceptual directions in the motor learning literature will be presented.

Cognitive processes operate sequentially and serially to help produce skilled movement-performance. Some of them change in relative importance as skill is acquired. It would be impossible to describe here in detail how these operations work, and so, a number of them are referred to briefly later in the chapter. Special emphasis is placed on example topics: *goal-image formation, goal-expectancy formation,* and *directing and controlling the act.*

The final section of the chapter addresses some practice and training considerations. Especially treated is the function of error-making in the learning of skills. The primary question raised is: What is the best learning strategy—to learn from making mistakes or to discourage the commission of errors? As the role of cognitive processes in the learning of various categories of tasks becomes revealed, the alternative and best strategies to enhance the operation of these processes can also be investigated and determined.

The ultimate idealistic objective of any training program might be to encourage learners to formulate strategies to cope with expected and unexpected events. These strategies should help in problem-solving and adaptive behaviors, as relationships between events are discovered and rules applied. External guidance is not always possible, and, in fact, may not always be desirable.

LEARNER STRATEGIES

Cognitive strategies represent, according to Gagné (1974), one of five principal categories of learning outcomes (learned capabilities). The others are verbal information or knowledge, intellectual skills, attitudes, and motor skills. Cognitive strategies are defined by Gagné (1974) as

> skills of self-management that the learner acquires, presumably over a period of years, to govern his own processes of attending, learning, and thinking. By acquiring and refining such strategies, the student becomes an increasingly skillful independent learner and independent thinker. As goals of education, cognitive strategies are often accorded the highest priority by educational philosophers [p. 4].

Dansereau (Chapter 1) has described learning strategies as learner-based techniques or processes associated with the acquisition, manipulation, and utilization of academic or technical material. He believes that there are primary and secondary strategies. Examples of the former are imagery usage, mnemonic techniques, and means–end analyses. Examples of the latter, which support and promote the use of primary strategies, are relaxation techniques, incentive structuring, and techniques to promote attention.

Whereas Dansereau has been primarily concerned with the application of strategies to cognitively oriented learning situations and Gagné has distinguished motor skills from from cognitive strategies, I contend that many strategies related to the learning of cognitive materials are similar to those involved in the mastery of motor skills. In addition, cognitions and strategies unique to psychomotor behaviors can be identified. In the following discussion of some of the cognitive processes involved in motor learning strategies will also be addressed. But first, let us briefly review two types of categories of motor tasks, as the demands and learner strategies for each are dissimilar.

Self-Paced and Externally Paced Activities

A self-paced activity is one that learners can initiate when ready. Trainees respond to a fixed object or static environment in a situation that permits them to progress at their own rates of speed. Typing a letter, assembling or disassembling a weapon, or hitting a golf ball are examples of self-paced activities.

An externally-paced activity requires a person to respond instantaneously to unexpected situational demands. Responses must be adapted to circumstances. Anticipation time and decision-making time may be very brief. Representative activities are often found in sport, such as rallying in tennis and handball. Another illustration would be a marksman aiming at a moving target.

The self-paced strategy suggests less concern for quickness in perceptual adjustments toward the activity and more concern for the appropriate sequence of responses. Because the cues or objects of concern are stable, the trainee has time to be alerted prior to performance. "Pressured intellectualization" of the task is at a minimum. When there are many potential variations of input, especially unexpected in nature, response demands are great. For a self-paced activity, the individual has time to preview the situation and to respond when ready (within reason). He paces himself during the activity rather than being paced. **The main focus in practice is on response consistency.**

Many possible situations exist with regard to externally paced activities in which the trainee might have to perform. Practice conditions are more complicated than for a self-paced task. Owing to situational uncertainties and the speed with which adjustments must be made, there appear to be many alternative practice possibilities. Practice should probably begin under standard, most probable conditions. Externally paced activities can be modified so as to possess self-paced properties, enabling learners to gain appropriate lead-up skills. After adequate competence is shown, practice situations should be varied. **The emphasis in practice is on familiarity with a wide array of situations and cues, with response adaptability of concern.** Response consistency is the objective with self-paced activities. Repetitious practice occurs until the act can be performed as if by habit; perceptual need is minimized and the ability to reproduce the same act continuously and with stability is emphasized. Reactions in externally paced skills cannot be fixed, but, rather, depend on circumstances.

Many activities contain self-paced as well as externally paced characteristics, and training techniques should reflect such considerations. Further analysis of psychomotoric activities indicates that some are *open loop* and others are *closed loop*. In an open-loop task, information generated about the performance comes at termination of the performance. When playing a composition on the piano which requires rapid finger movements, performance results are obtained at the outcome of performance (a series of notes). There is no time to use feedback to correct and adjust the finger movements. It is as if a motor program (e.g., Keele, 1973) has been preplanned, to run off for a period of time, and than another program is activated, and so on.

In a closed-loop task (which proceeds at a slower rate), the individual is able to utilize knowledge about performance to make continual adjustments through constant monitoring in order to match responses to input cues (e.g., Adams, 1971). Continual feedback while driving a car encourages proper adjustments for effective performance. In a sense, closed-loop tasks suggest peripheral nervous system control (feedback from sense receptors), whereas open-loop tasks suggest central nervous system control (the storage of programs, schemata, or plans in the brain).

Trainees must deploy the proper strategies for feedback usage (interpretation and application) to master closed-loop skills. For open-loop skills, they must learn to become less consciously aware of the situation, to develop, store, and retrieve programs pertinent to task demands.

CONCEPTUAL DIRECTIONS

The Past

Whatever research and theory in motor learning existed before the 1950s was behavioristically oriented. For the most part, then and even now, investigations and training programs embraced formal, associative learning conditions. In other words, the emphasis was on the design of situations to produce expected behavioral changes, with little regard for internal, or organismic, variables and the way individuals differ. Furthermore, the involvement of learner *cognitions* and learning *strategies* in the acquisition and performance of motor skills had been greatly underrated and overlooked.

Perhaps the major portion of the motor learning research, excluding the past decade, has tended to emphasize practice condition variables, such as the distribution of practice in relation to rest over time, the learning of a task in its entirety or fractionated into its parts, and various forms of knowledge of results. Training programs, illustrating behavioristic theory and a heavy reliance on standard environmental-manipulation training procedures, were virtually insensitive to the learning processes common among learners as well as to individual difference factors. Rather, the attempt was to implement the findings of laboratory research undertaken on such contrived tasks as the pursuit rotor (which requires the subject to track a small disk on a movable turntable with a stylus) and to design formal, simplistic training programs.

The development and acceptance of cybernetic, information processing, and control models as a viable means for studying human behavior led to specific inplications for and applications in the motor skills area. Stressed were self-regulatory and monitorial mechanisms in the form of feedback loops (e.g., Adams, 1968), perceptual, decision-making, and information storage and retrieval processes (e.g., Welford, 1968), and internalized hierarchical control functions over performance (e.g., Miller, Galanter, & Pribram, 1960). Such theoretical advances have led to a scholarly analysis of those processes and functions involved in the acquisition of skill, and to the development of systems models. Systems models of human motor behavior highlight the components and their functions.

Contemporary Conceptual Models

The three conceptual approaches to understanding human behavior relevant to the learning of motor skills will be briefly described. Each approach overlaps with the other and yet contains unique emphases, with implications for instruction related to motor skills. The first to be discussed is the *cybernetic approach*. One of the highlights of cybernetic theory is the belief in the role of feedback; self-regulatory and self-monitoring, which the learner can use to help guide learning and to improve skill. In typical introductory psychology classes held in the past, discussion invariably centered around S–R concepts, associationism, and behavioristic theory. A stimulus becomes conditioned to a particular response, and the learner presumably has very little control over the situation. If there is one thing that cybernetic theory has shown us it is that there is a great deal of control individual learners can exert over circumstances, many ways in which they can self-monitor and self-regulate activity. With the acquisition of skill, they learn to depend less on external influences and more on internal control and regulatory processes.

Information processing theory is complex and, in some ways, is related to cybernetic theory. Both theories were developed after World War II. Tremendous reliance in the theory is placed on the role of perception, attention, and decision making. A great deal of consideration is given to the channel capacity of a person: How much information can be dealt with at any given time? When are we overloading the system? When do we underload the system? When do we fatigue or bore the system? How can we optimize information? What do we know about attention spans? How can we maintain the attention of the learner? How do learners selectively discriminate among available information?

A common tendency is to examine the output side of behavior. But we rarely think of the way people in general can process information, and the way individuals differ due to handicaps in their systems (visual, auditory, learning disorders, and the like). In information-processing theory, the emphasis is on the input and transmission side of behavioral analysis.

Skilled motor activity is a function of Input (sensory and perceptual functions) × Central processing (decision and command functions) × Output (motor functions). The integration of these processes leads to more purposeful behavior. Plans of action, or programs, need to be established. Complex learning is obviously much more than the association of a particular response to a given cue.

In *adaptive models,* a human-to-computer analogy is made. Higher-order executive programs and lower-order programs are identified as they relate to the processes necessary to perform a task. In other words, the beginner will have to conceptualize some sort of movement plan and there will be certain kinds of lower-order programs that need to be executed if the higher-order plan is to be fulfilled. As a person becomes more skilled, that person is capable of trying to create an image or movement plan that is of a higher order. This process in the selection of routines will improve as skill is increased. With adaptive models, there is concern for the notion of the relationship of higher- and lower-order plans. This consideration has been most helpful for the understanding of the nature of skilled performance and the formulation of appropriate sequential instructional guidelines.

How do people tend to perform ongoing acts and yet be able to think ahead of strategies and tactics? The basketball player who dribbles the basketball with seemingly no attention paid to it is thinking ahead about tentative circumstances. With less attention necessary for the ongoing activity, cerebral processes are freed to think ahead—to anticipate. Adaptive models provide us with useful information about the analysis of behavior, especially as we proceed from lower- to higher-order behaviors.

Another example may be found in tennis. The executive program may be termed, "Serve and rush to the net," and obviously this program would be demonstrated by a higher-skilled performer. The beginning tennis player is panicked about merely throwing the ball straight up in the air and he prays that ball contact is good, let alone worrying about rushing to the net. The highly skilled performer is able to formalize a complex movement plan, so to speak, about not only hitting the ball and hitting it into the court correctly, but rushing to the net simultaneously as well. These, of course, are the independent lower-order kinds of behaviors that need to be learned if the executive plan is to be realized as well. Task analysis and person analysis (level of skill) would suggest the appropriate executive program that needs to be conceptualized and developed.

One of the models that I have developed represents an attempt to mesh together cybernetic, information processing, and adaptive models in order to identify the component parts of the human behaving system, how they are interrelated, and then how they function in such a way as to determine behavioral output. The schematics are presented in Figure 4.1. Familiarity with research on learning processes, functions, and mechanisms, and understanding how people are similar in behaving processes, leads to the more effective advisement that instructors and trainers can provide as they work with learners to develop their skills. This is a generalizing model. It is an effort to identify processes in general that are associated with all people and with all types of behaviors.

If we look at how people may differ from each other, we must consider a host of other variables (see Figure 4.2). It is readily apparent that people are dissimilar. Each has a unique behaving system because there are variations in abilities and

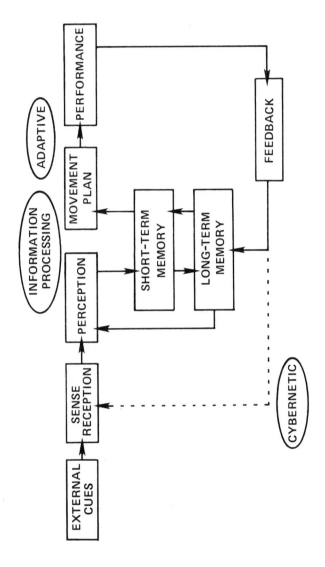

Figure 4.1. Impact of concepts from information processing, adaptive, and cybernetic models on the human behaving system.

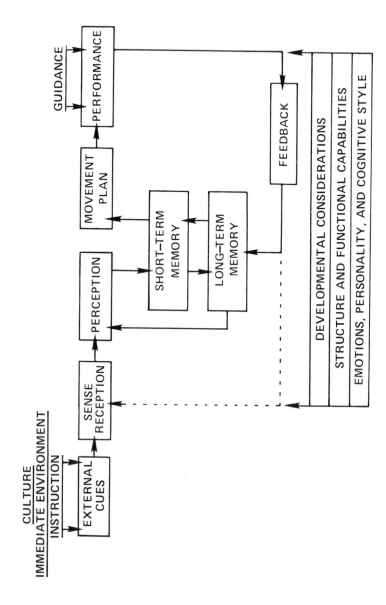

Figure 4.2. Factors that contribute to individual differences in human behaving systems.

capabilities due to genetics and experiences. There are differences in developmental factors, past learning and training experiences, and the way we are influenced by social and cultural factors. People from different cultures have special kinds of interests, attitudes, and motivations to perform and persevere at various kinds of activities.

And so, if we really want to have a dynamic picture of the human behaving system, and to recognize the way people in general behave and the way they are influenced differentially, Figure 4.2 indicates the kinds of factors we must consider. This type of perspective is not only useful to theoreticians and researchers, but can be translated into more appropriate learning environments and better teaching procedures.

SOME REFLECTIONS

If one major point has evolved from the formulation of contemporary conceptual models, it is the emphasis on the role of cognitions and perceptions in the learning and performance of complex motor skills. Likewise, current directions in cognitive psychology contrast traditional behavioristic thinking as to the active role learners play in expectations, perceptions, decision-making, interpreting feedback, making attributions to performance, arousal, memory and retrieval, and other processes.

Taken together, the next step would seem to be a thorough analysis of the cognitive aspects of motor skill learning, with implications for learner strategies and training programs. As Adams (1976) has suggested, "Actually, motor behavior is draped with more cognitive activity than most are willing to admit [p. 89]." This, of course, is especially true at the beginning stages of learning motor skills.

Previous research with motor skills has indicated the popularity of simple movement tasks requiring movement accuracy, speed, or both. These tasks are novel and unique. They have not been typically experienced by subjects prior to laboratory testing; consequently, their value in determining the "true" or "pure" effects of environmental manipulations on performance and learning is not to be denied, since subjects typically start at a theoretical zero baseline in performance expectancy.

The tasks are rather easy to administer and score. They yield trends in the data in a short period of time, and they involve primarily movement behavior. But there are limitations in their usage and important questions may be raised concerning the application of such data to so-called real-life motoric activities. For instance, the terms *motor skill, psychomotor skill, perceptual motor skill,* and the like, although often used interchangeably in the literature, invariably refer to laboratory activities that are highly movement oriented. The tasks require repetition and simple movements. The learning-ceiling effect is realized very quickly. Consequently, there exist obvious limitations to the value of this research in impacting on instruction.

The rationale for considering and understanding the cognitive aspects of motor learning, and furthermore, the identification of learner strategies, may be derived from the following suppositions:

1. Research and ideas associated with motor learning and training programs, despite some contemporary approaches, have generally reflected little concern for the cognitive features in motor learning, alternative cognitive strategies, and overall personal involvement in performance, and have emphasized, instead, the physical or observable movement behavior.

2. When compared to laboratory tasks and laboratory conditions, real-life complex psychomotor tasks demand not only refined movement responses to specific cues, but typically (a) are complex and take a considerable amount of time and effort to learn well; (b) make demands for instantaneous decision-making to unpredictable cues; (c) involve the effective use of tactics and strategies to solve familiar and nonfamiliar circumstances; (d) require the appropriate use of emotions under highly stressful or arousing conditions; and (e) call for a series of actions of continuous or serial behaviors that lead to a culmination in performance determined as appropriate or inappropriate according to established criteria.

3. On-the-job performance requires not only routine and familiar behavior but also adaption, adjustment, and accommodation to unexpected or unfamiliar situations.

4. Training programs, within time constraints, can only offer experiences with a limited number of tasks under certain conditions.

5. Training programs need to be developed that can provide learners with coping behaviors and learning strategies appropriate for on-the-job anticipated or nonanticipated situations.

6. Changes in cognitive involvement from initial to terminal levels of achievement in motor performance, and cognitive processes involved in the moment-to-moment execution of goal-directed activity can be described conceptually and identified systematically for the purpose of describing cognitive strategies that might be evoked from learners in an effective training program.

7. Research needs to be extended to more real-life settings as well as to laboratory settings that come closer to simulating the "actual" instead of the artificial and the constrained.

8. Instructional procedures, including learner modules in training programs, group and individually based, can be formulated on the basis of the aforementioned material.

Many occupational and other daily activities make tremendous demands on the information-processing capabilities of the human organism, instantaneous signal detection, the appropriate use of cognitive strategies and rule applications, and the demonstration of a goal-oriented serial sequence of responses, taken all together as to determine ultimately effective movement behavior. The analysis of real-life skills suggests their extreme complexity. This has been verified by the factor analytic studies of Fleishman and his colleagues (e.g., Fleishman, 1957, 1972a, 1972b; Fleishman & Hempel, 1954; Fleishman & Stephenson, 1970) for over 20 years, the experimental work undertaken and reviewed by Fitts and Posner (1967), Welford (1968, 1972), and Whiting (1969, 1972), the task analysis models proposed by Fleishman (1970), Robb (1972), and Singer and Dick (1974), and the conceptual overview models proposed by Adams (1971), Gentile (1972), Keele (1973), Schmidt (1975), Singer (1975), Welford (1960, 1968), and Whiting (1969).

Furthermore, psychomotor activities have been categorized in various ways, with implications for task analysis and training possibilities. Singer (1975) has identified discrete and continuous, as well as self-paced, mixed-paced, and externally paced characteristics. Kriefeldt (1972) has also considered open-loop and closed-loop task characteristics. It is especially those skills that require quick anticipation, judgments, decisions, and responses to unpredictable cues, termed by Poulton (1957) and Gentile (1972) as open skills, by Knapp (1963) as perceptual skills, and by Singer (1972, 1975) as externally paced skills, that are of concern with regard to relevant training procedures.

Trainees need to learn foundational and fundamental skills as well as strategies and rules applicable to a variety of circumstances. Performance in skills is dependent upon the ability to create a plan to accomplish a goal, with images and programs that contain a serial set of flexible actions which are appropriate for familiar and novel settings. Adaptive behavior is an often overlooked yet an extremely important feature of skilled performance.

The typical motor-skills training and instructional program is conceived of as the learning of specific responses to designated cues. A heavy emphasis in on repetition of movements. If the practiced task is the only concern, this procedure is quite acceptable. Yet it does appear that the long-term expectations of many programs is to enhance the probability of the learner being able to apply knowledge and skills to new and related situational demands. It is hoped that positive transfer will occur.

Cognitive involvement, in the form of learning how to formulate rules and strategies to cope with tasks that are newly introduced, will no doubt enhance the probability of successfully confronting future, related activities. The learner should realize how to analyze tasks. Prerequisite and component tasks build up to complex task mastery. Identifying subtasks, learning how to do them and eventually putting them all together constitutes a strong portion of ultimate achievement. Remedial adjustments appropriately follow error identification.

New learnings must be continually tied to old learnings. Establishing task relationships to replace learning in sequential isolation will probably be an effective training medium for long-range goals, especially when it appears that the learner is expected to experience a variety of situations, not merely the situational tasks practiced in formalized programs. Time limitations in training programs often do not permit experiences in the assortment of tasks and situations related to the overall activity. Therefore the importance of selecting the most appropriate learning tasks, seeing the relationships of tasks to each other, applying correct strategies and rules to newly introduced ones, and rectifying errors through problem-solving, is apparent.

One objective of any program should be the development of self-learning techniques. Extra cue and instructor dependency must be minimized since the availability of an external source instruction becomes limited once training programs are terminated. The individual may be alone or will receive limited guidance. Learners who can analyze tasks and self-prescribe procedures that will enable them to accomplish their goals obviously have an advantage. The role of cognitions, for example, analysis, judgement, and problem-solving, should never be underestimated in learning motor tasks. Beyond mere recognition of this fact, practice sessions should reflect the way cognitions should be involved in motor performance.

COGNITIONS AND THE
PROCESS OF SKILL ACQUISITION

Cognitions are involved in a variety of ways in learning and performing psychomotor skills. The skill level of the person and the nature of the activity must be considered. Cognitions play a major role in determining the effectiveness of an activity at any given time.

A series of phases related to cognitive intervention, control, and direction can be identified. This series begins with an internalization of the goal (getting the idea) and proceeds to the use of feedback for evaluative and improvement purposes.

Furthermore, these cognitions can be analyzed as they change in influence, involvement, and direction as a person acquires skill. Although such changes never occur in discrete stages, Fitts and Posner (1967) have conveniently identified three that encompass the process of acquiring skills: early or cognitive (Phase I); intermediate or associative (Phase II); and final or autonomous (Phase III).

In the first stage, the trainee is consciously and actively attempting to understand learning activities and environments, and to make appropriate responses to situational demands. In most cases, learners are too aware of the surrounding cues, of which many are irrelevant, and they lack a knowledge of what they must accomplish to be successful. They have difficulty learning what to do and how to do it. The problem increases substantially when skill level is low and task complexity is high.

Once the learner has grasped what needs to be done (Phase I), the emphasis then turns to strategies—the second stage. With a reasonable goal-oriented image formulated, how should practice proceed? A multitude of trade-off decisions confront the learner and instructor (e.g., whether to emphasize speed or accuracy, whole or part learning methods, learning through guidance or trial and error, experiencing simulators or the "real thing," and the like). Alternatives need to be determined, analyzed, and decided upon.

In the final stage, the trainee has attained a level of task mastery sufficient to perform with apparent automaticity. Immediate performance does not require much regulation, monitoring, and control. The higher centers of the nervous system are freed and the trainee can learn other skills and anticipate possible occurrences in order to create appropriate strategies. Automaticity within a framework of potential adaption to nonpredictable occurrences is a desirable endstate. With task proficiency comes less overt verbalization; for if anything, this process can be a hindrance to fluid performance.

It is readily apparent that whether we address the nature of a person's involvement with an activity at any one time, or a person's changing involvement as skill is acquired, an understanding of the role of cognition leads to the identification of many learning considerations and alternative strategies. In turn, task analysis, person analysis, program objectives, and resource and time availability will indicate the ways in which cognitive strategies are associated with the learning of psychomotoric activities, the number of alternative viable strategies, and ones that might be best suited for the circumstances.

The beginner appears to invoke cognitions for the following reasons.

1. To understand goals and to create an internalized image (covert verbalization), a process that could be termed *goal-image formation*.
2. To recognize similarities in the characteristics of the present task and situation with previous experiences (generalizability).
3. To recall related behaviors to the present task (to remember related cue–response associations and procedures; to retrieve information effectively).
4. To perceive the nature of the activity in the context of the environment, with situational demands and costs and payoffs relevant to decision-making.
5. To identify and select at any given time the most relevant and minimal cues to which to respond.
6. To concentrate in a relaxed state, demonstrating the desirable arousal level (the effect of cognitions over emotions).
7. To maintain the ideal motivational state and attitudes for optimal performance, task preference, and task perseverance (the effect of cognitions over emotions).
8. To establish goals and expectations that are high and specific, but attainable—a process that could be termed *goal-expectancy formation*.
9. To make correct response decisions (amplitude, speed, accuracy, direction).
10. To use problem solving, analysis, and adaptive behaviors when required.
11. To rehearse mentally prior to, during, and/or after performance (depending upon the situation and desirability of rehearsal).
12. To adapt to stress (cognitive control over and regulation of emotions).
13. To evaluate ongoing performance to monitor, regulate, and adjust performance, and evaluate the results of performance for future accommodations.
14. To attribute performance outcomes to the appropriate reasons (ability, energy expended, task difficulty, and luck).

The more advanced performer uses many of these same processes in the same manner without conscious attention and in a more sophisticated form. Of course, one of the basic differences between the novice and the highly skilled is that the latter does not have to think as much. It seems that with the development of skill, higher-order programs can be executed since the system is freed from the need to be consciously attentive to lower-order considerations. The automation of skill permits acts to be run off quickly, smoothly, and efficiently. But it must be emphasized that automated or nonthinking behavior is not always appropriate. There must be flexibility and adaptability in the system so that adjustments can be made when necessary.

In going through the list of cognitions, it becomes apparent that strategies need to be used by trainees to activate processes that will enhance learning. The objectives of the training program and the type of task (e.g., self-paced or externally paced) will also influence learner strategies. Space limitations do not permit an elaborate or detailed analysis of the many cognitive considerations related to the acquisition of skill. Some of them have been selected as representative to be described here to some degree. They include "goal-image formation," "goal-expectancy formation," and "directing and controlling the act."

Goal-Image Formation

A trainee must create an image of what is to be done in order for practice to proceed in a meaningful manner. The trainee must determine what is supposed to be achieved. This may be thought of as the first stage in the intellectualization of the learning of a motor skill.

How can information best be presented to enhance skill acquisition and retention? Attempts have been made to conceptualize associative learning in terms of imagery. As Paivio (1970) indicates, people may have difficulty encoding from word or picture to symbolic mediator or decoding from the mediator to the response. The presentation of cues or information can be concrete or abstract, visual or verbal, in a meaningful context or in isolation (Rohwer, 1970). Rohwer recommends that learners be taught to use verbal and visual kinds of elaborative activities. The transformation of information into a meaningful and memorable form serves as an internalized representation of the to-be-performed skill, to trigger it and to be used as a comparator.

Intuitively, we may be able to suggest a variety of ways in which trainees may form goal images. For instance, Rohwer (1970) suggests that attempts at imagery are more effective when verbal tags are applied to and stored with the images. Although verbal mediators may tend to confuse and to impair the performance of young children, more mature learners can intellectualize the relevant aspects of each image with words. If task components and verbal mediators will not overload a trainee's processing system, an instructional strategy in which visual and verbal communication are used should prove beneficial.

Actually, the things we learn are usually mediated by words. The trainee may have to learn instructions and directions to know how and what to perform. Not only are there words from external sources (instructors) but words spoken to oneself during activity. This latter theoretical state has been termed *verbal mediation* and has also been referred to as *conceptualization, ideation,* and *thought processing.*

The ability, then, to succeed in motor performance may very well be somewhat related to the ability to apply external and internal words to motor acts. If verbal labels are to be attached to movement, there is the expectancy that the learner can understand the choice of terms, phrases, labels, or descriptors used by the instructor. Unfortunately, this is not always the case.

Sometimes verbal mediation processes interfere with the potential production of skilled movement. Consider, for example, the person who thinks too much and becomes confused, and thus delays acting or improperly reacts to a particular situation. Movements to be executed quickly, accurately, and successfully must be cued properly, but too much attention to the act itself or to too many cues can have disastrous effects.

A mature trainee is capable of simultaneous storage of both pictures and words. This allows for an instructional strategy consisting of live or videotaped models, combined with verbalization of the skill. Zimmerman and Rosenthal (1974) concluded that modeling, when accompanied by a verbal rule, produces the highest level of acquisition and generalization. In other words, learners exposed to modeling exhibited the highest level of skill proficiency and retention and transfer of a skill when compared to other learners. A person learning from a model accompanied with a verbal description of the skill no doubt readily adapts previously-acquired skills in such a way as to learn new skills rapidly.

In support of this finding, Landers and Landers (1973) concluded that subjects who were exposed to an expert model performed better on a motor skill task than subjects who were not exposed to the model. If the trainees view the instructor's performance attentively, they will increase their potential to perform the task proficiently. It is not necessary, however, for the model to be present throughout the total learning period. Landers (1975) found that the temporal positioning of a model prior to and midway through the learning period was sufficient for superior motor performance over no model at all.

Modeling procedures represent one way in which to communicate the intended goal. Whatever means are employed, attentiveness and concentration are required on the part of the learner. These are behaviors that must be acquired. They are associated with quality performance in readying the learner for the experience, and in promoting quality performance during actual practice. Imagery, attentiveness, and concentration, as well as many other processes become less consciously directed and more automatic as trainees become more proficient in performing the tasks. In other words, just as the skills themselves are learned, the art of concentration is also acquired.

The goal image is more easily defined and activities are learned more quickly when trainees can generalize from previous, related experiences. Recognition of similarities from past behavior to present, and recall of appropriate decisions, strategies, and acts are cognitive processes that enhance present learning and performance. Generalizations assist in the early stages of practice. But there is no substitute for specific task practice if high levels of proficiency are to be attained.

In summary, the ability to form the appropriate image depends on previous experiences related to the present task, methods used to strengthen the image, concentration, and attentiveness. Although the instructor can use a variety of procedures to aid goal-image formation, in the long run, the learner should be self-directed and capable of using available information for this purpose. Let us now turn to performance expectations, which affect motivation and the analysis of personal and situational factors.

Goal-Expectancy Formation

There is no doubt that each learner develops performance expectations based on past successes and failures and an interpretation of present demands. These expectations may be quantitative (e.g., a specific score) or qualitative (e.g., good or bad). Goal levels may be high or low, general or specific, very attainable or remotely attainable.

Whereas the learning of cognitive material does not usually promote continual self-testing and feedback (except with computer-managed instruction and programmed material), the opposite is true with motor skills. Continual active engagement in the learning process provides feedback for the motor learner. This feedback is useful for motivational, directional, corrective, and goal-setting purposes.

Aspiration and expectancy levels continually change with repeated experience in an activity, assuming the participant is allowed to set the goals. Goals serve as motivators because they give one something to aim for, thereby making the task more interesting and challenging. Goals can also be established by someone other than the person performing the task. In either case—with self-projected or externally imposed goals—performance is usually better when clear goals exist than when goals are vague and general or virtually nonexistent. Lock and Bryan (1966a) used a task requiring complex coordination and concluded that the existence of specific goals produced higher levels of performance than did nonspecific goals. These results were confirmed in subsequent research (Locke & Bryan, 1966b, 1967).

The **reason** for the effects of performance goals was investigated by Locke and Bryan (1967). They found trying for a specific goal to be the main source of **interest** in the task.

A reasonable positive relationship appears to exist between goal level and performance level. Reasonably high, specific goals seem to facilitate performance. Apparently, the activation of cognitive processes in this manner enhances motivation and contains a directive function. If the trainee has some control over establishing and achieving goals, the perception of internal locus of causality leads to a greater commitment to performance (Singer, 1975), a higher level of intrinsic motivation (Deci, 1975), and thus to better performance.

Expectancy is defined in the research literature as a cognitive interpretation of the likelihood of success in a particular task—that is, an assessment of subjective degree of difficulty. Such assessments could be considered as a generalized prediction for success or failure, based on previous experience with similar tasks; or, such assessments could be a specific prediction from performance on the same task at a previous occasion (Rotter, 1966).

According to attribution theory (see, e.g., Weiner, 1974), estimates of expectancy are determined by the perceptions of the task, (for example, the ease or difficulty of the task) and perceptions of personal attributes (for example, ability, effort, and luck). Researchers using cognitive tasks have demonstrated that attributions to the factors of ability and task difficulty have a greater effect on expectancy shifts than attributions to the unstable factors of luck and effort. Many other relationships have also been drawn. It is possible that attributes, expectancy, and performance may be related as described in Figure 4.3.

It might be speculated, as we have at Florida State University (Singer & McCaughan, 1978), that successful performances may be attributed to stable, internal factors. These, in turn, influence expectancies for future performance by raising the level of aspiration, which might produce a greater degree of persistence and effort at a task, finally resulting in improved performance. An attributional analysis during skill acquisition (virtually all the research in this area is with cognitive materials) may assist in understanding the persistence and intensity of persons with differential achievement dispositions to aid prediction of task learning and performance.

A key to effective training programs lies in understanding personal motivational tendencies. We need to analyze cognitive processes in a way that might reveal the underlying decision-making and motivational processes of the individual. This would assist in making predictions of future performance as well as providing valuable personal information that could be useful for instructors who wish to use techniques that could influence attributes and achievement expectation, and ultimately motor performance.

Perhaps one of the most important statements in this regard has been made by Flanagan (1973), who writes, "Research in the last decade has made it quite clear

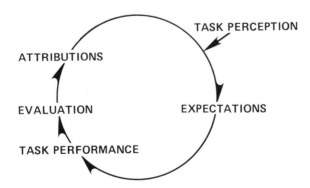

Figure 4.3. The relationship of expectancies and attributions to performance.

that the most effective force for motivation is progress toward a valued goal [p. 554].'' Furthermore, Flanagan suggests that progress in achieving goals should be much more effective without external systems of incentives and awards, and when the person develops a plan of action and has taken responsibility for executing it.

In conclusion, achievement expectancies are related to a host of situational and personal variables. These expectations are tied in to achievement itself, and therefore, many experiences in a training program should be interpreted as personally rewarding and successful in leading to future goals. Self-understanding of potential causative factors of performance and the establishment of realistic, high, but attainable goals should promote performance output.

Directing and Controlling the Act

Cognitive processes not only set the stage for performance, in terms of orienting and preparing the trainee as we have just seen, but also guide the plan of action. Yet, beginners and skilled performers differ in the degree and type of conscious involvement in the performance of a movement act. What is responsible for this change? The location and degree of attentional requirements, the development of error detection and correction mechanisms, and the use of memory, coding, and retrieval systems and processes are among the important considerations. The trend toward the consideration and analysis of processes involved in skills learning (as contrasted with the many years of task-oriented analysis) can be observed in the thinking and writing of numerous contemporary scholars (e.g., Stelmach, 1976).

As Glencross (1975) rightfully states, instruction can be more effective if an understanding of the information is required of the trainee at each stage of skill learning. ''Such information must resolve the uncertainty for the learner in terms of what decisions he should make in order to achieve the desired outcome [p. 50].'' When a person performs erroneously, it could be due to a wrong decision (inappropriate plan of action) or to an inappropriately developed plan. Obviously, performance output ideally matches the input. With experience, the learner develops a hierarchical structure of plans, programs, or schemata, enabling correct responses to specific cues, assuming anticipation, retrieval, and decision-making processes function correctly. Consequently, it appears that a related series of cognitive processes are active in the production of skill, that possibilities for achieving goals and the goals themselves become more elaborate and sophisticated, and that automaticity or redirected cognitive involvement also occurs as skill increases.

Another change of function in the automation of skills is the greater reliance on internal cues rather than external ones. The beginner is more attentive—perhaps too attentive—to environmental conditions and situational cues. Advanced learners appear to have constructed a better internalized state (the use of sense receptors in self-regulation and control and the refinement of programs and preprograms). A benefit of this circumstance is that it allows a person to attend to secondary or simultaneous demands of the same or another task. Many times during the performance of a task, cognitive decisions must be made with regard to other events.

Experimentally, this behavior is investigated with a paradigm called *secondary task loading*. In other words, a second task is executed at the same time a primary task is performed, and outcomes are compared with single task performances.

The effect of secondary task loading on the performance of a primary task (decisional stress) has been examined in a variety of circumstances. For instance, Eysenck and Thompson (1966) found that pursuit rotor performance declined proportionately to the intensity of the secondary task demands (foot-pedal responses). In the last of a series of studies designed to evaluate vehicular driver capacity (Brown, Tikner, & Simmonds, 1969), it was reported that specific perceptions related to car driving ability were impaired in the presence of secondary tasks, such as using a car phone. Some investigators have analyzed their findings within the framework of the single-channel hypothesis (e.g., Craik, 1948; Welford, 1959). The term "single channel" functionally describes the central decision mechanism that must be allowed a finite time to process one stimulus and its response before response to a second one is possible. However, certain empirical data (e.g., Allport, Antonis, & Reynolds, 1972) suggest that the human system need not only be a sequential processor of information but on occasion and under certain circumstances can be considered as a parallel processor (multichannel) of information.

For instructional and learning purposes, it is important to analyze task demands or the demands of concurrently performed tasks, the nature of these demands, and how performance can be improved. What learning strategies can we employ, considering the limitations of the human processing system? The more there is to do at one time, the more stress and demands are placed on the person.

Whatever the task, *selective attention* to the minimum number of appropriate cues is an important consideration for success. This is a perceptual and concentration problem that confronts learners in all types of situations. Selective attention is the process whereby attention is focused on certain aspects of the environment, with perception the end result (Marteniuk, 1976). Analogous to a practice effect, selective attention improves as different situations are encountered. According to Norman (1969), if a highly pertinent item is present in the information received by the trainee, it will be recognized and selected. Highly skilled performers, through experience, are able to make predictions from the information available about events that will probably occur.

In the previous discussion, it should be realized that the concept of selective attention is also related to other psychological concepts, for example, perceptual set, arousal, capacity, and effort (Wickens, 1976). Processes and mechanisms associated with these concepts should be in the ideal state of function for acceptable performance. This is true regardless of the nature of the task, although different types of tasks make different personal demands.

In self-paced, open-loop skills, variability in performance is discouraged and the attempt is to practice toward automation. In externally paced, closed-loop skills, adaptability to situational demands suggests the need for a repertoire of responses and the capacity to handle a high load of information. Therefore, performance in skills is dependent upon the ability to create a plan to accomplish a goal within time constraints, with images and programs that contain a serial set of flexible actions appropriate to familiar and novel settings.

The automation of skills, as pointed out by Jones (1976) may be a desirable end-state for performance in some cases but not in others. Closed skills, which have little variability in their demands, would appear to benefit from repetitive practice, which leads to habitlike performance. In open-loop skills, either automation or flexibility in behavior could be preferable, depending on circumstances. Some evidence (e.g., Hartnett, 1975; Mannell & Duthie, 1975) indicates that the more task performance is automated, the more difficult it is to make adjustments where necessary. In other words, the higher the level of programming, the less flexibility is demonstrated in rapid performance. Additional time is apparently needed to reject an habituated behavior (which might be inappropriate) in favor of the correct one.

Training procedures should be sensitive to the question of when to automate and when not to automate. Strategies to automate versus those to create adaptive behaviors would be dissimilar, as are the demands on the information-processing system and subsequent response patterns. As we can see, cognitive processes and strategies can be examined according to task classification as well as personal capabilities as movement control is considered.

PRACTICE CONSIDERATIONS FOR
LEARNER STRATEGIES

Although it would be ideal for learners to be able to manage their own learning, a major role of instructors is to assist learners in developing appropriate behaviors and strategies. There are those who would call for the application of psychoinstructional design principles[2] to approach situations and needs in a systematic manner. Presumably, instruction can then proceed in a logical and orderly manner for the fulfillment of stated goals and objectives.

A number of macrostrategies (general themes or philosophies of instruction) and microstrategies (specific considerations or tradeoffs in particular aspects of the skills learning situation) can be described. These considerations and the resultant decisions as to how to practice for perfection are made by instructors, learners, or both. Seidel (1971) has warned that improved instruction, grounded on the application of better instructional strategies based on learning theories, can occur only when a bridge is built from laboratory research (from which theories are developed) to the real world, including course materials and individual student differences. What is needed is a "global view of the informational requirements of the instructional system [Seidel, 1971, p. 3]." And certainly, there are scholars like Glaser (1976) who are quite optimistic about establishing a prescriptive science of instructional design.

Microstrategies embrace such procedural considerations as whether to practice skills in wholes or parts; in one sequence or another; under real or simulated

---

[2]See, for example, Chapters 15 and 16 in Snelbecker (1974) for an overview.

conditions; emphasizing speed, accuracy or both; and the like. The instructor considers situational manipulations, techniques for supplying reinforcers, incentives, knowledge of results, and so on, if they should be supplied and if so, to what extent and in what form. These and many others represent microstrategy concerns, and are necessary to be addressed by learners and instructors alike. However, they will not be discussed here. I prefer to consider the "larger" issues, or macrostrategy possibilities.

For example, we might question the content of training programs. On the one hand, to what extent should they contain specific information and skills, to be taught and learned in a very specifically prescribed manner? And on the other hand, to what extent should rules and strategies be taught in order to assist the trainee to develop generalizable problem-solving skills in preparation for possible future task demands? Intuitively, it seems that the positive influence on **product** (specific information and skills) as well as **process** (adaption and trouble-shooting behavior) are desirable outcomes of training programs. Since the first outcome is obvious in its importance and evident as the goal of many programs, I will deal with the second outcome, which is more difficult to quantify.

In order to adapt more readily and easily, one must apply the appropriate learning approach to the activity and the situation. Rules and strategies, if constructed correctly and usefully, should enable the learner to adapt what has once been learned to new but related circumstances. This type of transfer effect occurs when the individual has learned how to analyze tasks, to develop internalized guidelines for solutions that are not learned only by rote, and to formulate rules and strategies associated with the successful undertaking of a cluster of tasks, even though direct experience may only have been offered on one task in one situation.

The establishment of rules and strategies allows the trainee to identify task and situation relationships, that is, to tie new learnings back to old learnings (Gagné, 1970). Identifying such relationships leads to improved overall skill potential; learners should be able to cope with a variety of situations, not merely the situations and tasks practiced in formalized training programs (Singer, 1975). Gagné (1970) prefers the learning of abstract rules and concepts (with the intention of applying them to future-related tasks) to the learning of specific content by traditional methods. The trainee who can analyze tasks and self-prescribe procedures becomes a self-learner (Gagné & Briggs, 1974), and is at an advantage compared with other learners.

Following this line of logic, the implications for training programs are evident. Instructor dependency should be minimized, for guidance may not be available once formalized training is completed. The development of self-learning techniques might be one of the major objectives of any instructional or training program.

Maximal versus Minimal Guidance

I have been somewhat idealistic about minimizing instructor control in the learning situation. And yet, the nature of the learning experiences should reflect intended trainee outcomes. A more careful analysis of the tradeoffs involved in highly guided versus problem-solving learning is now in order.

Instructional designers have recognized a broad spectrum of approaches toward instruction that range from discovery or problem-solving methods to more authoritarian, formal programs (e.g., drill methods). Other strategies range on the continuum between these two extremes, incorporating aspects of both. A representative approach of this nature in the skills area might include a demonstration of the desired behavior, guided trials, and then "do-it-yourself" trials with sporadic guidance until the intended behavior or behaviors are attained.

The guided approach for the learning of cognitive materials is probably best represented by programmed techniques. Programmed learning controls the learner through step-by-step reinforced progressions. Skinner (1968), a pioneer in the development of programmed instruction, contends that it is better to learn something correctly the first time than to undo past error-filled experiences and then relearn. The discovery method approach to instruction allows for and encourages experimentation and exploration for solutions to problems. The method encourages reflective thinking and self-direction.

A distinguishing factor in these approaches is the function and desirability of error-making in the process of learning. In the learning of skills, as contrasted with the learning of other matter, a real issue as to "whether to err or not to err" (Singer, 1977) can be identified. Those who advocate the discovery method believe that learners can profit from their errors. Errors are presumed to aid in the development of problem-solving abilities applicable to future, related learning situations. Possibly a greater activation occurs on the part of the learners in the process of learning. From another point of view, we might consider guided learners as being asked to use minimal thought processes whereas problem-solving learners are continually required to activate higher-order cognitive processes and coping strategies.

The advocates of error minimization in the acquisition of skill believe that the learning of an inappropriate behavior will impair later learning, resulting in unlearning and relearning. Schulman and Keislar (1966) write that the occurrence of errors results in (a) interference effects that are resistant to extinction and (b) emotional problems, more specifically, frustration. Prompted and guided learning are favored by them, as is reinforcing and corrective feedback information.

As to which technique yields better performance, early studies (Macrae & Holding, 1965, 1966) indicated a preference for guided learning. However, the effect of guidance on learning decreased as the number of learning trials increased. Macrae and Holding (1966) concluded that guidance becomes more effective as task complexity, such as those tasks related to military maneuvers, increases.

Studies involving the retention and transfer of psychomotor skills based on acquisition through different instructional strategies have been limited. Prather and various associates used a complex perceptual motor skill (range estimation as used by airplane pilots) to investigate transfer effectiveness of trial-and-error learning as compared with prompted learning. Heavily prompted learning led to a significant advantage over trial-and-error learning in early trials. With the addition of more trials and with performance reaching asymptote, there was little difference in performance as a result of the training methods used (Berry, Prather, & Jones, 1971; Prather, 1971). A comparison between the two instructional strategies showed that the trial-and-error method produced greater transfer than the error-free method (Prather, 1969, 1971; Prather & Berry, 1970). The greater amount of experience produced by the error-free learning would seem to enable the learner to perform better in other highly related motor tasks.

In the first psychomotor skills study in which trials to a learning criterion were employed, Singer and Gaines (1975) indicated that prompted learners maintained a significant advantage in both the number of learning trials and task completion time over the trial-and-error group at the conclusion of the learning period. However, analysis of the transfer data yielded a significant difference favoring the trial-and-error group in time to criterion. It was concluded that those subjects learning under problem-solving conditions were able to approach the transfer situation in the successful performance of a new task in fewer trials and less time than that required by subjects learning under prompted conditions. The implication for enhancing trainee performance on various complex and highly related tasks is intuitively obvious.

Certain conclusions are warranted as evidenced by the research in this area. The instructional strategy employed to teach a motor skill must depend on the purpose for learning that skill. If it is a new skill, and high proficiency is desired in a short time, then guided learning seems to be the appropriate choice. If the task is to be recalled and transferred to a new situation at a later date, then some method of problem-solving strategy should be employed (Singer, 1975). Finally, after an initial task is learned, the learning of a second and related task is favored under problem-solving conditions (Singer & Gaines, 1975; Singer & Pease, 1976).

It can be inferred from the research evidence that early training may best benefit trainees through some means of guided learning. As the trainees advance further, it is probable that they will not be exposed to all the potential circumstances that may occur. At this point, some method of trial-and-error learning would be best. The vast number of experiences occurring during this type of learning period would enable trainees to develop the appropriate strategies they need to adapt to novel situations.

CONCLUDING COMMENTS

Cognitions are involved in different phases of the execution of an act. The appropriate strategies need to be enacted if success is to be realized. Although many training programs are geared for the preparation of personnel to perform psychomotoric tasks, little consideration has been given to the necessary and appropriate learner strategies that need to be taught and experienced by the trainees. Such strategies should indicate (a) a sensitivity to research, theory and the application of both to the formation of effective strategies; (b) an awareness of task analysis procedures and occupational demands; (c) the possibility of considering individual difference factors in learner styles, rates of learning, and motivation; and (d) the need for learners to develop such capabilities as trouble-shooting, adaption, problem-solving, and rule application.

Imposed training often fails to teach learners to think, to develop alternatives, to problem solve, and to evaluate. And in general, it often fails to motivate them. For instance, cognitions are involved in forming images, plans, goals, intentions, or "getting the idea" of what is to be done. They are also reflected as they interact with attitudes in the form of task expectations. Expectations, performance level, and attributions (causations of performance attributed to internal or external variables) appear to be interrelated, according to cognitive motivational theory, perhaps best illustrated in attribution theory as proposed by Heider (1958) and extended by Weiner (1974).

During actual practice, cognitions are associated with selective attention to the minimal correct cues, mental rehearsal, control over arousal level, and problem solving, if indeed this is encouraged. With training, skills are performed as if automatic. Proficiency is determined by the capability to achieve predetermined goals, either through an automatic run of a program or with the modification of behavior through effective use of internalized feedback to adapt to unpredicted or unusual circumstances.

The performer has to learn how to use corrective processes, to detect errors in performance, and to self-regulate behavior. With experience and information certainty comes automaticity in performance as well as the time and ability to anticipate and invoke strategies. The organization of movements at high skill levels is reflected by "more flexible, expedient, and economic methods [Bernstein, 1967, p. 127]." Some activities require sequential behavior under specified conditions. Potentially few variations in performance are acceptable. For other activities, a greater flexibility is permissable, indeed perhaps desirable, in the execution of their serial parts.

Consequently, cognitions in the form of rules, strategies, plans, and the formation of programs are closely allied to the production of skilled movement. Skilled behavior is emitted as a function of the sophistication of cognitions, response repertoire, and the resources of the physical system.

Assuming the validity of this premise, those cognitive processes involved in the execution of an activity need to be identified and clarified. Distinctions must be made according to task classification, performer's level of skill, and other individual difference factors. Training and learner strategies, as associated with these considerations, can be described and ordered in priority fashion to accommodate learners in achieving skills and knowledges appropriate for occupational demands. Singer and Dick (1974) have made some recommendations in this regard (see Figure 4.4). A logical next step would be the packaging of modules that encompass strategies applied to the learning of skills. These would be individual-centered and developed based upon the research collected in field situations.

Job analysis, training goals, and training programs must be compatible. Since a limited amount of content can be oriented toward specifics within the training time,

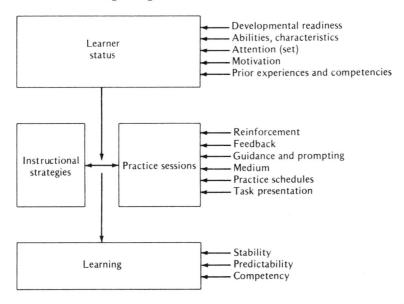

Figure 4.4 The intermix of learner status, practice, and strategy variables in the learning process. [From R. N. Singer & W. Dick, *Teaching Physical Education: A Systems Approach.* Boston: Houghton Mifflin, 1974. Reprinted with permission.]

the question is: What kinds of learner *processes* can be activated, what can the learner learn *how to do,* in order to generalize to and accommodate occupational demands?

Much thought has been given during the past decade as to whether different instructional methods should be related to learner characteristics. It seems plausible to me that certain learners might prefer one form of presentation or instructional technique, whereas other learners might accomplish more under alternative circumstances. Typical of this type of research is the work of Tallmadge and Shearer (1971), who instructed and tested Navy enlisted men. The literature embracing the relationship of instructional approaches to individual difference factors in students has usually been termed *aptitude treatment interaction* (ATI), and Tobias (1976) offers a recent overview on the current state of affairs. The research data indicate conservative optimism for the possibility of identifying the important interactions as well as implementing such considerations into learning strategies programs.

REFERENCES

Adams, J. A. Response feedback and Learning. *Psychological Bulletin,* 1968, *70,* 486–504.
Adams, J. A. A closed-looped theory of motor learning. *Journal of Motor Behavior,* 1971, *3,* 111–149.
Adams, J. A. Issues for a closed-loop theory of motor learning. In G. E. Stelmach (Ed.), *Motor control: Issues and trends.* New York: Academic Press, 1976.

Allport, A. D., Antonis, B., & Reynolds, P. On the division of attention: A disproof of the single channel hypothesis. *Quarterly Journal of Experimental Psychology,* 1972, *24*, 225–235.

Bernstein, N. *The coordination and regulation of movements.* New York: Pergamon, 1967.

Berry, G., Prather, D., & Jones, G. Effect of prompting and feedback on the learning of a perceptual skill. *Proceedings of the 79th Annual Convention of the American Psychological Association,* 1971, *6*, 589–590.

Brown, I. D., Tikner, A. H., & Simmonds, D. C. V. Interference between concurrent tasks of driving and telephoning. *Journal of Applied Psychology,* 1969, *53*, 419–424.

Craik, K. H. W. Theory of the human operator in control systems. *British Journal of Psychology,* 1948, *48*, 142–148.

Deci, E. *Intrinsic motivation.* New York: Plenum, 1975.

Eysenck, H. J., & Thompson, W. The effects of distraction on pursuit rotor learning, performance and reminiscence. *British Journal of Psychology,* 1966, *57*, 99–106.

Fitts, P. M., & Posner, M. *Human performance.* Belmont, Calif.: Brooks, Cole, 1967.

Flanagan, J. C. Education: How and for what. *American Psychologist,* 1973, *28*, 551–556.

Fleishman, E. A. A comparative study of aptitude patterns in unskilled and skilled psychomotor performers. *Journal of Applied Psychology,* 1957, *41*, 263–272.

Fleishman, E. A. On the relation between abilities, learning, and human performance. *American Psychologist,* 1972, *27* 1017–1032. (a)

Fleishman, E. A. Structure and measurement of psychomotor abilities. In R. N. Singer (Ed.), *The psychomotor domain: Movement behavior.* Philadelphia: Lea & Febiger, 1972. (b)

Fleishman, E., & Hempel, W. E., Jr. Changes in factor structure of a complex psychomotor test as a function of practice. *Psychometrika,* 1954, *19*, 239–254.

Fleishman, E. A., & Stephenson, R. W. *Development of a taxonomy of human performance: A review of the third year's progress.* Washington, D.C.: American Institutes for Research, 1970.

Gagné, R. *The conditions of learning.* New York: Holt, 1970.

Gagné, R. Educational technology and the learning process. *Educational Researcher,* 1974, *3*, 3–8.

Gagné, R., & Briggs, L. *Principles of instructional design.* New York: Holt, 1974.

Gentile, A. M. A working model of skill acquisition with application to teaching. *Quest,* 1972, *17*, 3–23.

Glaser, R. Components of a psychology of instruction: Toward a science of design. *Review of Educational Research,* 1976, *46*, 1–24.

Glencross, D. J. Information processing and skill training. *Australian Journal of Sports Medicine,* 1975, *7*, 48–51.

Hartnett, O. M. Error in response to infrequent signals. *Ergonomics,* 1975, *18*, 213–223.

Heider, F. *The psychology of interpersonal relations.* New York: Wiley, 1958.

Jones, J. G. *Automation of skill: Its pros and cons.* Paper presented at the International Seminar in Motor Learning in Physical Education and Sport, Wingate Institute for Physical Education and Sport, Netanya, Israel, April 1976.

Keele, S. W. *Attention and human performance.* Pacific Palisades, Calif.: Goodyear, 1973.

Knapp, B. *Skill in sport: The attainment of proficiency..* London: Routledge & Kegan Paul, 1963.

Kreifeldt, J. G. A dynamic model of behaviors in a discrete open-loop self-paced motor skill. *IEE Transactions on Systems, Man, and Cybernetics,* 1972, *SMC-2,* 262–273.

Landers, D. M. Observational learning of a motor skill: Temporal spacing of demonstrations and audience presence. *Journal of Motor Behavior,* 1975, *7*, 281–288.

Landers, D. M., & Landers, D. M. Teacher versus peer models: Effects of model's presence and performance level on motor behavior. *Journal of Motor Behavior,* 1973, *5*, 129–139.

Locke, E., & Bryan, J. The effects of goal-setting, rule-learning, and knowledge of score on performance. *American Journal of Psychology,* 1966, *79*, 451–457. (a)

Locke, E., & Bryan, J. Cognitive aspects of psychomotor performance: The effects of performance goals on level of performance. *Journal of Applied Psychology,* 1966, *50*, 286–291. (b)

Locke, E., & Bryan, J. Performance goals as determinants of level of performance and boredom. *Journal of Applied Psychology,* 1967, *51*, 120–130.

Macrae, A. W., & Holding, D. H. Method and task in motor guidance. *Ergonomics,* 1965, *8,* 315–320.

Macrae, A. W., & Holding, D. H. Rate and force of guidance in perceptual motor tasks with reversed or random spatial correspondence. *Ergonomics,* 1966, *9,* 289–296.

Mannell, R. C., & Duthie, J. H. Habit lag: When "automatization" is dysfunctional. *Journal of Psychology,* 1975, *89,* 73–80.

Marteniuk, R. *Information processing in motor skills.* New York: Holt, 1976.

Miller, G. A., Galanter, E., & Pribram, K. H. *Plans and the structure of behavior.* New York: Holt, 1960.

Norman, D. *Memory and attention.* New York: Wiley, 1969.

Paivio, A. On the functional significance of imagery. *Psychological Bulletin,* 1970, *73,* 385–392.

Poulton, E. D. On prediction in skilled movements. *Psychological Bulletin,* 1957, *54,* 467–478.

Prather, D. The effects of trial-and-error or errorless training on the efficiency of learning a perceptual-motor skill and performance under transfer and stress. (Doctoral dissertation, University of Arizona, 1969.) *Dissertation Abstracts International,* 1969, *30,* 2385A. (University Microfilms No. 69-20, 790.)

Prather, D. Trial-and-error versus errorless learning: Training, transfer and stress. *American Journal of Psychology,* 1971, *84,* 377–386.

Prather, D., & Berry, G. Comparisons of trial-and-error versus highly prompted learning of a perceptual skill. *Proceedings of the 78th Annual Convention of the American Psychological Association,* 1970, *5,* 677–678.

Robb, M. D. Task analysis: A consideration for teachers of skills. *Research Quarterly,* 1972, *43,* 362–373.

Rohwer, W. Images and pictures in children's learning: Research results and educational implications. *Psychological Bulletin,* 1970, *73,* 393–403.

Rotter, J. Generalized expectancies for internal versus external control of reinforcement. *Psychological Monographs,* 1966, *80* (1, Whole No. 609).

Schmidt, R. A. A schema theory of discrete motor skill learning. *Psychological Review,* 1975, *82,* 225–260.

Schulman, L. & Keisler, E. *Learning by discovery—a critical appraisal.* Chicago: Rand McNally, 1966.

Seidel, R. J. *Theories and strategies related to measurements in individualized instruction* (HumRRO Prof. Pap. 2-71). Alexandria, Va.: Human Resources Research Organization, March 1971.

Singer, R. N. *Coaching, athletics, and psychology.* New York: McGraw-Hill, 1972.

Singer, R. N. *Motor learning and human performance* (2nd ed.) New York: Macmillan, 1975.

Singer, R. N. To err or not to err: A question for the instruction of psychomotor skills. *Review of Educational Research,* 1977, *47,* 479–498.

Singer, R. N., & Dick, W. *Teaching physical education: A systems approach.* Boston: Houghton, 1974.

Singer, R. N., & Gaines, L. Effects of prompted and problem solving approaches on learning and transfer of motor skills. *American Educational Research Journal,* 1975, *12,* 395–402.

Singer, R. N., & Pease, D. A comparison of discovery learning and guided instructional strategies on motor skill learning, retention, and transfer. *Research Quarterly,* 1976, *47,* 788—791.

Skinner, B. F. *The technology of teaching,* New York: Appleton, 1968.

Snelbecker, G. E. *Learning theory, instructional theory, and psychoeducational design.* New York: McGraw-Hill, 1974.

Stelmach, G. E., (Ed.). *Motor control: Issues and trends.* New York: Academic Press, 1976.

Tallmadge, G. K., & Shearer, J. W. Interactive relationships among learner characteristics, types of learning, instructional methods, and subject matter variables. *Journal of Educational Psychology,* 1971, *62,* 31–38.

Tobias, S. Achievement treatment interactions. *Review of Educational Research,* 1976, *46,* 61–74.

Weiner, B. *Achievement motivation and attribution theory.* Morristown, N.J.: General Learning Press, 1974.

Welford, A. T. Evidence of a single-channel decision making mechanism limiting performance in a serial reaction task. *Quarterly Journal of Experimental Psychology,* 1959, *11,* 193–210.

Welford, A. T. The measurement of sensory motor performance: Survey and reappraisal of twelve years' progress. *Ergonomics,* 1960, *3*, 189–230.

Welford, A. T. *Fundamentals of skill.* London: Methuen, 1968.

Welford, A. T. The obtaining and processing of information: Some basic issues relating to analyzing inputs and making decisions. *Research Quarterly,* 1972, *43*, 295–311.

Whiting, H. T. A. *Acquiring ball skill: A psychological interpretation.* London: Bell, 1969.

Whiting, H. T. A. Overview of the skill learning process. *Research Quarterly,* 1972, *43*, 266–294.

Wickens, C. D. The effects of divided attention on information processing in manual tracking. *Journal of Experimental Psychology,* 1976, *2*, 1–13.

Zimmerman, B., & Rosenthal, T. L. Observational learning of rule-governed behavior by children. *Psychological Bulletin,* 1974, *81*, 29–42.

5

Artificial Intelligence and Learning Strategies[1]

JOHN SEELY BROWN, ALLAN COLLINS, and GREGORY HARRIS

In this chapter we examine the different kinds of knowledge and strategies necessary for "understanding" in three radically different domains—namely, stories, solutions to mathematical problems, and electronic circuits. From analyzing the understanding process in these different domains, some surprising similarities have emerged concerning the role of *planning knowledge* and the strategies governing the application of that knowledge for synthesizing a deep-structure analysis of a story, a math solution, or a circuit. Insights gained from these similarities are applied to the problem of teaching learning strategies to students and of developing an expanded theoretical basis for further research in learning strategies.

The field of artificial intelligence grew out of the attempt in the late 1950s to build computer programs that could carry out tasks requiring human intelligence. The goal was to build machines that could understand language, recognize objects in scenes, act as intelligent robots, solve problems, play games such as chess, teach students about different subjects, etc. These problems have not been completely solved, but there has been a steady accumulation of tools and techniques in artificial intelligence such that the programs designed to carry out these tasks have become increasingly sophisticated (Bobrow & Collins, 1975; Schank & Abelson, 1977; Winston, 1977).

[1]This research was supported by the Advanced Research Projects Agency, Air Force Human Resources Laboratory, Army Research Institute for the Behavioral and Social Sciences, and Navy Personnel Research and Development Center, under contract number MDA903-76-C-0108 and by the Personnel and Training Research Programs, Psychological Sciences Division, Office of Naval Research, and Advanced Research Projects Agency, under contract number N00014-76-C-0083, Contract Authority Identification Number, NR 154-379. Views and conclusions contained in this document are those of the authors and should not be interpreted as necessarily representing the official policies, either expressed or implied, of the above-named groups or of the United States Government.

In order to build these programs, artificial intelligence has developed a variety of formalisims that in turn provide a new basis for analyzing cognitive processes. These formalisms are used to express structural and procedural mechanisms and theories about human problem-solving, planning, representing knowledge, and understanding text by computers. Our belief is that the cognitive and artificial intelligence theories expressible in these formalisms can begin to provide a domain-independent, theoretical foundation for research in learning strategies.

With the development of these formalisms, there has been renewed interest in what it means exactly to "understand" a piece of text, a set of instructions, a problem solution, a complex system, etc. This has repeatedly led to the realization that "understanding" requires different kinds of knowledge **not** explicitly referred to in the text or problem solution, as well as *strategies* for governing how this *implicit knowledge* should be used in synthesizing a *structural model* of the meaning of the text or problem solution. This model, which we call a *deep structure trace,* is a complex hypothesis about the plans and goals of the characters in the text or the person who solved the problem.

The intent of this chapter is to explore the role of the different kinds of knowledge needed in the understanding process and to examine those insights we have gained about learning strategies through the recognition of the tremendous amount of tacit knowledge that must be exploited by students as they try to understand something. This is especially relevant for learning strategies, because in analyzing comprehension tasks in a variety of **divergent** knowledge domains, we have begun to see some surprising similarities in the kinds of strategies and knowledge used in these different domains. This suggests that there may be general learning strategies that will enhance a student's comprehension abilities over a wide range of content areas. Rigney (1976) has claimed that "The approach to teaching students cognitive strategies has been through content-based instruction and maybe that is wrong and should be reversed; that is, content independent instruction." Rarely has anyone tried to make explicit or formalize the different kinds of strategies and knowledge needed for understanding something in even one content area—let alone in different ones. Perhaps that is why we have not seen powerful generality along the learning strategies dimension from content-based instruction.

One goal of a learning strategies curriculum might justifiably be first to teach the student all of the abstract, tacit knowledge and strategies that underlie problem solving and understanding for a particular content area, and then later to show the student the generality of these strategies across content areas. Alternatively, a curriculum might teach the knowledge and strategies in a content-independent form, and then show how they apply to different content areas. Either approach would help the student to acquire more readily an understanding of a particular domain of knowledge. Transferring these skills would also have a significant effect on students' ability to acquire other quite separate domains of knowledge.

It has sometimes been suspected that presenting a topic to students in the clearest way can be counterproductive in the long run, since they do not have to struggle with understanding the concept, and walk away expecting that real-world situations will always be crisp, clear, and easy to grasp. At first glance, this would seem to argue against articulating the tacit knowledge involved in understanding a concept or performing a task, since it might make "understanding" too easy and compartmental. However, it is precisely this lack of attention to tacit knowledge that often causes "optimal" presentations of a concept to have this effect. If a concept is explained without explicit reference to the complex processes necessary to understand it, then the student will not be able to reconstruct the process alone. However if a concept is presented by showing successively how to refine one's understanding of the concept (or, more metaphorically, how to experiment with the concept in order to "debug" one's own understanding of it), it will not be counterproductive.

Before proceeding, let us restate our premises from a slightly different viewpoint. We believe that (a) by explicating the underlying domain-independent cognitive processes, strategies, and knowledge that students must use to "understand" a new situation, text, set of instructions, solutions to a problem, etc. and (b) by finding ways to teach students a general awareness of these processes along with some learning strategies based on those processes, we can provide them with a foundation for acquiring new knowledge and perhaps, more importantly, diminish their fear of being confronted with new conceptual material that cannot be instantly understood. How detailed these learning strategies must be in order to be effective is, of course, an open question. But simply making students aware of the existence of some very simple strategies that are involved in synthesizing an understanding can be surprisingly useful. For example, the act of understanding, in itself, can become less mysterious with the realization that comprehension is an active process requiring the *formation and revision of hypotheses* about the meaning of a given event or situation.

In this regard, we are reminded of an apocryphal story of a teacher who gave a young student a problem to work out. After several minutes of attempting (and failing) to solve it, the student asked for help, and was told to return to his chair and to THINK about it some more. At this point the student broke into tears, exclaiming that everybody tells him to "think," but he doesn't have the slightest idea of what that means! Naturally, he felt terribly frustrated. "Thinking" was something that he could not see, feel, or touch. It seemed to him that everyone assumed he knew the secret to this magical process. When he was told to think about something, all he could do was stare blindly at the problem and panic. He kept wondering why no one would tell him the secret. Today, schools are flooded with experimental programs to teach students to "think" (à la problem-solving), but where are these students being taught how to **understand** something new on their own, let alone what it means to "understand"?

In the next three sections we will analyze the knowledge and strategies underlying three radically different domains: understanding stories, problem-solving in mathematics, and understanding electronic circuits. We will proceed by describing the cognitive processing of a person performing these three tasks in terms of artificial intelligence concepts. This analysis is not meant to be definitive. Rather, it is suggestive of a kind of analysis and concern that might be beneficial to learning strategists. We will conclude the chapter with a discussion of the central ideas that have emerged from studying the invariances over these disparate domains. We will also specify the implications this analysis has for a learning strategies curriculum, and suggest some techniques that might be useful in teaching these strategies.

UNDERSTANDING A STORY

We will begin with story understanding, since this is the domain that has been analyzed most thoroughly and because it is easier to understand the artificial intelligence terminology in a familiar context. At the same time, we think the reader may find it surprising how much problem-solving knowledge is involved in the comprehension of a story. We have chosen an Aesop fable called *Stone Soup* that requires a fair amount of problem-solving to interpret both the characters' actions and the author's intentions.

Stone Soup

A poor man came to a large house during a storm to beg for food. He was sent away with angry words, but he went back and asked, "May I at least dry my clothes by the fire, as I am wet from the rain?" The maid thought this would not cost anything, so she let him come in.

Inside he told the cook that if she would give him a pan, and let him fill it with water, he would make some stone soup. Since this was a new dish to the cook, she agreed to let him make it. The man then got a stone from the road and put it in the pan. The cook gave him some salt, peas, mint, and all the scraps of meat that she could spare to throw in. Thus the poor man made a delicious stone soup and the cook said, "Well done! You have made a silk purse from a sow's ear."

Surface Structure and Deep-Structure Traces

The story recounts a set of events that occurred as the poor man solved the problem of obtaining food. This set of events is the *surface structure trace* of the story. They are the result of the man's problem-solving activity.

To understand this story in any deep sense, the reader must construct an interpretation of these events of the following type (Adams & Collins, 1977):

1. The poor man is prevented from obtaining his initial goal.
2. He uses clever means to get part way to the initial goal.
3. He then uses an even cleverer means to reach the initial goal.

This understanding of the story is not a simple trace of how the events in the story are linked up, but rather a *deep-structure trace*; that is, it is not at all obvious from the surface form of the story. The reader must reconstruct from the surface events how the poor man solved the problems he faced in the story.

The reader must utilize many different types of knowledge in order to construct such an interpretation of *Stone Soup*. We will try to illustrate them and then we will briefly try to recount how a skilled reader uses these different kinds of knowledge to understand the story at several different levels.

Basic World Knowledge and Schema Theory

A large amount of *basic knowledge* about the world is necessary to understand *Stone Soup:* (*a*) that servants work in large houses of wealthy people, are paid with room and board and small amounts of money, and want to please their employers; (*b*) that maids clean and take care of the residence and play the role of butler if there is none; (*c*) that to make soup a cook slowly heats a base of some meat, bones, or vegetables plus other ingredients in water over a low fire; (*d*) that fables are short stories with a moral, designed to explain people's motivations or actions; and (*e*) that a moral is the summary of a story structure, usually in terms of what a person should do in a given situation, and usually in the form of a proverb or maxim. These are English descriptions of a small part of the basic knowledge readers have about these concepts.

Schema theory (Bartlett, 1932; Minsky, 1975; Rumelhart & Ortony, 1977; Winograd, 1975) provides a very general formalism for representing different types of knowledge, including the basic knowledge just described and the planning knowledge to be described. One of the fundamental notions associated with schemata is that they have various *slots* for variables (Minsky, 1975) that can be filled with different values. For example, the slot of the master can be potentially filled by any adult and the place where the cook heats meals can be filled by a stove, oven, fireplace, etc. Associated with each slot are *default values,* which will be assumed if no value is specified. For example, the default value for a master is the owner of the house, and the default cooking place is a stove. Thus associated with any slot is information about the range of values that can fill that slot plus the most likely values to fill it for particular predictable contexts.

Means–Ends Analysis

Means–ends analysis is a procedural formalism developed by Newell and Simon (1963) in the General Problem Solver (GPS) that was designed to simulate human problem-solving. Means–ends analysis operates as follows: If there is a method to reach a goal directly, then that method is applied. If there is none, then a subgoal is generated that reduces the difference between the present state and the goal. If there is a method to reach the subgoal directly, then this method is applied; otherwise a subsubgoal is generated, etc. Often, a potentially useful method cannot be directly applied because the prerequisites for that method have not been met. In this case, a new subgoal is generated that tries to alter the given state of affairs so as to enable the application of this method.

In *Stone Soup* the man is hungry and is trying to achieve the goal of obtaining food. First he applies the method of begging for food but fails. However he does achieve the prerequisite of attracting the attention of someone in the house. He then pursues the subgoal of getting into the kitchen near the fire, which reduces the difference between his current state and his goal. Then he pursues the second subgoal of getting the cook to help him make soup, further reducing the difference.

As Newell and Simon argue, people solve problems in everyday life and understand the actions of other people in terms of the means–ends strategies described here.

Applying means–ends analysis to a problem-solving situation produces a tree structure of goals and subgoals. The tree structure for *Stone Soup* is illustrated in Figure 5.1. The events in the story are the *terminal nodes* in the tree structure—the begging, the asking permission, the going inside to the fire, etc. The deep-structure trace is the structure of goals and subgoals above the terminal nodes.

Several researchers (Mandler & Johnson, 1977; Rumelhart, 1975, 1977) have developed *story grammars* to specify the structure of well-formed stories. These story grammars are formalisms for specifying the possible *target structures* that a story's deep-structure trace must fit. In fact, they define the set of tree structures that means–ends analysis would produce. Thus, they are compact representations for the target structure that a reader must construct in order to understand a story. Story grammars are specific to the domain of stories, but there are similar target structures that guide understanding in other domains.

Planning Knowledge

The problem-solving strategies based on means–ends analysis provide a domain-independent method for constructing plans. Abelson and Schank (Abelson, 1975;

```
Goal: Become fed
  Subgoal: Obtain food
    Method: Beg → Fails
    Subgoal: Get inside
      Subgoal: Con maid for permission to go inside
        Method: Ask permission to dry himself → Succeeds
      Subgoal: Move inside
        Method: Walk (Default value) → Succeeds
    Subgoal: Obtain soup
      Subgoal: Con cook into giving him soup
        Subgoal: Con cook into helping him make soup
          Subgoal: Con cook for permission to make stone soup
            Method: Bargain recipe for permission → Succeeds
          Subgoal: Get pan
            Method: Ask cook → Succeeds
          Subgoal: Get stone
            Method: Go out to road → Succeeds
          Subgoal: Cook soup
            Method: Heat stone in water filled pan → succeeds
          Subgoal: Con cook into adding scraps of food
            Method: Bargain his contributions for hers → Succeeds
      Subgoal: Ingest soup
        Method: Drink (Default value) → succeeds
```

Figure 5.1 Nested tree structure of goals and subgoals for *Stone Soup*.

Schank & Abelson, 1977) have developed a *deltact theory* to account for the way that people construct social plans. In particular, they are trying to specify in formal terms the goals and methods that apply in a social context using means–ends analysis.

A deltact does two things: It permits the factorization of the differences between a situation and an arbitrary social goal into a few familiar categories, and it gathers together all the methods that might make each difference category reducible in an actual situation. A deltact is a class of acts that reduce a certain difference to achieve a social goal. That class is broken into *methods,* which are ordered to suggest which to try first. A method of a deltact is something that is done (a segment of a plan) plus the preconditions under which it may be expected to reduce the deltact difference as promised. The plan segment can be as vague as a goal to satisfy or as specific as a goal + deltact + method already learned. The claim is that with this *planning knowledge,* elaborate plans can be constructed (such as those of the man in *Stone Soup*), and complicated sequences of actions can be understood.

Some aspects of deltact theory can be illustrated in terms of *Stone Soup.* Two deltacts serve high level goals in the story:

1. The man's goal of obtaining food is accomplished by a ΔHAVE (a change of possession).
2. The goal of getting into the house is accomplished by a ΔPROX (a change of proximity).

Each of the deltacts has a formal definition: A ΔHAVE has five variables, an *actor* causes an *object* to change possession from the *possessor* to the *receiver* by some *means.* In *Stone Soup* the poor man causes soup to change possession from the cook to himself by some unspecified means. There is an ordered set of methods for obtaining a ΔHAVE. The methods are ASK; INFORM REASON; BARGAIN OBJECT; BARGAIN FAVOR; THREATEN; OVERPOWER; STEAL. In *Stone Soup* the poor man first tries to ASK to obtain food from the maid, but ends up using a BARGAIN FAVOR with the cook; buying is a special case of BARGAIN OBJECT, where the object bargained is money. The methods are ordered according to the priority in which they should be used in constructing a plan, but the order changes in different contexts.

Each of these methods is formally defined as an act with various prerequisites and results (Charniak, 1975; Schank & Abelson, 1977). In Schank and Abelson's theory an ASK has the following prerequisites:

1. The asker is near the askee.
2. The askee knows the information.
3. The askee wants to transmit the information to the asker.

The result is that the askee transmits the information to the asker, which in turn causes the asker to have the information. When any precondition for applying a method is not satisfied, then a deltact can be used to propose a plan for obtaining the required precondition. This is how subgoals are generated in the theory.

Essential to *Stone Soup* is the notion of a CON. A CON has the same structure of prerequisites and results as does a method, but the actual act involved in a CON may be any of the methods that Schank and Abelson (1977) describe. In conning the maid, the man used an ASK, whereas in the case of conning the cook he used a BARGAIN FAVOR. What the reader knows about a CON is its result—X gets nearer his goal (G1)—and its prerequisities:

1. X must have a goal G1.
2. Y must have a goal (G2) to prevent X from obtaining G1 and a plan for G2 that X and Y believe will work.
3. X must perform some act that Y thinks is directed toward a different goal (G3) and that helps X obtain G1 without Y giving up either the goal G2 or the plan for it.

To identify a CON in reading a story, the reader must match the preconditions of any act in the story against the prerequisites of a CON, and find (or guess) all of the participants by name.

Deltacts illustrate the notion of a difference. They facilitate the reduction of differences by suggesting methods for the means–ends analysis that will reduce some or all of the differences that have been noticed in a pair of actual and desired situations.

Means–ends analysis operates by *searching* among the known means or methods for those that will attain the ends that are sought, expressed in terms of such differences. This analysis depends on two pieces of planning knowledge: an index of the known methods in terms of descriptions of the differences they can be expected to reduce, and a technique for computing the differences from a given situation plus goal so that a method indexed by that difference can be applied.

Strategic Knowledge for Understanding

Strategic knowledge refers to knowledge that the reader uses to drive the process of trying to make sense out of the story. It is the most elusive kind of knowledge because it is not at all apparent in any trace the readers may leave of their understanding (such as a summary of the story). Perhaps for this reason there are no explicit theories of what comprises this knowledge.

We will list a few general principles that skilled readers must use in understanding stories, as a first attempt toward specifying what some of this knowledge must look like:

1. The deep-structure trace constructed by the reader should make a well-formed story. (Things such as episodes should begin and end.)
2. The deep-structure trace should somehow accommodate every event in the story.
3. Every slot in the schemata used to understand the story should be filled, preferably by values specified in the story, or by default values that do not contradict anything in the story.

4. Authors write stories for particular purposes and the reader should construct an interpretation of the author's intentions as well as an interpretation of the events in the story.
5. The reader should reread to synthesize a new interpretation of the story, if any of the strategic conditions (such as the preceding four) are not satisfied.

Principles such as these must be operating as a skilled reader tries to make sense of the story, but there may be many more such principles.

Constructing and Revising Hypotheses about Deep-Structure Traces

With this glimpse of the various kinds of knowledge needed to understand a story, we will briefly describe how a skilled reader synthesizes this knowledge to understand *Stone Soup*. Comprehension involves a notion of *variable binding,* where elements in the story are bound to slots in different knowledge structures. Where a value is not specified in the story, it must be assigned a default value. For example, when the man begs for food, this is bound to the method ASK, which in turn is bound to the goal of pursuing a ΔHAVE to obtain food. The reader makes the default assumption that the man's ultimate goal is eating to alleviate his hunger, rather than giving the food to his dog, for instance. The way objects and events in the story invoke different pieces of knowledge to suggest hypotheses is called *bottom-up processing.* For example, the poor man's begging for food suggests he wants to eat. In contrast, the way that knowledge schemata compete to provide the best hypothetical account for the input data is called *top-down processing.* For example, the goal of getting inside the house competes with that of getting dry as an explanation of why the man asked permission to dry himself by the fire. Taken together these two processes allow the reader to piece together the large amount of structure necessary to integrate the structural fragments in the text (Adams & Collins, 1978; Rumelhart & Ortony, 1977).

The skilled reader uses bottom-up and top-down processing to formulate hypotheses about the deep structure underlying the various events as they are encountered in the story. As suggested earlier, the reader makes the inference that the man wants food because he is hungry. The default method of obtaining food is buying it— BARGAIN OBJECT—but this is not possible since the man is poor. The ASK is thwarted by the maid's refusal. There are a number of alternative methods but apparently the man goes off to beg elsewhere. He then returns to ask if he can dry himself by the fire. Apparently he has changed his top-level goal in the means–ends analysis structure. This change agrees with the fact that it is raining, and drying himself could be a reasonable lower-order goal in the man's goal structure. Thus an intelligent reader at this point may be led into constructing an incorrect hypothesis as to why the poor man asks to dry himself by the fire.

When the man suggests making stone soup, the reader may construct a second incorrect hypothesis. The apparent goal is that he wants to teach the cook a new recipe. There are several clues, however, that allow the reader to formulate a different hypothesis about the man's goal:

1. Stones are not in the variable range of things from which one normally makes soup.
2. Stones have no food content.
3. Because the man helped make the soup the reader infers that he gets to eat it. This satisfies the original top-level goal that the reader constructed for the man's coming to the house in the first place.

These three facts should lead the reader to construct a **new** goal structure in which making the stone soup is a subgoal, beneath the higher level goal of eating. In this new structure, making stone soup is a BARGAIN FAVOR for the subgoal ΔHAVE to obtain food. This nesting of the goal structure eliminates an un-motivated change of goals. Until this revision is made, the third strategic principle we have named—no important slots left unfilled—is violated because there is no purpose for the change of goals.

In view of this restructuring, the reader should also be able to revise the earlier incorrect hypothesis as to why the man wanted to dry himself by the fire. To do this, the reader must notice that the man needed a ΔPROX to get into the kitchen, where he could bargain with the cook to obtain food. Thus asking to dry himself by the fire can be subsequently interpreted as a CON: It moved the man closer to the initial goal of eating that the maid had prevented. However once the maid thought the action was directed toward the goal of getting dry, she allowed the poor man to achieve his subgoal. By restructuring these two acts under the one goal of obtaining food, the reader has produced a tree structure that fits the constraints on a well-formed story according to Rumelhart's (1975) story grammar.

Knowing that this story is a fable, the skilled reader should infer that the story has a moral, a prescription for how to behave in a given situation. The reader can convert the deep-structure trace to a moral something like the following: If one method fails, you can often reach your goal by a more circuitous one that is clever but not immoral. There are several underlying aspects to this moral: initial failure, persistence or repeated trying when you fail, changing methods when you fail, devising multistep plans, using clever means such as a CON, not using immoral means such as THREATEN, OVERPOWER, and STEAL, and, finally, succeed-ing. The avoidance of immorality can only be realized from the reader's knowledge of the alternative methods the man did not use. This ability to evaluate another person's plan derives from the reader's own ability to plan.

Furthermore, if the reader knows that the points of fables are often proverbs, he might be able to select the correct one for *Stone Soup*. This is done by matching the various aspects of the deep-structure trace of the story against the deep-structure trace of any candidate maxims. For example, "If at first you don't succeed, try, try again" matches the two aspects of failure and repeated trying. "Where there's a will there's a way" matches four aspects fairly well: persistence, changing methods, using a circuitous (multistep) plan, and ultimate success. Neither of these proverbs matches perfectly or includes the cleverness aspect, but that's why we have fables.

By tracing the process of understanding through different stages, we have tried to show: (*a*) the problem-solving processing necessary to forming hypotheses about the underlying structure; (*b*) the way the reader must construct revised hypotheses from the incorrect ones; and (*c*) how notions of means–ends analysis, goals, and methods for achieving those goals are integral to the understanding and evaluation of social events in the world. In particular, we have hinted at the duality between problem-solving and understanding where we, in part, achieve an understanding of this fable by recapitulating a hypothetical trace of how the beggar was achieving his goals, what his methods and intentions were at each step, and so on.

As readers, we must actively invoke our own problem-solving strategies in synthesizing a deep-structure model or understanding of this story so as to be able to bridge the gaps between each line in the story. Hence, we see that even in simple stories, readers cannot expect to be given or told everything. Indeed, readers must participate, so to speak, in the event that they are trying to understand. This often happens almost unconsciously since the planning knowledge and problem-solving strategies needed to participate are thoroughly ingrained in our heads. However, understanding less common events (instructions, systems, etc.) requires an active invocation of this knowledge, as we shall see in considering the less natural domains of mathematics and electronics.

UNDERSTANDING ELEMENTARY MATHEMATICS

In the previous section, we discussed how higher-order knowledge in the form of plans, methods, and hypothesis-construction strategies in the area of social interactions must often be used in order to understand even simple stories. In this section, we will sketch out an analysis of the understanding of a solution to an exercise in elementary mathematics that directly corresponds to our preceding analysis of story comprehension. The correspondence is between the strategies and processes used to conjecture and fill in the unmentioned plans in a story and those used to fill in the motivations for the steps in a solution to a math problem. In both cases, the lines comprising the surface structure of the story or solution must be augmented by the understander before a deep-structure trace constituting an understanding can be generated.

While studying mathematics, probably everyone has experienced at one time or another the phenomenon of the almost magical nature of mathematic proofs or solution paths—the steps leading to a solution—that are encountered in most mathematic textbooks. Somehow the critical lines of a proof or critical steps in a solution seem to be pulled out of thin air, leaving one in awe of how these steps were ever conceived of or selected. Although each step of the proof, or solution, seems plausibly true as it is read, the proof as a whole is hard to remember; one could not summarize it except by reciting it verbatim from memory—much like what one does for a story which makes no sense, or a magic act in which the trick remains unknown. Worse, the proof as a whole does not seem to bear more than a coincidental resemblance to other proofs that are presented "on the same subject." For students to develop the skills to understand, as opposed to rotely memorizing, a new solution—let alone skills to create their own solutions—the sense of what makes one proof or solution like the others is needed. In short, the answer is "there," but a student who does not know what to look for cannot really see it.

For the rare student who **has** seen how it all fits together, a newly "worked solution" seems well-planned, a deliberate sequence of steps culminating in the desired result. The steps are often so directly justified and self-evident that after a while, the student begins to speak of steps "falling right out" and "moving toward the solution"—spatial metaphors. These metaphors are the inarticulate allusions to habits of thought in which the same knowledge is used in solution after solution. This planning and strategic knowledge is identical in structure and function to that used in story understanding.

To demonstrate this thesis, let us start with a concrete example drawn from Bundy (1975). Consider the task of solving the following equation:

$$\log(x + 1) + \log(x - 1) = 3.$$

We seek all the expressions for x that make this equation true. (These logarithms are in base 2.) How are we to proceed? Observe that knowing all the basic mathematical transformations (e.g. commutativity, associativity) gives us no information as to what **direction** we should move or what transformation we should apply. Indeed, this basic knowledge tells us nothing more than the **legal** transformations that **can be** made on the expression. We know we can rewrite this equation in at least a dozen different ways, but which ones will move us closer to achieving the goal of solving the equation? For example, we could use the commutativity transformation:

$$A + B = B + A$$

which generates a host of new expressions such as

$$\log(1 + x) + \log(x - 1) = 3,$$

or

$$\log(x + 1) + \log(-1 + x) = 3,$$

or

$$\log(x - 1) + \log(x + 1) = 3.$$

Or we could use a transformation applying to logarithms such as:

$$\log A + \log B = \log(A\,B), A > 0, B > 0;$$
$$\log(-A) + \log(-B) = \log(A\,B), A < 0, B < 0,$$

which generates:

$$\log(x + 1)\,(x - 1) = 3, x > 1,$$

and so on.

Before proceeding, we encourage you, the reader, to generate your own solution. As you do so, try to keep track of *why* you applied a particular transformation, what kind of difficulties you experienced, and how you decided when to abandon an unsuccessful approach toward solving the equation. Now let us flip the coin from the typical problem-solving process to the almost totally overlooked (in mathematics) understanding process. What follows is one of the many possible solution paths to this problem. Read through this solution and then step back and think about what it means to understand or summarize it in a way that might help someone else generate a solution to another problem.

Example 1

1. $\log(x + 1) + \log(x - 1) = 3.$

2. $\log(x + 1) \cdot (x - 1) = 3, \quad x > 1.$

3. $\log(x^2 - 1) = 3.$

4. $x^2 - 1 = 2^3 = 8.$

5. $x^2 = 8 + 1 = 9.$

6. $x = \sqrt{9} = \pm 3.$

7. But $x > 1$, so $x = 3$ only.

As we skim over this solution, each step *by itself* seems to be almost obvious, but what about its overall structure? Can we scrutinize it as easily as we can the *Stone Soup* fable? Can we fill in the underlying motives or plans that directed the unfolding of this solution? To see that each step of this solution path indicates to the initiate a separable, distinct decision and has its own motivating piece of an overall plan for the solution (that is, to see that there must exist some deep-structure trace for solutions to math problems and that it plays a determining role in what steps were taken), compare the surface-structure trace given in Example 1 with that given in Example 2 for a slightly different problem statement.

Example 2

1. $\log(x) + \log(x - 2) = 3.$

2. $\log(x) \cdot (x - 2) = 3, \quad x > 2.$

3. $(x) \cdot (x-2) = 2^3 = 8.$

4. $x^2 - 2x = 8.$

5. $x^2 - 2x - 8 = 0.$

6. $(x + 2) \cdot (x - 4) = 0$.

7. $x + 2 = 0$ or $x - 4 = 0$.

8. $x = -2$ or $x = 4$.

9. But $x > 2$, so $x = 4$ only.

Although this is the same problem with $(x - 1)$ substituted for x of Example 1, some of the steps to solve the equation were different in each case. Why?

Planning Knowledge and Means–Ends Analysis

Bundy (1975) has constructed an initial taxonomy and theory of the planning knowledge involved in solving a wide class of elementary equations such as this one. His theory involves two types of knowledge: first, there are *planning rules* for associating transformations that are applied with situations that arise in means–ends analysis; and second, there is strategic knowledge that selects the order of the application of these rules. Integrating these two types of knowledge results in a problem-solving procedure which Bundy calls the *Basic Method*; that is, a schema for an instance of a means–ends analysis strategy for seeking a solution. In the following, we give examples of such planning knowledge, cast as Bundy rules:

Isolation: *Given a single occurrence of the unknown in the equation, apply a set of mathematical transformations that removes whatever functions surround this occurrence, so that it stands in isolation.*

This covers any set of steps that selects the outermost function dominating the occurrence, selects an axiom that eliminates it by introducing its inverse on the right-hand side, and so on until the unknown sits by itself on the left-hand side of the equation.

Simplification: *Place expressions in canonical form.*

This covers adding and multiplying by zero, multiplying by one, logarithm of one, zero or one as an exponent, evaluation of terms with no unknowns, cancellation of factors across a quotient sign, etc. It is often enabled by the isolation strategy.

Collection: *Given more than one occurrence of the unknown, select a transformation that reduces the number of occurrences of the unknown, thereby making the isolation strategy applicable.*

This covers such steps as summing terms, adding constant exponents of products of power of the same expression, etc.

Attraction: *Given more than one occurrence of the unknown, apply a transformation that simply moves two occurrences of the unknown closer, to enable some transformation for the Collection strategy.*

This covers such steps as finding common denominators for the sum of fractions, nonelementary applications of legal transformations, etc.

> **Splitting:** *Given a complicated expression or subexpression, split it into a functional composition of some less complicated expressions, to enable the composed expressions to be treated separately.*

This covers factorization, completing the square, cancellation of terms across an equals sign, etc.

> **Check:** *Given additional relationships that might hold, check whether they do.*

This covers substitution of answers or expressions into a previous step, the extra case analysis for division by zero, indeed it includes almost any deliberately redundant processing, such as multiplying out the square that has been completed.

Basic Mathematical Knowledge

These planning rules for mathematical problem-solving help specify which basic mathematical knowledge—the kind taught laboriously in most elementary mathematics curriculums—should be applied at each step in the solution. This is the knowledge of what one may and may not do (that is, performing the same operation on both sides of an equation, multiplying by an expression equal to 1, adding an expression equal to zero, transposing commutative operands, distributive law for multiplication, adding exponents in multiplication, etc.), the basic mathematical skills of algebra that make the difference between a sloppy victim of careless mistakes and a loyal upholder of the deductive laws of mathematics. Basic knowledge is not sufficient for flexible, independent mathematics—the kind of flexibility and independence derived from the ability and confidence to plan on one's own.[2]

Deep-Structure Traces

The preceding sections have discussed some of the basic mathematical and planning knowledge needed to tie together the individual steps of a solution into a coherent deep structure, revealing the motivations and plans that lie beneath the surface of the solution path. But how is one to synthesize this structure? Before

---

[2] In fact, perhaps one of the causes for a math student "bending the law" when he gets lost is that (a) he is told he has to get from here to there, but he does not see how; (b) the paradigmatic math proof is usually given with unjustified leaps (i.e., referring only to the basic knowledge), but since he did not follow its thread when it was presented, he assumes nobody expects there to be one; (c) by not using planning knowledge, he views the process of constructing a proof as one of jumping forward from the premises and backward from the conclusions: and (d) he may as well jump from one such sequence of jumps to another whenever the expressions look sufficiently similar.

Solve the quadratic equations $x^2 - 2x = 8$ (Line 4) by

SPLIT (4)—into one equation for each root
   by: express as $f(x) \cdot g(x)$ ch 0
      by: ATTRACT (4)—towards desired form above
         by: SIMPLIFY (4)—into $ax^2 + bx + c = 0$
         by: SPLIT: $8 \rightarrow 0 + 8$
        and: ATTRACT: move the 8 over, switching sign yielding (5): $x^2 - 2x - 8 = 0$
      and: SPLIT (5)—into $(ax + b) \cdot (cx + d) = 0$
        by: factoring (5), yielding (6): $(x + 2) \cdot (x - 4) = 0$.
  and: use the product-zero rule, yielding (7): $(x + 2) = 0$ or $(x - 4) = 0$,
and solve the linear equations.

Figure 5.2. Deep-structure trace for Steps 4–7 of Example 2.

exploring this issue, let us first show both a top-level summary of planning knowledge that might have been used for solving Example 1 (see page 119) and a more detailed example of the deep structure trace for Example 2 (see page 119).

For Example 1, we may briefly note that Steps 4–6 reflect the successful application of the planning rule for Isolation. This was made possible by the prior application of the Collection planning rule, which in turn was enabled by the correct application of the Attraction rule.

We can see in Example 2 that Steps 4–7 are motivated by the desire to split the quadratic into cases corresponding to its two roots; that this becomes possible if we could express it as a product of expressions of the form $(ax + b)$ set equal to zero (as was done to get from Steps 6 to 7); and that this would become possible if we were able to express our quadratic as $ax^2 + bx + c = 0$ and then factor it. So the deep-structure trace underlying steps 4–7 is shown in Figure 5.2.

But what kind of reasoning–strategies did we use to synthesize this deep-structure trace from Steps 4 through 7 of the solution?

CONSTRUCTING AND REVISING HYPOTHESES ABOUT DEEP-STRUCTURE TRACES

Note the three patterns cited in the deep structure trace shown in Figure 5.2: $f(x) \cdot g(x) = 0$, $ax^2 + bx + c$, and $(ax + b) \cdot (cx + d)$. Each of these patterns is related to a small chunk of basic algebraic knowledge that specifies what basic operations and truths can be linked to this pattern, such as the product-zero rule: $f(x) \cdot g(x) = 0 \rightarrow f(x) = 0$ or $g(x) = 0$. These patterns play a pivotal role in that they link fragments of the deep-structure trace to elements in the surface-structure trace via *hypotheses* that the understander forms. For instance, when one sees (by comparing the right-hand sides of Steps 4 and 5) that one side of the equation is *being made zero*, one might be able to apply the product-zero rule, which splits the equation into two simpler equations. This rule requires some instantiation of the pattern $f(x) \cdot g(x) = 0$, which is found when it is searched for further down the line of the proof, identifying step 6 as an important *clue* in our reconstruction of the deep-structure trace, since it confirms our hypothesis that this particular kind of split was attempted.

Our next hypothesis-formation subtask is to determine how step 6 is different from step 4 and how and why it got that way. (We indent one level in the deep-structure trace—Figure 5.2—since this is a subtask.) Step 4 is a *quadratic*, which means it is a close relative of a three-termed polynomial in x—$ax^2 + bx + c$. This minihypothesis is easily confirmed (all the terms of step 4 are of the form ax^2 or bx or c), but it is crucial to making sense of step 6 because one of the many ways to express a quadratic is the next pivotal pattern—$(ax + b) \cdot (cx + d)$. This pattern matches step 6, so we now know that the jump from step 4 to step 6 included *placing a quadratic in the form* $(ax + b) \cdot (cx + d)$. And that is another basic knowledge schema, for it tells the understander that *one converts* $ax^2 + bx + c$ *into* $(ax + b) \cdot (cx + d)$ *by* factoring (provided the roots exist).

Now there is a reason to look for $ax^2 + bx + c$ in the surface-structure trace, which we find at step 5. Note that not every proposed surface-structure element must be visible in forming a hypothesis; often a little basic knowledge is needed to see that what one is looking for is implied in what was there explicitly (e.g., a few steps were skipped, or the representation given is not in canonical form, etc.) This is what the understander will have to do if and when he or she explores just how the square was completed and whether the jump from step 5 to step 6 was valid. But in this case the understander was fortunate to find $ax^2 + bx + c$ directly, and has only to note that the 8 came from the right-hand side to get a zero, thereby splitting 8 into $0 + 8$.

The overall process at work here for handling the understander's hypotheses is controlled by a group of strategies for taking information from the solution path that dictates possible new hypotheses, and for connecting existing hypotheses together in ways that are consistent with basic mathematical knowledge and planning knowledge for algebra. These are *bottom-up* and *top-down* activities, respectively. From this hypothesis-growing-and-merging process, we can construct a model of how the problem was solved, what motivation lay behind selecting each step, and what the overall plan was behind solution of the problem.

Of course, the purpose of this planning knowledge is usually to help solve a problem rather than enhance one's understanding of a particular solution; however, without recourse to it, understanding the solution path is nearly impossible. This top-down bottom-up hypothesis formation process is indeed a complex one—one that may seem more difficult than solving the problem in the first place. That this is so indicates, in part, how little experience we have in "reading" and understanding novel mathematical solutions (or proofs).

How Does This Relate to the Stone Soup Fable?

If a reader has trouble understanding the "point" of the *Stone Soup* fable, it is apt to be because of a failure to perceive the existence or structure of the planning knowledge used by the global problem-solving strategies being invoked by the beggar. Less likely, but still possible, the troubled reader might never have learned the planning knowledge comprising the "social" plans and methods underlying each particular isolated action of the beggar. In story understanding, the individual schemata of planning knowledge, the plans and methods, are more apt to be recognized in a piecemeal fashion than the global hypothesis-handling strategy that weaves these schemata into a coherent model of what is really happening in the story.

However, in understanding (or generating) the solution path for solving an equation, the troubled student is apt to be completely unaware of either the existence, content, or use of the planning knowledge (in the form of, say, Bundy rules) that lies between the lines of the solution path and that provides the rationale for tying the individual steps together into a coherent plan. By being both unaware of this higher-order knowledge and of the hypothesis formation/revision strategies that use it, the student is deprived of the basic apparatus to **make sense** out of a solution or proof (a necessary but not a sufficient condition), and is therefore likely to believe that understanding math is a difficult and mysterious process, even after having mastered all the basic knowledge of math (i.e., when the transformations are applicable and how they are done). The end result is that whatever mathematical knowledge the student does manage to absorb is in the form of heavily encoded procedures that are rotely memorized and mechanically applied in order to solve special classes of problems. As a student is likely to experience it, learning mathematics consists of categorizing or linking problem characteristics to rotely memorized procedures that "solve" them. Lacking the insight to see how each individual procedure naturally follows from applying some simple higher-order knowledge, the student has little basis for understanding the semantics of the procedure, and therefore cannot reliably generalize or apply the procedure to slightly different problems.

To summarize the point of this section, we have seen that the cognitive process of understanding elementary mathematics does conform to our regularities:

1. There is a surface-structure trace that results from the sequence of applications of mathematical transformations and laws.
2. There is a deep-structure trace that recapitulates the understander's best guess as to what motivated the steps that were made.
3. There is a well-known literature of basic knowledge, consisting of axioms, notations, transformations, and the like, that serves to define the composition of the surface-structure trace by saying what may follow directly from what, and to suggest all the possible ways that the surface-structure trace may be extended to intermediate steps when a jump has been made.
4. There is a body of planning knowledge, consisting in part of Bundy-style rules, concepts for types of equations given as patterns that may be matched. These serve to define the interrelations among trace elements (particularly those involving trace elements that do not appear in the surface-structure trace, for example, the schema for factoring), and to suggest further

bases for constructing hypotheses that would connect up with those the understander has found so far.

The fundamental coin of math understanding is the body of *hypotheses* about the deep-structure trace. Teachers never talk about them, but they reflect the mental steps that every student takes when reading the lines of a proof and trying to piece it together. The strategies the student uses (which threads to pursue before others, which logically-based predictions to make from the ones he accepts), as well as the different tools for handling hypotheses (how to confirm one, how to extend one, how to suggest one) are something teachable, like all "study habits," and are surely something most people could import wholesale from their deep familiarity with social attribution and planning. We think it might even be the case that some people do just that, once they grasp the planning knowledge underlying mathematics.

We think that people have not thought of math this way before; that if they had, a teaching methodology that cites the planning knowledge explicitly and gives practice in its application would have evolved and ameliorated the mathematical illiteracy that presently offers such a stark contrast to people's familiarity with the analogously structured knowledge for social goals and attribution. Although most people find mathematics hard to understand (as compared with fables and other stories), its formal nature enables us to be substantially more precise about the planning knowledge, hypothesis formation strategies, etc., underlying the act of understanding than in the domain of general text understanding.

UNDERSTANDING ELECTRONIC CIRCUITS

In the last two sections we illustrated some of the important theoretical constructs and processes involved in understanding some event, story, mathematical solution, etc., while stressing the surprisingly invariant nature of these concepts and processes over two radically diverse domains. It might seem to be belaboring this point by delving into yet a third knowledge area—understanding electronic circuits—but it was from witnessing student technicians struggling and failing to "understand" a novel circuit that we first began to wonder what higher-order knowledge (knowledge besides basic electronic laws and concepts) were actually needed to enable a technician to understand a new circuit well enough to troubleshoot it. As we began to explore this issue by explicitly representing the tacit knowledge that a skilled troubleshooter uses in "comprehending" a new circuit schematic and then analyzing the protocols of both expert and student technicians using this knowledge, we discovered the strong similarity between this activity and that of story comprehension. In fact, comprehending a circuit schematic is a slow and conscious effort, with eye fixations complementing verbal protocols. Thus we had an unparalleled experimental setting for probing the understanding process. After discovering the strong correspondence between these two diverse domains of knowledge—story understanding and circuit schematic understanding—we questioned: (*a*) if other domains, equally diverse, would support this correspondence (and hence we began to examine the process of understanding mathematical solutions) and (b) if these "comprehension" skills were sufficiently domain-independent to enable us to find ways to teach them to technicians using the more intuitively understandable domain of, say, stories, and then transferring them to the domain of electronic troubleshooting (admittedly a bizarre idea).

Just as with student technicians, most of us will find the jargon and technical underpinnings of electronics rather unnatural. Therefore, in the remainder of this section we shall lapse into technical details only when absolutely necessary, and focus our attention primarily on the relationships between this domain and story understanding.

Surface Structure and Deep-Structure Trace

In story understanding, the basic elements of the surface structure were easy to identify since an element of the surface structure was basically a line or group of lines in the text. Identifying the basic elements in the circuit schematic involves segmenting the two-dimensional diagram into its primitive functional constituents (e.g., a transistor with its biasing network). Sometimes this segmentation is explicitly indicated with functional block diagrams superimposed on top of the schematic.

The deep-structure trace of a circuit, which is the result of the understanding process, captures the underlying teleology and causal mechanisms of the circuit. It should contain the information necessary to explain how the circuit works and why it works as it does, with each component of the schematic (or constituent of the surface structure) playing some role in the purposeful design of the circuit. Initially, one would expect the deep structure trace of a fable, for example, to have little in common with that of an electronic device. However, such is not the case. One of the key conceptual processes used in "reading between the lines" of a story consists of the skillful application of social attribution theory—a theory of social plans, motives, intentions—for providing the grist for filling in the plot of the story.

We have begun to appreciate that schematic understanding has its own *attribution* theory. The mental glue used for cementing the constituents of a circuit schematic are the designer's *plans*. Constructing an understanding of a circuit schematic requires one to realize a sequence of plans and subplans, in which fulfilling each piece of a higher-order plan generates a subplan. Therefore, understanding a novel schematic involves recapitulating, to a limited degree, the problem-solving activity that hypothetically went into designing it. Each function block or component becomes associated with a piece of a plan which, in turn, is a piece of a higher-order plan, continuing up the planning tree until a top-level plan is reached. This plan accounts for all of the components in the circuit—much like the moral explicates the fable. Understanding schematics, therefore, requires access to both the planning knowledge and the problem-solving strategies that expand and refine these plans, just as understanding stories requires access to, for example, what is involved in CON.

Planning Knowledge

In the last several years there has been a flurry of activity in the discovery, the representation, and the use of plans in circuit design, circuit understanding, and teaching (A. L. Brown, 1976; J. S. Brown, Rubinstein, & Burton, 1976; deKleer, 1977; Goldstein, 1974; Goldstein & Miller, 1976; Rich & Shrobe, 1976; Sussman, 1973). A detailed discussion of this knowledge is beyond the scope of this chapter but to give the reader some idea of its scope we will illustrate some of the planning knowledge underlying one class of circuits—regulated power supplies. For our purpose here, this planning knowledge is meant only to facilitate understanding circuits, as opposed to designing them from scratch, and therefore there is little need for extensive mathematical details. What is more important here are those aspects of the planning knowledge that provide guidance in uncovering which particular plan underlies a given circuit (such as the knowledge about a CON that helps us **recognize** a variant of a CON as opposed to performing a CON).

An active regulated power supply is most likely to be constructed from one of three top-level plans types:

1. Series-regulated plan.
2. Shunt regulated plan.
3. Switching regulated plan.

Each one specifies a connected set of circuit plan "elements"; recursively each element can be constructed from one of a set of subplan types.

In Figure 5.3a we present a diagram of the set of connected elements in the series-regulated plan. The top-level plan is, by definition, abstract. It specifies the top-level functional elements, their interrelationships, and the various constraints that each element must meet relative to the design goals of the top-level plan. Since there are many ways to realize each of these elements, the plan at this level of abstraction covers a large variety of series-regulated power supplies. An actual circuit appears only when each of the top-level functional elements is expanded according to a repertoire of lower-level plans for realizing that element (see Figure 5.3b).

Plans at any level of abstraction are multifaceted specifications embodying several other kinds of knowledge. These can be brought together to form a *plan schema*. The kinds of knowledge in a plan schema are illustrated in a subplan schema for the "regulating element" of the series-regulated plan shown in Figure 5.4. If other, alternative realizations of this element existed, then each would also have a corresponding plan schema. Of course, these plans may consist of functional descriptions that require a still lower level expansion before an actual series-regulated power supply becomes fully specified.

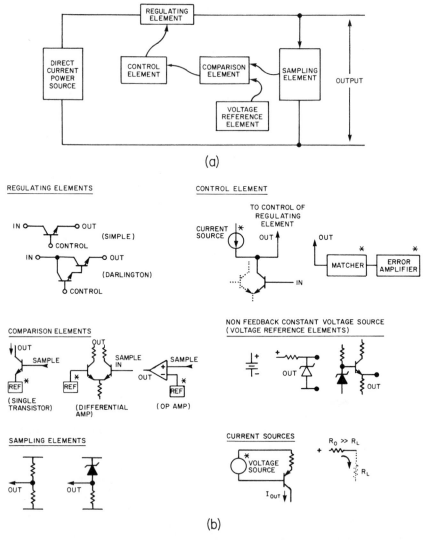

Figure 5.3. (a) Top level series-regulated plan. (b) Lower level subplans. (Various possible expansions for each of the functional elements of the top level plan. [Asterisks denote elements that are, in turn, instantiated by still lower level plans.] Only the circuit form is shown here; the annotations are omitted for simplicity.)

According to our theory, understanding a circuit schematic involves using this planning knowledge to propose a sequence of design (problem-solving) steps that will eventually culminate in the given schematic. This planning knowledge, which is so tightly structured that it could even be viewed as a *planning grammar*[3] (much

---

[3]A concept originally used by Goldstein (1976) to formalize basic problem-solving methods as augmented transition networks.

Stereotype form:

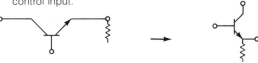

CONTROL

Input/Output (I/O):   The current through the in–out line changes as a function of the control input.

Viewpoints: 1. May be seen as electronically controlled variable resistance forming, together with the load, a voltage divider across the power source.
2. May be seen as an emitter follower by including the load resistance, as shown below.

Recognition features   Transistor is in series with the load in a closed path across the
for parsing a schematic: power source. There are no other significant impedances in this path

Commentary: Transistor must be operating in its active region.

Typical faults and their   Example: Control terminal open would cause the current refer-
manifestations: enced in the I/O behavior slot to be independent of the control. (Note that the global symptoms of the fault are then determined by "lifting" the altered I/O behavior up through the teleology of the higher-order plans.)

Knowledge and meta-   The regulating element has an input driven by the power source
phors for understanding   and an output delivering current to the load. The control input
the teleology of the plan: mediates power flow similar to how a valve mediates flow in a pipe.

Boundary conditions: Surrounding circuits must provide sufficient current to control input and maintain emitter base junction forward-biased and collector base junction reverse-biased. There is a lower bound on output current below which the element ceases to operate.

Teleology: (Basically none since this plan has only one component—unless we discuss the junctions in the transistor.) Ordinarily, teleology would describe how the elements of the plan function together so as to achieve the I/O behavior. For example, in the plan scheme of the series-regulated plan the teleology would specify how the elements function together as a feedback control system to achieve the goals of the I/O slot; whereas the "Knowledge and metaphors . . ." slot contains the conceptual knowledge about feedback.

Figure 5.4. A simplified example of the kinds of knowledge in the subplan of the regulating element.

like a story grammar), captures the set of abstract plans and methods that could be used to construct (up to some level of detail) any one of a potentially infinite number of circuits pertaining to some generic class of electronic devices. The challenge of understanding a particular circuit schematic involves discovering a sequence of plans (and subplans, ad infinitum) that will eventually account for the way each surface structure fragment becomes an integral part of the overall plan.

Without knowing this planning grammar for the generic device being examined, the process of understanding a schematic is as difficult as understanding a fable from a foreign culture. By knowing this planning grammar, the understanding process becomes one of examining the schematic in a bottom-up way, isolating fragments of the schematic and guessing what part of a lower-level plan it might match. This bottom-up process constantly interacts with the top-down process for conjecturing the nature of the high-level plan. The process is complete and the circuit understood when the two ''meet,'' accounting for all the components in the schematic.

Hypothesis Formation and Revision

Strategies for facilitating this comprehension process not only concern how to apply the higher-order knowledge in the form of plans but also how to coordinate and allocate processing resources between top-down hypothesizing about a possible global plan and bottom-up processing of the data contained in the schematic. Understanding how to coordinate these two approaches is critical, since it is often difficult to know how to interpret a fragment of the schematic without the advantage of using a conjecture about how to view it that finally stems from some top-level plan. The person trying to understand a circuit must often be willing to make **educated** guesses about how some fragment of the circuit might be functioning in terms of some high-order plan, and then attempt either to verify or reject that guess.

An ''Understanding'' Scenario

Rather than provide a theoretical description of the hypothesis-formation-and-revision process, we have included in what follows an annotated trace of a subject, having access to the planning knowledge, describing his process of understanding a particular voltage-regulated power supply. The protocol has been described in a way that (we hope) the casual reader can skim, gleaning the flavor of the process to sufficient depth so as to be able to perceive its relationship to the understanding process for fables, etc.

Event 1

An initial scan is made of the schematic (see Figure 5.5) and immediately the pair of transistors Q3,Q4 leaps out as an instance of the Darlington plan. (The Darlington transistor pair is such a common device that it is not unreasonable for an electronics technician to be able to pick it out nearly instantly.) This leads to the conjecture that this pair of transistors is an instance of a Darlington schema which

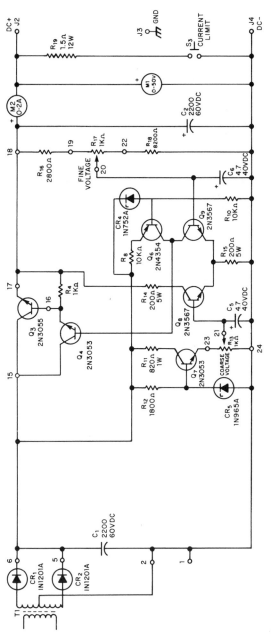

Figure 5.5 Circuit schematic for a regulated power supply.

functions as the regulating element in the series-regulated plan for feedback/ regulated power supplies.

*This conjecture follows from two facts: The first is that we know this circuit is some kind of regulated power supply and the second is that the only top-level plan of the three (i.e., SRP SP SWP) which **naturally** uses a Darlington subplan as an element is the series-regulated plan (SRP). Additional support for this conjecture comes from the fact that the Darlington pair lies along a path in series with the load—a clue sought for in the recognition knowledge part of the plan schema; as well as satisfying the topological constraints imposed by the series-regulated plan.*

Event 2

Continuing to scan the schematic, zener CR4 is detected in series with the resistor R10. This grouping satisfies one of the intermediate level plans for a nonfeedback constant voltage source and is therefore conjectured to be the voltage reference element under the hypothesized Series-Regulated plan.

Note how the initial hypothesis about the top-level plan is beginning to affect how a low level element is interpreted.

Event 3

Next, the pair of transistors Q8,Q9 are superficially examined and guessed to be the kernel of the plan for a differential amplifier.

This low level conjecture seems reasonable since the Series-Regulated plan calls for a Comparing Element which can be realized by a Differential Amplifier plan.

Event 4

Believing this, the bank of resistors R16,R17,R18 is guessed to be an instance of a voltage divider plan which serves as the sampling-element in the series-regulated plan.

*This again seems reasonable except for the fine-voltage control which is not expected as a component in the sampling-element. But this **objection** to a piece of contradictory evidence is temporarily ignored, perhaps because there is a coarse voltage adjusting element which is not connected to the fine control in an obvious way (i.e., no known plan schemata account for this).*

Event 5

At this point, all active components (e.g., transistors, diodes) have been accounted for in the schematic except for zener CR5 and transistors Q6,Q7. Hence, there could be something amiss. There is only one element of the series-regulator plan that is still unfulfilled, namely the control element, and since transistors Q6 and

Q7 do not appear to be topologically close, it seems doubtful that they can be made to instantiate any of the potential control element plans.

Note the use of heuristic knowledge about topology to accrue more evidence that something might be wrong with the current deep structure trace-hypothesis.

Event 6

This causes a reexamination of what has been accounted for thus far by the current hypothesis (which is a prelude to a hypothesis revision step). It seems that interpreting CR4,R10 as the voltage reference element cannot possibly be correct since it does not feed into the comparing element as dictated by the top-level series-regulated plan. Further examination reveals an even more important clash: under this interpretation, one side of the differential amplifier plan has no input and the other side has two contradicting inputs.

Enough evidence has certainly been accrued to call for a revision of the current hypothesis but should the whole hypothesis be abandoned and, if not, what parts of it can be saved and the remainder intelligently revised?

Event 7

Feeling confident that the conjecture about the role of Q8, Q9 is correct, (he feels he can save this part), a decision is made to reconsider the two inputs of the comparing element. (Note that he determines where the two inputs should be from the differential amplifier plan.) There is little doubt that the low-level conjecture about instantiating the sampling element with R16,R17,R18 is correct, since this string of resistors is such a usual realization of that element.

Event 8

A match is attempted of the unrecognized active devices topologically connected to Q8. In fact, CR5,Q7 trivially matches a low-level plan for constant voltage sources which only leaves Q6,CR4 unexplained.

This process combines both a bottom-up data-driven grouping with a local top-down hypothesis expectation.

Event 9

It is hoped that these remaining devices will satisfy one of the control element plans. Since the **hypothesized** output of the differential amplifier is directly connected to the input of the regulating element, that rules out viewing the control element as a matcher (one of the possible plans for the control element). Hence this leads to viewing it as a constant current source (i.e., the *other* known plan for the control element).

If this does not work then another major revision is called for. But now after he concentrated all his processing resources on this goal, it becomes

clear how to match these remaining components to one of several possible
plans for a constant current source.

Event 10

Now all the active components have been grouped together and consistently interpreted as elements in subplans within the context of the overall series-regulator plan.

> *The resulting deep-structure trace-hypothesis can now tie together all the*
> *knowledge associated with each plan schema yielding a teleological*
> *model (structured by the top-level plan) of how the circuit works and how*
> *to troubleshoot it. For example now that devices (CR5,Q7) have been*
> *successfully accounted for as instantiating one of the constant current*
> *source plans, the role or purpose of CR5 can be determined from*
> *additional knowledge in the given plan.*

This scenario captures the essence of how one person made sense of a novel schematic. It does not describe very much of the problem-solving effort that went into fulfilling each plan in terms of satisfying any constraints required by the laws of electronics. Rather it focused on satisfying topological constraints dictated by the plans themselves. In part, this was to show how this higher-order planning knowledge can, in fact, be useful to technicians (who do not have the electronic theory needed by circuit designers) and, in part, it was to show that the problem solving required to handle these issues goes beyond our means–ends analysis scheme and involves a collection of more sophisticated problem-solving strategies.

In concluding this section, it might be of interest to note that the above-mentioned understanding process involving a hypothetical recapitulation of a sequence of design-plan steps has been used as the primary explanatory methodology for teaching student technicians why a *given* piece of equipment works, that is, what its underlying teleological model is (J. S. Brown *et al.,* 1976). In this scenario, we first present a simplified model-design of the circuit, examine why this simplified circuit fails to perform satisfactorily, and then examine how that failure might be patched or modified and so on until this hypothetical sequence of design patches finally yields the given circuit.[4] In this way, the student understands what each component's role is, either in terms of its role in the simplified circuit model, or as a patch around some understood shortcoming of that model.

SUMMARY OF THEORETICAL CONCEPTS IN
COMMON OVER THE THREE DOMAINS

In the last three sections we have examined what kinds of knowledge and strategies are used in the understanding process over three diverse domains. Al-

[4]A pedegogical idea inspired by Sussman's research in electronics (A. L. Brown & Sussman, 1974).

though each domain has its own idiosyncratic and domain-specific knowledge, there is a fair amount of invariance over the domains. In this section we summarize the underlying concepts in this theory of "understanding."

The *surface-structure trace* is an information structure that spells out what actually happens in the story, solution path, etc. It is a sequence of the reported or described elements of the behavior to be understood. Since one can never describe everything about a behavior, there will always be gaps in the information that the surface structure trace provides; one of the measures of how thoroughly the behavior has been understood will be the ability to fill in these gaps.

The *deep-structure trace* is an information structure that spells out the decisions that were made and that resulted in the particular behavior. It is composed recursively from the following elements.

Goals—desired situation, usually described in the same terms as the behavior. A goal always occurs in a deep structure trace in contrast with another actual situation. This contrast is factored into differences that the decision maker hopes to reduce. Hence, the deep-structure trace also contains:

Deltacts—reducible difference categories. The reason a difference is abstracted as a category and given a deltact name is that the understander knows some

Methods—how various things may be achieved; the means to an end. Methods are attached to one or more deltacts. ("To get less hungry [deltact] try eating [method].") Methods are where the recursion comes in. A method may consist of reducing certain differences or adopting certain other goals, as well as some fully specified behavior. By having methods that use goals and deltacts, a wide range of possible behaviors may be regarded as pursuing a particular method.

The deep-structure trace is an explanation of the surface structure trace; one of the measures of how thoroughly it has been understood will be the plausibility and completeness of this explanation. It is an information structure, and the processes that produce it may be quite different in form from the problem-solving process it traces. We believe that understanding proceeds by assembling hypotheses about the two traces of behavior and of problem solving.

We use the term *means–ends analysis target structure* for a familiar pattern of deep-structure trace elements used in building up hypotheses. Means–ends analysis describes the purposive aspect of the deep-structure trace. The target structure guides the construction of the deep-structure trace, filling in for certain parts of the pattern with known behavior from the surface-structure trace or with other (presumably confirmed) hypotheses. (The part filled in is called a "slot.") Thus, the means–ends analysis target structure yields a *basic hypothesis* about the deep-structure trace that may be revised in light of other details.

When revising an hypothesized deep-structure trace, there are constraints on what may be changed, and on what must be changed, in addition to deciding which kind of change should be made. We will use the term *planning knowledge* for the *rules* that specify how deep structure trace elements may be combined. The planning knowledge defines the target structure for: (*a*) understanding the behavior as a unified whole; (*b*) the plausibility of the deep-structure trace; and (*c*) the habits as to which combinations to try and which basic hypotheses to suggest.

The understander must have a feel for the *problem-solving* processes that will explain or generate the behavior: The understander must know those processes involved in finding possible solutions in order to solve the problem without help. In effect the understander is being asked to "catch up" with the plans and motives underlying some behavior that has already happened, and must thus have a mastery of the *hypothesis-formation* processes available. These are the tools for getting from behavior to explanation. They enable the understander to know the range of other possible behaviors and plans; to fill in choices in the deep-structure trace that appear to have been glossed over; to understand and profit from conventions or restrictions in the planful behavior for a given domain; to select major deep structure elements to dominate the hypothesis; and to incorporate details into an hypothesis (either by substitution or by composition), etc.

Since these hypothesis-formation tools are incomplete and imperfect (to say nothing of the information that may be given to work on), it is equally important that the understander have a mastery of the *hypothesis-selection* process, since there will always be inconsistent, alternative hypotheses from which to choose. Some of the devices and criteria for making such a choice are: (*a*) the integrity, wholeness, or appropriateness of a plan; (*b*) its formal plausibility; (*c*) its consistency with the situations contrasted in the various goal elements; (*d*) the ease with which the planning knowledge (grammar) can splice it into larger, accepted structures; (*e*) the presence of confirming behavior for a plan; (*f*) predictions and consequences for further behavior; and (*g*) whether or not two hypothesis elements can be interchanged or combined.

An incorrect hypothesis can be salvaged: It may have been almost right, or the detailed understanding of most of its evidence may have been correct. For this reason, we have introduced the notion of **revising** the hypothesis to conform to the evidence. Revising a hypothesis consists of focusing criticism and responding with proposed improvements.

The hypothesis formation and elaboration process is dominated in a "top-down" way by a target structure or model, such as is given by means–ends analysis, the planning knowledge, the hypothesis manipulation procedures, and the basic deductive strategies taken together. The hypothesis proposal, confirmation, and revision processes are necessarily driven onward by the actual evidence available—the elements of the two kinds of traces—in a "bottom-up" way, for the fundamental direction of information flow is from behavior narrative to complete explanation. These two, one pulling, one pushing, strike a balance in the understanding of purposive behavior that we call *top-down/bottom-up processing*.

Herein lies the beauty of the model notion and its potential relevance to learning strategies: Without guessing in advance what the eventual explanation is going to be, the understander can use each new piece of evidence to drive deduction forward, while using the largely intensional target structure provided by the model to focus on the most viable explanation. Given the right distribution of knowledge between the representational framework and the principal target structure representation, the basic strategies can be expressed in a domain-independent way.

FORMULATIONS AND DELIVERY OF SOME NEW LEARNING STRATEGIES

Thus far, we have examined the understanding process over three diverse domains, describing the processes, strategies, and conceptual structures for each, and the invariances over these domains. Within each domain we have focused on the correspondence between the knowledge needed for problem solving and the knowledge needed for understanding. Without explicit awareness of the largely tacit planning and strategic knowledge inherent in each domain, it is difficult for a person to make sense of many sequences of behavior as described by a story, a set of instructions, a problem solution, a complex system, etc. Our premise was that before one could begin to formulate new learning strategies for enhancing a student's abilities to acquire an understanding of some new piece of knowledge (as opposed just to memorizing it rotely), these processes and tacit knowledge had to be made more explicit. Having partially accomplished this, the question naturally arises as to what impact this has on the formulation and teaching of learning strategies.

We suggest that the preceding theory be used to make as explicit as possible how "understanding" is an active process requiring the understander to synthesize, verify, and refine a deep-structure trace or hypothesis about the underlying motives, plans, and intentions that fit each separate piece of the "puzzle" into a coherent structure. Teaching this process can probably best be accomplished by focusing on the domain of knowledge in which the student is to specialize. The teacher should articulate for that domain the higher-order planning knowledge and the strategic knowledge for formulating and revising hypotheses about what something means. By carefully choosing a set of situations for the student to understand, each strategic rule can be instantiated, providing the student with practice in the coordination of the top-down, bottom-up hypothesis formation and revision process. Some situations might be devised to be inherently "garden path," where the students' most likely first guesses of the underlying meaning are apt to be wrong, requiring them to focus on how they detect that their guesses are wrong and how they then intelligently go about revising them.

Since this hypothesis-formation–revision process is so complex, it might be useful to construct a hypothetical understander in a film animation, who shows the process in an expert's head (in slow motion) as the expert goes about understanding some novel situation. At the very least, this will suggest to the student that understanding is not a simple process, but rather a complex and very active one.

After students have begun to master strategies for constructing and revising deep-structure traces over the given knowledge domain, their attention could be drawn to this same process as it applies to story comprehension. In this way, they could begin to witness the generality of what they have been taught, especially since the planning knowledge needed in story comprehension is usually well understood (albeit tacitly), as are the rudimentary strategies and processes of weaving together the lines of a story into a coherent explanatory structure.

There is one new kind of instructional technology we are developing that might provide a unique capability for exposing students to the underlying problem-solving strategies and knowledge for a domain in a way that is apt to be enticing and meaningful. We have been designing an "articulate expert" instructional computer system that explicitly contains all of the planning knowledge, basic knowledge, means–ends problem-solving strategies, as well as a limited class of hypothesis revision (debugging) strategies necessary for solving on its own a wide class of student-generated problems. The expert's articulateness is especially significant: Not only can it solve a problem, but it can also explain (at various levels of detail) *why* it performed each step. It can explain its overall plan of attack, how it formulated that plan, and why it did not do it some other way.

In other words, the student can pose a problem to this system and witness all the inner thinking, mistakes, and false attempts that an expert makes, thereby exposing the student to strategies and knowledge sources that are hidden by looking only at the final solution to a problem. We believe that by letting the student pose problems to the articulate expert and witnessing the unfolding of the plans of a problem solver, "understanding" a problem solution in a particular domain, can be enhanced. Then attention would be drawn to this same process as it applies to a second domain. These steps would then provide students the ability to generate their own learning strategies.

ACKNOWLEDGMENTS

We are indebted to Harry O'Neil whose suggestions on our first draft led us to such a major revision that this final form now bears little resemblance to it. We would also like to thank Marilyn Jager Adams, Bob Donaghey, and Ned Benhaim for their suggestions and assistance.

REFERENCES

Abelson, R. P. Concepts for representing mundane reality in plans. In D. G. Bobrow & A. Collins (Eds.), *Representation and understanding: Studies in cognitive science.* New York: Academic Press, 1975.

Adams, M. J., & Collins, A. A scheme-theoretic view of reading. In R. Freedle (Ed.), *Discourse processing: A multidisciplinary perspective.* Norwood, N.J.: Ablex, 1978.

Bartlett, F. C. *Remembering.* Cambridge, Eng.: University Press, 1932.

Bobrow, D. G., & Collins, A. (Eds.). *Representation and understanding studies in cognitive science.* New York: Academic Press, 1975.

Brown, A. L. *Qualitative knowledge, causal reasoning, and the localization of failures* (TR-362). Cambridge, Mass.: MIT, Artificial Intelligence Laboratory, 1976.

Brown, A. L. & Sussman, G. J. *Localization of failures in radio circuits: A study in causal and teleological reasoning* (Memo No. 319). Cambridge, Mass.: MIT, Artificial Intelligence Laboratory, 1974.

Brown, J. S., Rubinstein, R., & Burton, R. *Reactive learning environment for computer assisted electronics instruction* (AFHRL-TR-76-68). Air Force Human Resources Laboratory, October 1976.

Bundy, A. *Analyzing mathematical proofs (or reading between the lines)* (D.A.I. Res. Rep. No. 2). Edinburgh: University of Edinburgh, Department of Artificial Intelligence, May 1975.

Charniak, E. A partial taxonomy of knowledge about actions. *Proceeding of the Fourth International Joint Conference on Artificial Intelligence.* 1975, pp. 91–98.

deKleer, J. *A theory of plans for electronic circuits* (Working Paper 144). Cambridge, Mass.: MIT, Artificial Intelligence Laboratory, 1977.

Goldstein, I. P. *Understanding simple picture programs* (TR-294). Cambridge, Mass.: MIT, Artificial Intelligence Laboratory, 1974.

Goldstein, I. P., & Miller, M. L. *PAZATN: A linguistic approach to automatic analysis of elementary programming protocols.* (AIM-388), Cambridge, Mass.: MIT, Artificial Intelligence Laboratory, 1976.

Mandler, J. M., & Johnson, N. S. Remembrance of things parsed: Story structure and recall. *Cognitive Psychology,* 1977, *9*, 111–151.

Minsky, M. A framework for representing knowledge. In P. H. Winston (Ed.), *The psychology of computer vision.* New York: McGraw-Hill, 1975.

Newell, A., & Simon, H. A. GPS, a program that simulates human thought. In E. A. Feigenbaum & J. Feldman (Eds.), *Computers and thought.* New York: McGraw-Hill, 1963.

Rich, C., & Shrobe, H. E. *Initial report on a LISP programmer's apprentice* (TR-354). Cambridge, Mass.: MIT, 1976.

Rigney, J. *On cognitive strategies for facilitating acquisition, retention, and retrieval in training and education* (Tech. Rep. No. 78). Los Angeles: University of Southern California, 1976.

Rumelhart, D. E. Notes on a schema for stories. In D. Bobrow & A. Collins (Eds.), *Representation and understanding: Studies in cognitive science.* New York: Academic Press, 1975.

Rumelhart, D. E. Understanding and summarizing brief stories. In D. LaBerge & S. J. Samuels (Eds.), *Basic processes in reading: Perception and comprehension.* Hillsdale, N.J.: Lawrence Erlbaum Associates, 1977.

Rumelhart, D. E., & Ortony, A. Representation of knowledge. In R. C. Anderson, R. J. Spiro, & W. E. Montague (Eds.), *Schooling and the acquisition of knowledge.* Hillsdale, N.J.: Lawrence Erlbaum Associates, 1977.

Schank, R., & Abelson, R. *Scripts, plans, goals, and understanding.* Hillsdale, N.J.: Lawrence Erlbaum Associates, 1977.

Sussman, G. J. *A computational model of skill acquisition* (TR-297). Cambridge, Mass.: MIT, Artificial Intelligence Laboratory, 1973.

Winograd, T. Frame representations and the declarative-procedural controversy. In D. G. Bobrow & A. M. Colins (Eds.), *Representation and understanding: Studies in cognitive science.* New York: Academic Press, 1975.

Winston, P. H. *Artificial intelligence.* Reading, Mass.: Addison-Wesley, 1977.

6

An Instructional Systems Development Approach for Learning Strategies[1]

ROBERT S. LOGAN

The first purpose of this chapter is to examine the concept of learning strategies in terms of instructional systems development (ISD). Second, I will discuss tools and procedures for analyzing problems in learning strategies and for designing, developing, implementing, and controlling solutions to those problems.

Instructional systems development is a technique for breaking down complex instructional problems into smaller, more manageable problem areas which can then be usefully addressed by specialists. For example, one complex problem that is a goal of learning strategies research is the specification of individualization processes for the structure and presentation of instructional media and materials. Based on the belief that deficient or proficient learner characteristics can be compensated for or optimized by specific learning scenarios, we can analyze the problem of specifying individualization processes by addressing three smaller problem areas: (*a*) identification of learner characteristics, (*b*) development of instructional materials, and (*c*) collection and analysis of learner performance data. An ISD approach of analysis, design, development, implementation, and control may be applied effectively to these areas.

[1]Preparation of this chapter was supported in part by the Defense Advanced Research Projects Agency under contract number MDA 903-76-C-C0086 under terms of DARPA Order 3076. Views and conclusions contained in this document are those of the author and should not be interpreted as necessarily representing the official policies, either expressed or implied, of the Defense Advanced Research Projects Agency or of the United States Government.

141

A great deal of effort is beginning to be directed toward learning strategies research and development, as demonstrated by the chapters in this book. However, little attention has been directed toward the careful development and presentation of instructional materials. And yet, I believe, this is precisely where the success or failure of much learning strategies research finds a genesis or digs a grave.

This is because implementation and validation of most learning strategies consists of three steps: First, learner characteristics are identified; second, instructional materials are developed; and third, learner performance data are analyzed. The second step (developing instructional materials) is the key to the whole process. Learning strategies that compensate for or optimize a particular learner characteristic must be embedded in and presented through instructional materials. Learner performance data are collected and analyzed through the student's interaction with the instructional material. If instructional materials are not properly developed and presented in some controlled manner, the effectiveness of a learning strategy may remain in doubt.

All three steps in the implementation and validation of learning strategies are critical. But the step receiving the **least** attention in the past—and which therefore probably deserves the **most** attention in the future—is development of instructional materials in which learning strategies are successfully (and knowingly) embedded and through which learning strategies are effectively (and knowingly) presented.

The term "knowingly" is purposely used twice. An instructional materials developer is told to write an "alternative module" that would "compensate" for the specific weakness in the student's repertoire of learning abilities, aptitudes, attidues, interests, and motivations. Like penicillin, the alternative module is also referred to as a "treatment." When instructional materials developers ask for guidance, they are told, for example, to use their own judgment, or to use plenty of drill and practice, or to use small amounts of text, or to use numerous examples, or to use a few very clear examples, or to use black-and-white line drawings, or to use color photographs. How the advice should be put into practice is never made clear, and what specific procedures should be followed are never explained. And so the instructional material developer goes off with his ears ringing and writes the alternative module. It is tested, revised, and retested until it is "validated" as a working alternative module. Validation means that the material allows the student to achieve course or lesson objectives according to some criteria.

The virtue of such modules is that they work. Students take them, pass the tests associated with them, and eventually graduate. But the vice of such modules is that they deceive. Strategists analyze their data, do their regressions, and conclude that the modules did or did not compensate for the lack of a learning strategy or, perhaps, that they were good predictors of lesson completion times or criterion scores. However, whether the module works as it was intended to work is never discerned. Whether the learner performance data resulting from the module gives credence to the hoped-for prediction equation is unclear. These two things remain in doubt because, in part at least, a systematic approach was never taken from the starting point of analysis to the ending point of control.

The technique called *instructional systems development* (ISD) considers instructional problems in five phases: analysis, design, development, implementation, and control. It has been used in differing instructional environments and applied to a variety of instructional problems. An examination of the concept of learning strategies in terms of instructional systems development is one purpose of this chapter. A discussion of tools and procedures for analyzing problems in learning strategies and designing, developing, implementing, and controlling solutions to those problems is the second purpose of this chapter. I will discuss the development of instructional materials in which learning strategies are embedded and through which they are presented.

INSTRUCTIONAL SYSTEMS DEVELOPMENT PHASES

Instructional systems development is a general systems approach with multiple components that, given a certain set of constraints, is used to produce an instructional system. One example of an instructional system is a learning strategies research program. Instructional systems development is based upon a series of activities that are arranged in several phases, including analysis, design, development, implementation, and control (Baker, 1970; Bunderson, 1970; Butler, 1972; Civil Service Commission, 1969; Cogan, 1971; Peck & Tucker, 1973; TRADOC, 1975; Wong & Raulerson, 1974). The phases and activities in ISD are explained in what follows in order to relate the approach to the field of learning strategies. They are also presented in Figure 6.1.

Phase I. Analyze

A certain training or educational program is determined to be both desirable and feasible. For example, a needs assessment study may determine that a large proportion of foreign students are being admitted as undergraduate students in a university. The study may conclude that the current freshman English program fails to address the foreign students' needs, and may recommend that a new remedial English program be developed and implemented.

The preferred outcome that is to be taught is analyzed into a series of task statements. For example, one task statement in the remedial English program might be *conjugate verbs*. Statistical techniques and the judgments of subject matter experts are used to select a subset of the task statements for instruction. For example, it might be determined that a subset of task statements relating to written communication skills should be taught.

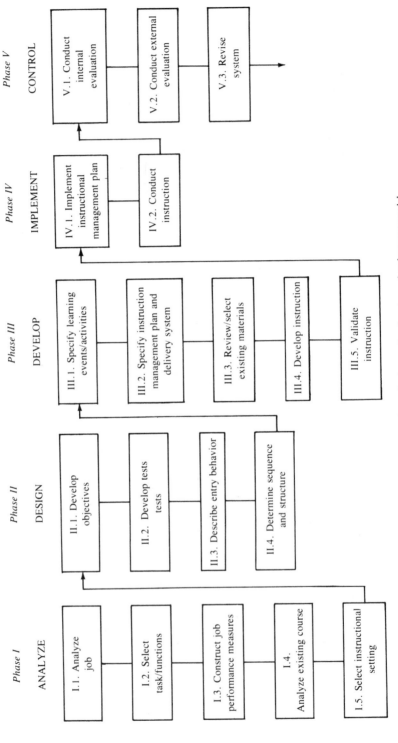

Figure 6.1. Interservice procedures for instructional systems development model.

144

Finally, the instructional setting for the new program is determined. For example, it might be concluded that the remedial English program could be offered most effectively in a formal classroom situation, such as a language laboratory. Or it might be that the best instructional setting would be a seminar, a correspondence course, or a self-study course with programmed instructional texts. Factors affecting this decision are length of course, type of course, student proficiency desired, personnel available to teach the course, and other operational constraints.

Phase II. Design

Phase II converts the tasks selected for instruction in Phase I into behavioral objectives that are to be achieved at the end of instruction by the students in the program. Behavioral objectives are **precise** statements of desired learning outcomes. They are precise because they contain a condition under which the outcome is executed, a measurable behavior, and a standard that indicates pass–fail status on an objective, absolute criterion.

Criterion-referenced measures based upon the behavioral objectives are devised for measuring learner performance in both cognitive and psychomotor domains, if desired. For example, a criterion-referenced measure might be used to assess a student's understanding of the principle of verb conjugation or whether that student can, in fact, conjugate a verb. Unlike norm-referenced tests, learner performance on criterion-referenced measures is judged against an objective, absolute standard rather than against some norm such as a class average.

A fourth step in the design stage is to characterize incoming students in terms of general ability, reading level, and prior experience. For example, some foreign students entering the remedial English program may be able to "conjugate verbs" when they arrive for instruction whereas others cannot. Numerous measures exist for identifying many different entry-level abilities, skills, and backgrounds.

The final step in the design stage is to construct a suitable sequence and structure of instruction. For example, having identified the fact that some foreign students are already able to conjugate verbs when they arrive for instruction, instructional designers can devise an alternative sequence of instruction that allows the students to bypass those parts of the instruction they have already mastered.

Phase III. Develop

Several activities occur in this phase. First, instructional media are selected on the basis of cost, available resources, and instructional requirements. Second, individualized materials are developed on the basis of data from Phases I and II. For example, examination of the task statements analyzed and selected for instruction in Phase I may reveal that some tasks statements or groups of task statements are more difficult than others. Knowing this, instructional materials developers can provide additional details or examples in those materials covering the more difficult task statements. If *conjugate verbs* is a difficult task step, information or examples covering that task statement may be expanded. Another way to individualize materials is to present the same instructional content in a different media, one that is more compatible with a student's learning characteristics. In either case, the object of the individualization process is to compensate for or optimize a student's weaknesses or strengths.

A third activity in this phase is decision-making concerning (*a*) management of students, instructors, and program administrators; (*b*) desired learning experiences and activities, and (*c*) the form and content of the instructional delivery system. For example, a decision might be made to have a self-paced instructional delivery system. Another decision might be whether to have only student self-examinations, to have mastery tests scored by a proctor, or to have a complete computer-managed instructional (CMI) system. Decisions made in the course of this activity are heavily influenced by institutional resources that support the program.

The last step in the development stage is instructional materials validation during small and large tryouts. Instructional materials are tested and revised in order to ensure that students using the materials can meet course and lesson objectives. Also, alternative instructional materials developed in accordance with student characteristics are evaluated to determine whether the materials meet the needs imposed by those characteristics. This is commonly known as *formative evaluation*.

Phase IV. Implement

The instructional and administrative staff is trained according to the requirements of the instructional management plan and delivery system. Procedures for record keeping, data collection, student counselling and tutoring, and other aspects of program administration are created. During implementation, periodic evaluations are made of the performance of both personnel and procedures. For example, if a separate room is reserved for test-taking, personnel manning the room should be instructed in the specific procedures for admitting students, scoring tests, releasing successful students for further instruction, and remediating students who fail to meet the stated criteria.

When the instructional media and materials are implemented in approved, large-scale courses of instruction, feedback is obtained on both system performance and effectiveness of materials. This activity has been called *summative evaluation*. Instructional systems development places somewhat more emphasis on system performance during summative evaluation, because replicable data collection and analysis methodologies and standardized administrative processes can make the difference between an accurate and an inaccurate evaluation. For example, if a fast track of instruction is being evaluated for *conjugate verbs,* we will have to administer the instruction to the students, collect data on it, and analyze it **in exactly the same manner** so there may be only one variable: the interaction between the student characteristic and the materials comprising the fast track of instruction.

Phase V. Control

Phase V consists of three activities. First, the procedures and materials evaluation begun in the previous stage is extended to a longer term by obtaining data from the system itself. This is called *internal evaluation*. Second, graduates of the new system are evaluated in terms of job performance or later instruction by obtaining data from job supervisors or administrators of later instruction. This activity is called *external evaluation*. For example, internal evaluation determines whether a foreign student can meet the lesson objectives for *conjugate verbs*. External evaluation determines whether the foreign student performs better in the freshman English program after having completed the remedial English program.

The third activity is to revise the system. The extent of system revision is determined by the answers from internal and external evaluation. For example, suppose two sets of performance data (course completion times, criterion scores, attitudinal data, or whatever) are obtained. The first set of data concerns performance of foreign students in the freshman English program prior to implementation of the remedial English program; that is known as *baseline data*. The second set of data concerns performance of foreign students in the freshman English program after implementation of the remedial English program. If the second set of data tends to show improvement over the baseline data, the conclusion may be that foreign students did benefit from the new program. Although this is a simplification of program evaluation, it is intended to show that evaluation of a learning strategy should be a longer-term exercise than one normally considers. This is because evaluation is based on the outcomes of many previous activities.

Negative answers to either the first or second of the three activities in this stage demonstrate that revision of the contents and/or procedures of the new program are necessary, and revisions may be required in any of the five phases of ISD. If the rationale for every previous activity is documented and available for reexamination, the revision process may be made an easier, more accurate process.

INSTRUCTIONAL SYSTEMS DEVELOPMENT CONSIDERATIONS

Since instructional systems development is obviously a detailed, task-intensive technique, potential users should ask themselves several questions:

1. What are the benefits of instructional systems development?
2. In what environments and institutions has it been used?
3. Are tools and procedures available which make it more easily adopted?

The remainder of this chapter is devoted to consideration of these questions.

Benefits

Instructional systems development has several benefits. First, it "works equally well to induce desirable teaching behavior in cognitive and in affective respects

[Peck & Tucker, 1973, p. 943]." Second, general instructional effectiveness is greatly increased through the design and development procedures, a careful selection of what is to be taught, the measurement and evaluation of instruction, and the revision of the instructional program until its objectives are met. Third, instruction can be offered in a much more time-efficient way than before. Finally, a systematic way of viewing costs of training and instruction is obtained, and whether additional resources are justified in view of the output may be considered. Demonstrated improvements in cost per student, time required to complete, and increased effectiveness have been obtained on large systems which use advanced simulators as well as areas of instruction that use no hardware at all (TRADOC, 1975).

Users

Instructional systems development has been used in both military and civilian environments for education and training program development. The Army first adopted ISD for training program development in an official regulation published in 1968 (Continental Army Command, 1968). Two years later, the Air Force published detailed procedures for ISD and followed that with a handbook for designers of instructional systems based on instructional systems development (Air Force, 1970, 1973). More recently, the ISD approach was extensively documented and approved for interservice use in a package including a four-volume manual, an adjunct instructional workbook, mediated workshop materials, and a workshop directors handbook (TRADOC, 1975).

Civilian institutions that use or have used instructional systems development include Federal agencies such as the Federal Law Enforcement Training Center and the Internal Revenue Service (Civil Service Commission, 1969). Commercial firms such as American Airlines, Eastman Kodak, Hughes Aircraft, IBM, and McDonnell Douglas also use instructional system development (Sullivan, Smith, & Filinger, 1974). Colleges and universities using the approach include Dallas Baptist College, Mt. San Jacinto College, Brigham Young, Illinois, Florida State, Illinois State, Pittsburgh, Stanford, Purdue, and Texas at Austin (Cogan, 1971; Sullivan et al., 1974).

Obstacles

Despite the extensive use of instructional systems development several obstacles to it exist (Cogan, 1971). First, ISD requires a strong, centralized management structure to obtain cooperation from potentially conflicting elements. Computer support personnel, evaluation teams, materials developers, instructional psychologists, other interdisciplinary elements of a large-scale instructional development effort do not readily lend themselves to a strong, centralized management structure.

Second, ISD assumes more or less the reputations of previous innovations. The history of education is replete with innovations that promised performance that could not be met and, if met, could not be maintained. As a result, ISD has its own healthy share of skeptics and doubters.

Third, ISD has perhaps no equal as a consumer of time. Funding for programs such as learning strategies is often of such short-term duration that not enough time is provided for properly evaluating and revising a program. Therefore, a certain residue of uncertainty about the program's effectiveness frequently remains. And, I believe, this is true not only of the "customer" for a learning strategies program, but also of its developers.

Fourth, ISD requires an extremely complex manning table. A manning table is a document listing the number of personnel required to develop, operate, and maintain a program as well as the specialties and expertise those personnel must have. The fact that ISD requires a complex manning table has special impact for a university-oriented learning strategies research program. The transient nature of student life, the wholesale changes of available students at each semester's completion or beginning, and the demands and pressures of student academic life work against maintaining a stable cadre of experienced personnel. In addition, the personnel required by ISD efforts are simply in short supply and training technologies applicable to the approach are not generally available (Hunter, Kastner, Rubin, & Seidel, 1975).

A fifth obstacle suggested by a Navy study (NTEC, 1976) concerns the nature of ISD; that is, whether it can be proceduralized. The argument is as follows: If instructional systems development can be proceduralized, then instructional designers can formalize models of instruction and techniques that laymen can follow and produce at lower cost, with the same results. If it cannot be proceduralized, then instructional designers themselves will have to develop each instructional program case-by-case, using subject-matter experts as information suppliers, and costs will be higher. The Navy study determined that the key to whether ISD could be proceduralized was whether common factors existed in the more than 100 methodologies developed to date. The study concluded that no common factors existed among the methodologies reviewed. As a result, no linear sequence of generally applicable, prescriptive procedures could be developed. The disagreement among ISD practitioners prevented it.

Another study, which identified authoring tools and procedures for ISD, did not agree with the conclusion of the Navy study (Logan, 1977). It was found that the basic issue of disagreement was the synthesis of the generally applicable, prescriptive procedures—regardless of linear or nonlinear sequence. The first reason for this conclusion was that few, if any, instructional designers took a cosmic view that considered both content and sequence of the whole process. The second reason was that general requirements for ISD were widely accepted—a different finding from the Navy study.

There was also little disagreement as to the content and sequence of procedures for conducting job and task analysis, developing behavioral objectives and criterion-referenced tests, and developing and validating instructional materials. These were the areas that the Navy study identified as most ill defined. (Job analysis is determining what job incumbents actually do on the job in terms of specific tasks. For definitions of other terms, see the explanation of phases and activities in ISD previously given.)

Finally, Logan (1977) found that for other ISD activities, such as selecting instructional settings, specifying an instructional management plan and delivery system, and revising systems, there are few disagreements, since few procedures existed in these areas at all. The reason for this was that these activities were subject to policy considerations rather than simply the evidential rightness or wrongness of a technical approach, and policy cannot be proceduralized.

In summary, common factors are found in ISD that can be applied to instructional development for learning strategies. The objective of the systems approach in ISD or learning strategies is improved instructional processes. Its product is an instructional system—a group of coordinated parts designed to achieve an instructional-oriented purpose. One coordinated part of a typical instruction system is development of instructional materials in which learning strategies are effectively embedded and through which such materials are effectively presented. This occurs as a result of the authoring process.

THE AUTHORING PROCESS

We can define the authoring process as a sequence of activities that obtains supportive information from analyses of jobs, tasks, incoming students, and existing courses and course materials; converts that information into instructional packages of a proper sequence, structure, and format that enables learning to occur; revises those packages during preliminary and large-scale tryouts on the basis of feedback from students, instructors, and administrators; and publishes those revised packages as finished products by which the largest number of students achieve the greatest number of objectives in the shortest possible time. These activities are concerned with both the use of existing materials and the development of standardized, transportable material development techniques.

Cogan (1971) argues that the heart of the educational technology endeavor lies in instructional materials. A similar argument is advanced from a writer's viewpoint by Slack (1973):

> The American Educational Establishment is waiting for The Big System to come down, Deus ex-machina data-wise, all solid-state and chrome-plate with tri-color consoles, tailfins and one-billion words storage. Maybe it can make the kids shut up and do the reading. Well, I'm here to tell you, they're waiting for Godot, and many's the riot that'll romp 'round the playground at old PS 501 before the computer comes to town. And when it does arrive, all nice and shiny, it'll be the dumbest computer you ever saw and will just sit over in the AV Department along with the rest of the teaching machines, unless somebody has written some might good stuff to go into it [p. 32].

The importance of a particular genre of effective instructional material such as programmed text over conventional teaching materials is that they "teach the student the capability of **doing** something, not of 'knowing' something [Gagné, 1973, p. 15]." **Doing** something can be measured, which provides evidence of a learning strategy's effectiveness. In short, it can be determined whether, according to some criteria such as completion times or scores or improved attitudes, a student achieved stated objectives during instruction or was able to perform in later instruction or, ultimately, in job situations.

But as important as using and developing effective instructional materials is, there are major shortcomings in both areas. For example, the Carnegie Commission (1972) noted the shallow penetration of quality materials into higher education and said "high priority must be placed, during the next two decades, upon the design and utilization of effective instructional programs suitable for use or adaptation by more than one institution [p. 47]." Lack of high-quality materials, overlooked materials, and lack of a standardized curriculums have been noted by several researchers as obstacles to the adoption of computer-related technology (Hunter *et al.*, 1975).

Similarly, procedures for developing new instructional materials remain typical of the "cottage industry" approach criticized by Molnar (1971):

> The large amount of uncoordinated research activities and the lack of pre-planned linkages between research and practice has led to the existence of an expensive cottage industry in educational technology which tends to retool every academic year. Researchers and educators frequently demonstrate a strong resistance to the use of someone else's innovation. It has been said that if there was a Nobel prize for educational research, we would have to nominate an entire generation of researchers for their co-discovery of the wheel [p. 7].

At least three factors have forced the development and application of unique, situation-specific methods to such things as job analysis, test and behavioral objectives construction, and implementation, evaluation, and revision of instruction. First, many educators feel very strongly that instruction should have a local, indigeneous quality (Demerath & Daniels, 1973). Second, instructional material development efforts are usually driven by a "raw empiricism" so that they

> are prepared on the basis of intuition, folklore, or experience and administered to members of the target population. If the students pass the test, the product is considered appropriate; if not, the materials are revised and tried again. This tryout-revision cycle is repeated until the product works or the developers run out of resources or time [Merrill & Boutwell, 1973, p. 96].

In addition, empirical revision rules are often compounded with changes in syntax, organization, and usage, and, therefore, comparison of alternative revision procedures is almost impossible (Baker, 1970).

The third factor forcing situation-specific development methods is that the authoring process itself has been studied piecemeal. Any attempt at synthesis has been limited to general handbooks on developing instructional systems. A Navy study

(NTEC, 1976) criticized the handbooks for telling the developers what to do but not how to do it. For example, numerous handbooks emphasize the importance of learning taxonomies but few discuss the application of them to actual instructional problems. The how-to aspect of the authoring process is the concern of authoring tools and procedures, a study of which is reported in what follows.

Authoring Tools and Procedures

An instructional systems development methodology was earlier defined as a general systems approach with multiple components which, given a certain set of constraints, is used to produce an instructional system. A learning strategies research program was given as an example of an instructional system. Authoring tools and procedures can be defined in terms of this methodology.

We may define an authoring procedure as a step or series of steps that operationally defines one component of the methodology such as instructional materials development. An authoring tool may be defined as an evaluated, self-contained product in a suitable format which is applied to the analysis, design, development, implementation, or control of one or more steps of a procedure such as development of behavioral objectives. Authoring tools and procedures, and clearinghouses for existing instructional materials were identified in a study by Logan (1977) in order to disseminate work that could facilitate analyzing, designing, developing, implementing, and controlling the ISD process.

In order to place the authoring tools and procedures in proper perspective, I will provide some background on the study.

Model

The Interservice Procedures for Instructional Systems Development (IPISD) model provided the structure for the authoring tools and procedures study (TRADOC, 1975). The IPISD model consists of 5 phases and 19 steps (see Figure 6.1). Each step has both an input and an output. For example, one phase in the model is "Develop"; one step in that phase is "Develop Instruction"; one input to that step is a review and selection of existing materials; one output of that step is an integrated series of new or adapted instructional materials and media. The steps and phases of the IPISD model are not necessarily done on a once-and-once-only basis, but rather provide for a continuing, iterative process of system development. The detailed discussion of phases and activities in ISD given earlier applies equally to the IPISD model.

Literature Search

A literature search was conducted of American and Canadian instructional systems from 1965 through 1976. The search included the areas of on-line and off-line instructional systems, instructional materials development and revision methodologies, design and installation of instructional materials, studies of media effectiveness, information-processing behavior of students, analyses of instructional tasks and job requirements, and revision procedures for instructional systems.

Computerized and manual searches of several data banks and libraries were conducted. Computerized searches were made of data banks in the Educational Resources Information Centers, the Defense Documentation Center, and other libraries. Manual searches were made of indexes, abstracting services, and bibliographies emphasizing instructional-oriented issues. In addition, a Selective Dissemination of Information service on specific topics in educational and instructional technology was used.

In total, over 5000 reports were read in full-text or abstract form and approximately 1400 practical, development-oriented documents were selected for inclusion in a computerized data base developed for the study.

Selection Criteria

Documents were selected for inclusion in the data base according to three criteria. First, selected documents had to fit the definition of either a tool or a procedure. Second, since the end result of the study was to be the identification and analysis of authoring aids usable in a military environment, selected documents had to report work developed in a military setting, or in the civilian sector and be suitable for adaptation to operational military training. Third, work discussed in a report or in a clearinghouse brochure had to be applied and evaluated or, if a procedure, at least applied.

The data base was analyzed in terms of authoring tools and procedures applicable to ISD activities. Printout listings of research reports were obtained describing authoring tools and procedures that had been applied and evaluated in military or civilian environments. In some cases, an additional printout identifying unevaluated applications was also produced. Appropriate authoring tools and procedures were then selected for a bibliography (Logan, 1977) on the basis of three guidelines:

1. Large pools of applied and evaluated reports allowed some early or obsolete work to be rejected.
2. Relative cost and availability made some authoring aids more suitable than others.
3. Approaches and concepts that had been widely used but not evaluated were occasionally chosen over narrower, more parochial work that had been evaluated.

Results

We must interpret the findings and conclusions of the study in light of two limitations. First, classification and categorization of reports were not subject to interjudge reliability tests. Second, the population of reports in the data base was created by applying operational definitions of authoring tools and procedures and an experimenter-derived classification scheme for report characteristics.

The raw data from the printouts were analyzed to determine the ISD activities for which there were no tools. Tools were considered as the most desirable authoring aid because they were readily transportable and required the least adaptation or restructuring by potential users. No tools were available in the following ISD activities taken from the IPISD model:

Select tasks/functions,
Construct job performance measures,
Select instructional setting,
Specify learning events/activities,
Implement instructional management plan, and
Conduct external evaluation.

Procedures were unavailable for two of these activities: *select instructional setting* and *specify learning events/activities.*

Since the authoring process is composed of four processes (information gathering, conversion, revision, and publication), authoring tools and procedures were drawn from those activities which analyzed, designed, developed, implemented, and controlled those processes. Available tools and procedures are noted below and grouped according to the phases and steps that comprise the IPISD model.

Analyze Job. An extensive Air Force occupational analysis program was begun in the 1960s that culminated in development of a very effective tool for computer-based job analysis. The Comprehensive Occupational Data Analysis Programs (CODAP) provides individual or group descriptions that specify the percentage of time spent on each task in a job, describes an actual job at different task levels such as apprentice or officer, derives individual and group job differences, and identifies specific types of jobs as they exist or should exist within a general specialty. Detailed descriptions of procedures, programming notes, and applications are provided by Archer (1966); Morsch and Archer (1967); R. E. Christal (1972), Weissmuller, Barton, and Rogers (1974a,b); Stacy, Weissmuller, Barton, and Rogers (1974); Mayo, Nance, and Shiegekawa (1975); Stacey and Hazel (1975); and R. E. Christal and Weissmuller (1975). Although the data described in these reports apply to Air Force technical training, the CODAP computer programs will manipulate data from other environments. The computer programs may be purchased inexpensively on magnetic tapes for use on a UNIVAC 1108 computer. Control card specifications are also available, which enable reprogramming for use on IBM 360/370 series computers.[2]

Existing task and job data in many career specialties are available from the Task Inventory Exchange (TIE, 1975). Specific task inventories may be purchased on a cost-recovery basis and cumulative task inventory directories are available at reasonable cost. The Task Inventory Exchange has published three task inventory directories through 1976.

Select Tasks/Functions. McKnight and Adams (1970) report detailed procedures by which a panel of experts select critical behaviors for driver education training from a possible pool of 1000 relevant behaviors. When a specific outcome is known, their procedures are useful for identifying critical behaviors that must be taught to help a student achieve that outcome.

---

[2] Available from Dr. R. E. Christal, Technical Director, Occupational and Manpower Research Laboratory, AFHRL/OR, Stop #63, Lackland Air Force Base, Texas 78236.

Powers (1971) added a phrase to the standard task statement which aided the selection of tasks for teaching physician's assistants. The phrase *in order to* is used to indicate an intended outcome of a task, and thereby group students according to the required levels of competence. As an elementary form of pretest, the phrase may be used to devise preliminary alternative learning paths for students with differing levels of competence.

Cline (1973) used a sophisticated, computer-based, multivariate statistical model to predetermine preferable aircraft assignments for Air Force pilots. Although not quite fitting the definition of a tool, Cline's model may be used to select subgroups for instruction. For example, it could be adapted to group foreign students who can conjugate verbs as opposed to those who can identify verb tenses. Then each group could be given the further specific instruction it needed.

Construct Job Performance Measures. Gael (1974) describes the selection and design of instruments used to measure job aptitudes and job proficiencies for several Bell System jobs. The instruments employed both knowledge and performance measures as well as simulation for evaluating clerical skills and performance. Although the measures themselves may not be generalizable as tools, their format is. The measures were developed in the form of self-paced programmed texts and examinations that are scored cumulatively.

Analyze Existing Course. Formal analysis of an existing Air Force course appears in the Specialty Training Standard, Plan of Instruction, and the Course Chart for *Inventory Management Specialist* (1975) and *Material Facilities Specialist* (1973, 1974). The documents provide codes for various levels of performance required at end of training and divide instruction into sequential segments. We can use them to distinguish among levels of performance (both cognitive and psychomotor) required for training and to sequence instruction accordingly. As examples of a clear and unequivocal statement of desired learning outcomes, these documents can provide a useful function for learning strategies development.

Develop Objectives. A programmed text by Rose, Balasek, Kelleher, Lutz, and Nelken (1972a,b) is designed to help teachers learn how to write performance objectives. One of the most comprehensive and literate how-to books on behavioral objectives, this programmed text covers the writing of behavioral objectives, cognitive objectives, psychomotor objectives, and performance objectives in the affective domain and at program and instructional levels. No matter what level or domain of learning outcome is desired, this book shows how to write it.

Barton (1973) presents a booklet that teaches how to recognize and write technically correct performance objectives. Validated over a 2-year period, the booklet is in programmed text format and contains numerous self-checks. The book is a handy primer or refresher course for the writing of performance objectives.

A reference wall chart (INSGROUP, 1975) identifies the structure of measurable objectives, discusses three applications of measurable objectives, presents several taxonomies of learning that are used to analyze objectives, and contains brief annotations for the learning taxonomies. Also on the chart are addresses where collections of objectives may be obtained. The chart is useful as a compact, inexpensive, ready-inference information package for behavioral objectives.

Develop Tests. The Center for the Study of Evaluation (1972), in conjunction with Research for Better Schools, Inc., analyzed and evaluated approximately 2600 tests for measuring higher-order cognitive, affective, and interpersonal skills. The tests are generally available to the public and provide a useful compilation of measures for determining entry-level behaviors and attitudes. For example, foreign students may have attitudinal as well as academic problems with a freshman English program. Measures identified and evaluated in the book from the Center for the Study of Evaluation[3] may be used to reveal both kinds of problems.

Swezey and Pearlstein (1974) developed a manual that thoroughly covers the design, use, and evaluation of criterion-reference tests. Four steps of the process are discussed: (*a*) develop adequate behavioral objectives, (*b*) develop a test plan and examine practical constraints, (*c*) build an item pool, and (*d*) select the final test items for instruction. Numerous examples of products of each step leave no doubt as to how criterion-referenced tests should be developed.

Stevens and O'Neil (1976) discuss procedures for generating test items by item transformation, that is, by varying sentences according to their syntactic structure. The test items can be used in multiple-choice or constructed-response tests. The procedures are extremely helpful for building a large pool of potential test items that measure student progress and performance on lesson objectives. With some adaptation, the procedures are also applicable to computer-generated test construction.

Describe Entry Behavior. Bierbaum and Planisek (1969) developed an index and procedure for determining the probable academic success of students seeking readmission after academic dismissal. It may be used to bar students from admission to an instructional program, or to determine whether to drop students from instruction or allow them to continue.

An interest inventory designed to measure the vocational interests of enlisted men entering the Air Force was developed by Ecternacht, Reilly, and McCaffrey (1973). Called the Vocational and Occupational Interest Choice Examination (VOICE), it is an instrument that was to be used in the development of an interest inventory for the Guaranteed Enlistment Program. For community colleges and other institutions with a specific audience, VOICE can be used to determine whether an existing program meets the needs and interests of prospective students. As a cautionary note, however, it should be noted that a rigid evaluation of VOICE scale reliabilities was not done.

Mockovak (1974) assessed the literacy requirements of Air Force career ladders in order to determine the reading demands placed upon trainees and job incumbents by instructional materials. This report is a good example of a procedure for determining the reading requirements of instructional programs. Also useful is a discussion of a validated conversion procedure that converted Airman Qualification Examination scores to estimated reading grade levels. The Airman Qualification Examination is a test that measures the general, mechanical, electronic, and administrative aptitudes of

---

[3]Available from the Graduate School of Education, University of California, Los Angeles, Los Angeles, California 90024.

Air Force enlistees. Presumably, the conversion procedure may be used by learning strategists to convert similar aptitude test score data to reading grade levels for other learning environments.

Determine Sequence and Structure. Dansereau, Evans, Wright, Long, and Actkinson (1974b) and Dansereau, Evans, Actkinson, and Long (1974a) developed and evaluated the use of multidimensional scaling (known as INSCAL) for describing the information structure of Air Force instructional materials and generating effective instructional sequences. This is the only useful procedure identified for determining instructional sequence and structure in terms of existing instructional materials. Successful application of other mechanisms for deriving learning or instructional hierarchies were not identified.

A checklist for determining students' positions along a curriculum scale was developed by the Bucks County Public Schools (1970). The simple checklist is useful as a manual backup to computer-based learning systems for assessing student performance and progress on a particular learning sequence.

Review/Select Existing Materials. An annotated listing of free or inexpensive curriculum materials obtainable from state education agencies is available from the U.S. Government Printing Office (1973). Various guides cover agriculture, distributive education, health occupations, home economics, technical education, and trade and industrial occupations. The guides list manuals and handbooks for administrators and teachers, as well as task-specific booklets for various phases and steps of instructional program development.

The National Network for Curriculum Coordination in Vocational–Technical Education (1975) develops, publishes, and distributes free curriculum guides and inexpensive curriculum support services from six regional curriculum management centers. The guides are available in brochure, booklet, and microfiche form. Many have been field-tested and are ready for use in such activities as data collection and analysis, instructional materials development, and, perhaps, identification of learner characteristics.

The Directorate for Audio-Visual Activities (DAVA, 1975) presents a detailed users guide that provides the required information for participation in the Defense Audiovisual Information Network and for use of their Audio-Visual Products Data Base. When media is an integral part of a specific instructional program, the use of the Audio-Visual Products Data Base should be considered for obtaining data or materials relevant to learning strategies research.

The Department of the Army (1975) provides a catalog of Army motion picture films and audiovisual aids for nonprofit use by government agencies, civic, religious, fraternal and educational organizations, schools, colleges, and universities. Materials from the catalog cover general subjects such as education, sports, and health. Whether you can use them for a learning strategies research program depends upon the particular application to and audience for the program.

Develop Instruction. Thiagarajan (1971) offers a programmed text that teaches the writing of programmed texts. Five stages of the programming process are discussed and a confirmation section at the conclusion of the book contains correct answers to the questions imbedded in the text. It is as clear and concise a guide to the writing of programmed texts as Barton's book is to writing performance objectives.

Deterline and Lenn (1972) developed a self-study course known as the Coordinated Instructional System for Training (CISTRAIN) that teaches a set of skills for designing, developing, and implementing instruction. The two-volume set includes a *Lesson Book* and a *Study Resource Materials Book*. Students are required to complete two lessons on the subject of their choice. CISTRAIN course completion times average 35 hours. The *Lesson Book* guides the student through the appropriate portions of the *Study Resource Materials Book*. All instructional articles, sample lesson materials, and procedural guides necessary for completing the course are in the *Study Resource Materials Book*. This book is often cited and is very useful for teaching students how to write instructional materials which effectively present a desired learning strategy.

Nesbit and O'Neil (1976) provide practical guidelines for editing programmed texts. The report contains a glossary of terms, explanations of three models for programmed texts, and guidelines for checking the lesson content and author's style. Examples of good and bad programmed text frames are given. Once the basics of how to write programmed texts are learned, this report presents specific guidelines for improving one's skills.

Validate Instruction. The use of computer-based test analysis and course evaluation questionnaires is reported by Aleamoni (1970). The system provides for (*a*) test scores, (*b*) analysis of scores for groups or individuals, (*c*) test-item analysis printouts, (*d*) item analysis data, and (*e*) analysis of course evaluation questionnaires, attitude scales, and other measures that have no known correct responses. This is a very complete system for analyzing student performance and attitudinal data. A manual and system documentation are also provided.

Abedor (1972) presents a formative evaluation model that functions in a practical, operational environment. Noting that multiple, iterative revisions of materials can be a monumental and costly effort, Abedor designed a formative evaluation model to generate large amounts of data on instructional problems in a one-shot trial of the prototype lesson. Abedor's approach to formative evaluation is especially appropriate for large-scale learning strategies research programs with long-term, continuing use of instructional materials.

Rayner (1972) developed a formative evaluation model that provides data not only for content but also for procedural changes to instructional materials development and administration. The provision for examination and revision of administrative procedures emphasizes the importance of standardized lessons and test-taking, and data collection and analysis.

Conduct Internal Evaluation. Bailey (1972) discusses the testing of manual procedures in the Bell System personnel subsystem. The procedures consist of six steps and provide data concerning the numbers and kinds of errors and the probable causes of errors for various job activities. The procedures may serve to troubleshoot and standardize data collection and analysis, and lesson and test administration.

Miller and Sellman (1973) developed a new student critique form for the Air Training Command that emphasizes the use of factor analysis. As demonstrated in the report, the technique can be used to manipulate large amounts of questionnaire data and generate reliable subscales for describing student attitudes toward instruction.

Conduct External Evaluation. Anastasio (1972) proposed a field-test evaluation of the PLATO and TICCIT systems that includes cost and educational analyses. Although the evaluation was never fully implemented, the discussion of achievement and attitude measures, and the Survey of Instructor Activities and Attitudes contained in Appendix A of the report are of interest to instructional strategists. Student achievement would be measured by standardized achievement tests, with addition of item-analysis and multiple-matrix sampling techniques for obtaining group measurements. Student attitudes would be measured by five standardized surveys and by measures developed by the Educational Testing Service. The five attitude surveys are (*a*) Student Instructional Report, (*b*) Comparative Guidance and Placement Program Student Questionnaire, (*c*) College Student Questionnaire— Part 2, (*d*) College and University Environment Scales, and (*e*) Student Reactions to College.

Like the student critique form developed by Miller and Sellman, the measures discussed by Anastasio provide student attitude data. But unlike the Miller and Sellman form, the measures reported by Anastasio are specifically designed for college students. Thus, the Anastasio measures may be more immediately useful to learning strategies in that environment.

CONCLUSION

It has been argued that a learning strategies research program is in fact an instructional system. Many of the problems arising from such a system can be minimized by applying the ISD principles of analysis, design, development, implementation, and control. A number of tools and procedures that address these principles are available for use in learning strategies research programs. These tools and procedures will facilitate the implementation and validation of such programs.

REFERENCES

Abedor, A. J. *Development and validation of a model for formative evaluation of self-instructional multi-media learning systems.* Paper presented at the meeting of the American Educational Research Association, Chicago, April 1972.

Air Force. *Instructional system development* (AFM 50-2). Washington, D.C.: Department of the Air Force, December 1970.

Air Force. *Handbook for designers of instructional systems* (AFP 50-58) (5 vols.). Washington, D.C.: Department of the Air Force, July 1973.

Aleamoni, L. M. *MERMAC: A model and system for test and questionnaire analysis* (Res. Rep. No. 330). Champaign: University of Illinois, Office of Instructional Resources, Measurement and Research Division, March 1970. (ERIC Document Reproduction Service No. ED 055 097)

Anastasio, E. J. *An evaluation of the demonstrations being conducted by the University of Illinois and the MITRE Corporation of their respective computer assisted instructional systems* (ETS PR-72-19). Princeton, N.J.: Educational Testing Service, 1972. (ERIC Document Reproduction Service No. ED 072 070)

Archer, W. B. *Computation of group job descriptions from occupational survey data* (Tech. Rep. PRL-TR-66-12). Lackland Air Force Base, Tex.: Air Force Systems Command, Aerospace Medical Division, Personnel Research Laboratory, December 1966.

Bailey, R. W. Testing manual procedures in computer-based business information systems. *Proceedings of the 16th Annual Meeting of the Human Factors Society,* 1972, pp. 395–401.

Baker, E. L. Generalizability of rules for empirical revision. *AV Communication Review,* 1970, *18,* 300–305

Barton, G. E. *Performance objectives: A self-instructional booklet.* Provo, Utah: Bringham Young University Press, 1973.

Bierbaum, G. A., & Planisek, R. J. *An index and procedure for readmitting the academically dismissed student.* Kent, Ohio: Kent State University, 1969. (ERIC Document Reproduction Service No. ED 063 555)

Bucks County Public Schools. *Intensification of the learning process: Diagnostic instruments—Learner state check list evaluation response form.* Doylestown, Pa.: Author, February 1970. (ERIC Document Reproduction Service No. ED 063 345)

Bunderson, C. V. *Instructional design, computers, and teacher education* (Memo No. 2). Austin: University of Texas, Computer Assisted Instruction Laboratory, December 1970.

Butler, F. C. *Instructional systems development for vocational and technical training.* Englewood Cliffs, N.J.: Educational Technology Publications, 1972.

Carnegie Commission on Higher Education. *The fourth revolution: Instructional technology in higher education.* New York: McGraw-Hill, 1972.

Center for the Study of Evaluation, *CSE-RBS test evaluations: Tests of higher-order cognitive, affective, and interpersonal skills.* Los Angeles: University of California, Graduate School of Education, 1972.

Christal, R. E., & Weissmuller, J. J. *New CODAP programs for analyzing task factor information.* Paper presented a the meeting of the Military Testing Association, Indianapolis, September 1975.

Christal, R. E. *CODAP: Input standard (INPSTD) and variable generation (VARGEN) programs* (AFHRL-TR-72-51). Lackland Air Force Base, Tex.: Air Force Human Resources Laboratory, Personnel Research Division, May 1972.

Civil Service Commission. *Instructional systems and technology: An introduction to the field and its use in federal training* (Training Systems and Technology Series, No. 1). Washington, D.C.: U.S. Civil Service Commission, Bureau of Training, June 1969.

Cline, J. A. A multivariate statistical model to predetermine preferable aircraft assignments: A feasibility study (Doctoral dissertation, Arizona State University, 1973). *Dissertation Abstracts International,* 1973, *34,* (University Microfilms No. 73-20, 494).

Cogan, E. A. *Systems analysis and the introduction of educational technology in schools* (HumRRO Prof. Pap. 14–71). Alexandria, Va.: Human Resources Research Organization, June 1971.

Continental Army Command. *Regulation No. 350-100-1.* Washington, D.C.: Headquarters, Department of the Army, February 1968.

Dansereau, D. R., Evans, S. H., Acktinson, T. A., & Long, G. L. *Factors relating to the development of optimal instructional sequences* (AFHRL-TR-53-51(II)). Lowry Air Force Base, Colo.: Air Force Human Resources Laboratory, Technical Training Division, June 1974. (a)

Dansereau, D. R., Evans, S. H., Wright, A. D., Long, G., & Acktinson, T., *Factors related to developing instructional information sequences: Phase 1* (AFHRL-TR-73-51(I)). Lowry Air Force Base, Colo.: Air Force Human Resources Laboratory, Technical Training Division, March 1974. (b)

DAVA (Directorate for Audio-Visual Activities). *Department of Defense audiovisual information system: A user guide for the audiovisual products data base.* Arlington, Va.: Author, Office of Information for the Armed Forces (OASD/M&RA), October 1975.

Demerath, N. J., & Daniels, L. A. *How to make the fourth revolution: Human factors in the adoption of electronic instructional aids* (Memo No. 75-3). St. Louis: Washington University, Center for Development Technology, December 1973.

Department of the Army. *Index of Army motion pictures for public non-profit use* (Pamphlet No. 108/4). Washington, D.C.: Author, Headquarters, May 1975.

Deterline, W. A., & Lenn, P. D. *Coordinated instructional system. Study resource materials book. Lesson book.* Palo Alto, Calif.: Sound Education, 1972.

Ecternacht, G. J., Reilly, R. R., & McCaffrey, P. J. *Development and validity of a vocational and occupational interest inventory* (AFHRL-TR-73-38). Lackland Air Force Base, Tex.: Air Force Human Resource Laboratory, Personnel Research Division, December 1973.

Gael, S. Employment Test validation studies. JSAS *Catalog of Selected Documents in Psychology*, 1974, *4*, 95. (Ms. No. 711)

Gagné, R. M. Educational technology as technique. In *Introduction to educational technology* (Educational Technology Review Series, No. 1). Englewood Cliffs, N.J.: Educational Technology Publications, 1973.

Hunter, B., Kastner, C. S., Rubin, M. L., & Seidel, R. J. *Learning alternatives in U.S. education: Where student and computer meet.* Englewood Cliffs, N.J.: Educational Technology Publications, 1975.

INSGROUP. *Objectives for instructional programs, Reference Wall Chart.* Huntington Beach, Calif.: INSGROUP, 1975.

Inventory management specialist and inventory management supervisor. Specialty training standard 645XO. Washington, D.C.: Department of the Air Force, Headquarters, August 1975.

Logan, R. S. *A survey and analysis of military computer-based training systems: A two-part study* (Vol. 1). *A survey and annotated bibliography of authoring aids for Instructional Systems Development* (Rep. No. MDC E1570). St. Louis: McDonnell Douglas Astronautics Company-East, February 1977.

Material facilities specialist. Course chart 3ABR647X0-1. Lowry Air Force Base, Colo.:Lowry Technical Training Center, School of Applied Aerospace Sciences, Department of Logistics Training, September 1973.

Material facilities specialist. Plan of instruction 3ABR647X0-1. Lowry Air Force Base, Colo.: Lowry Technical Training Center, School of Applied Aerospace Sciences, Department of Logistics Training, January 1974.

Mayo, C. C., Nance, D. M., & Shiegekawa, L. *Evaluation of the job inventory approach in analyzing USAF officer utilization fields* (AFHRL-TR-75-22). Lackland Air Force Base, Tex.: Air Force Human Resources Laboratory, Occupational and Manpower Research Division, June 1975.

McKnight, A. J., & Adams, B. B. *Driver education task analysis* (Vol. 2). *Task analysis methods. Final report* (HumRRO Tech. Rep. 72-13). Alexandria, Va.: Human Resources Research Organization, 1970. (ERIC Document Reproduction Service No. ED 075 624)

Merrill, M. D., & Boutwell, R. C. Instructional development: Methodology and research. In F. N. Kerlinger (Ed.), *Review of research in education* (Vol. 1). Itasca, Ill.: Peacock, 1973.

Miller, G. G., & Sellman, W. S. *Development of psychometric measures of student attitudes toward technical training: Norm group report* (AFHRL-TR-73-15). Lowry Air Force Base, Colo.: Air Force Human Resources Laboratory, Technical Training Division, October 1973.

Mockovak, W. P. *Literacy skills and requirements in Air Force career ladders* (AFHRL-TR-74-90). Lowry Air Force Base, Colo.: Air Force Human Resources Laboratory, Technical Training Division, December 1974.

Molnar, A. R. *The future of educational technology research and development.* Washington, D.C.: National Science Foundation, 1971. (ERIC Document Reproduction Service No. ED 054 642)

Morsch, J. E., & Archer, W. B. *Procedural guide for conducting occupational surveys in the United States Air Force* (PRL-67-11). Lackland Air Force Base, Tex.: Air Force Systems Command,

Aerospace Medical Division, Personnel Research Laboratory, September 1967.

National network for curriculum coordination in vocational-technical education. Washington, D.C.: Department of Health, Education, and Welfare, Office of Education, 1975.

Nesbit, M., & O'Neil, H. F., Jr. *Guidelines for editing programmed instruction.* Austin: University of Texas Press, 1976.

NTEC (Naval Training Equipment Center). *Instructional Systems Development: Conceptual analysis and comprehensive bibliography* (Rep. No. NAVTRAEQUIPCEN IH-257). Orlando, Fa.: Author, February 1976.

Peck, R. F., & Tucker, J. A. Research on teacher education. In R. M. W. Travers (Ed.), *Second handbook of research on teaching.* Chicago: Rand McNally, 1973.

Powers, L. *The systems approach to functional job analysis: Task analysis of the physician's assistant* (Vol. 1). *Task analysis methodology and techniques.* Winston-Salem, N.C.: Wake Forest University, Bowman Gray School of Medicine, 1971. (ERIC Document Reproduction Service No. ED 059 378)

Rayner, G. T. *An empirical study of a methodology for the revision of systematically designed educational material* (Tech. Rep. No. 24). Tallahassee: Florida State University, Computer-Assisted Instruction Center, March 1972. (ERIC Document Reproduction Service No. ED 067 877)

Rose, B. K., Balasek, J., Kelleher, J., Lutz, J. L., & Nelken, I. *A programmed course for the writing of performance objectives. A constructed response linear program.* Bloomington, Ind.: Phi Delta Kappa, Commission on Educational Planning, 1972. (ERIC Document Reproduction Service No. ED 073 528) (a)

Rose, B. K., Balasek, J., Kelleher, J., Lutz, J. L., & Nelken, I. *Writing performance objectives. Instructor's manual for teachers and administrators. To be used with a programmed course for writing of performance objectives.* Bloomington, Ind.: Phi Delta Kappa, Commission on Educational Planning, 1972. (ERIC Document Reproduction Service No. ED 073 529) (b)

Slack, C. W. Who is the educational technologist?—And where is he? In *Introduction to educational technology* (Educational Technology Review Series, No. 1). Englewood Cliffs, N.J.: Educational Technology Publications, 1973.

Stacey, W. J., & Hazel, J. T. *A method of determining desirable task experiences for first-line supervisors* (AFHRL-TR-75-23). Lackland Air Force Base, Tex.: Air Force Human Resources Laboratory, Occupational and Manpower Research Division, August 1975.

Stacey, W. D., Weissmuller, J. J., Barton, B. B., & Rogers, C. R. *CODAP: Control card specifications for the UNIVAC 1108* (AFHRL-TR-74-84). Lackland Air Force Base, Tex.: Air Force Human Resources Laboratory, Computational Sciences Division, October 1974.

Stevens, J. C., & O'Neil, H. F., Jr. *Suggestions for development of test items.* Austin: University of Texas Press, 1976.

Sullivan, O. J., Smith, E. A., & Filinger, R. H. *A survey of the present state-of-the-art in learning center operations.* (AFHRL-TR-74-11). Lowry Air Force Base, Colo.: Air Force Human Resources Laboratory, Technical Training Division, February 1974.

Swezey, R. W., & Pearlstein, R. B. *Developing criterion-referenced tests* (Rep. No. 287-AR18(2)-IR-0974-RWS). Arlington, Va.: U.S. Army Research Institute for the Behavioral and Social Sciences, Unit Training and Educational Technology Systems Area, Performance Measurements and Standards Work Unit, March 1974. (NTIS No. AD-A014 987)

Thiagarajan, S. *The programming process: A practical guide.* Worthington, Ohio: Charles A. Jones Publishing Co., 1971.

TIE (Task Inventory Exchange). *Brochure.* Columbus: Ohio State University, Center for Vocational Education, 1975.

TRADOC (Training and Doctrine Command). *Interservice procedures for instructional systems development* (5 vols.) (TRADOC Pamphlet 350-30). Fort Benning, Ga.: Combat Arms Training Board, August 1975.

U.S. Government Printing Office. *Vocational education. State instructional materials for office occupations.* Washington, D.C.: Author, 1973.

Weissmuller, J. J., Barton, B. B., & Rogers, C. R. *CODAP: Source program listings for the UNIVAC 1108* (AFHRL-TR-74-83). Lackland Air Force Base, Tex.: Air Force Human Resources Laboratory, Computational Sciences Division, October 1974. (a)

Weissmuller, J. J., Barton, B. B., & Rogers, C. R. *CODAP: Programmer notes for the subroutine library on the UNIVAC 1108* (AFHRL-TR-74-85). Lackland Air Force Base, Tex.: Air Force Human Resources Laboratory, Computational Sciences Division, October 1974. (b)

Wong, M. R., & Raulerson, J. R. *A guide to systematic instructional design.* Englewood Cliffs, N.J.: Educational Technology Publications, 1974.

7

Learning Strategies: A Theoretical Perspective[1]

JOSEPH W. RIGNEY

At our laboratory, research on instructional systems has been organized in relation to an analysis of elements and functions making up these systems, illustrated in Figure 7.1. This is intended to serve as a road map of areas where research and development should be done on these systems. In the section of Figure 7.1 labeled "external facilitation" the terms *content bridges* and *cognitive strategies* are intended to distinguish between material specific to a particular subject matter and more general procedures that facilitate acquisition, retention, and retrieval across different categories of subject matter. Cognitive strategy will be used to signify operations and procedures that the student may use to acquire, retain, and retrieve different kinds of knowledge and performance. These operations and procedures may be cognitive information processing, as in mental imagery, or may be cognitively controlled, as in skimming through a textbook to identify major points. Cognitive strategies involve representational capabilities of the student (reading, imagery, speech, writing, and drawing) selectional capabilities (attention and intention) and self-directional capabilities (self-programming and self-monitoring).

A cognitive strategy is composed of two parts: (*a*) a cognitive orienting task and (*b*) one or more representational, selectional, or self-directional capabilities. The term *orienting task* will be used throughout this chapter to designate methods for inducing the student to perform particular kinds of operations. The term *orienting directions* was used in the same way by Frase (1969).

[1]This research was supported by ONR contract number N00014-76-C-0838, and by ARPA order number 2284. The support and encouragement of Harold F. O'Neil, Jr., Cybernetics Technology Office, ARPA; and of Marshall Farr and Henry Halff, Personnel and Training Research Programs, ONR, is gratefully acknowledged. Views and conclusions contained in this document are those of the author and should not be interpreted as necessarily representing the official policies, either expressed or implied, of the Defense Advanced Research Projects Agency or of the United States Government.

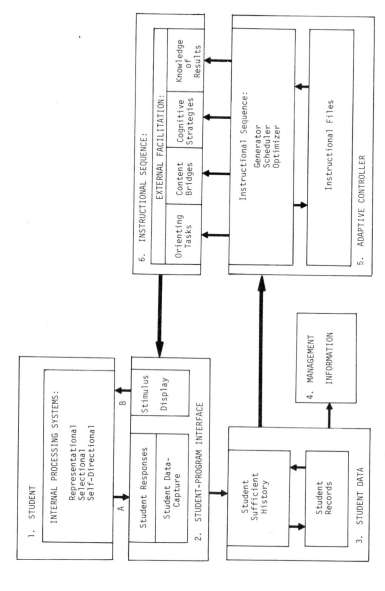

Figure 7.1 Outline of major sybsystems in an automatic instructional system.

Some additional definitional considerations are necessary at this point. Although cognitive strategies are always performed by the student, initiation of their use may come from the student's self-instructions or from an instructional system. The processing operations students perform constitute a cognitive strategy that may or may not be apparent to them. It seems likely, in fact, that many students fall into ways of learning—possibly as a consequence of haphazard reinforcement of which they are not aware. Furthermore, an instructional system can be designed to teach students to use some cognitive strategies without making them aware that the operations they are performing are, in fact, cognitive strategies. If orienting tasks are categorized as student assigned (SA) or instructional system assigned (ISA), then these distinctions can be summarized in Figure 7.2.

The distinction presented in Figure 7.2 between detached and embedded strategies requires clarification. A detached cognitive strategy is described independently of the subject matter. Instructions to use mental imagery or instructions to think of analogies would be examples. An embedded cognitive strategy is not explicitly identified independently of the subject matter. Instead, the instructional system is so designed that the student must use particular processing resources in order to accomplish the orienting tasks in the subject matter. For example, questions often are used to force students to do deeper semantic processing in long-term memory. Another example would be requiring students to multiply three-digit numbers in their heads, which would force them to use a form of mental imagery to keep track of intermediate products and carries.

Some instructional systems are now designed to realize Combination D of Figure 7.2. Their designers seek to induce students to use effective cognitive strategies by the design of the orienting tasks in relation to the subject matter to be taught, and by the design of other conditions, which together constitute an instructional strategy. Not all instructional strategies, it should be noted, are designed to induce students to use cognitive strategies. They may instead be concerned with optimal allocation of trials or of time for learning content (Chant & Atkinson, 1975). It will be a premise of this chapter that Combination A of Figure 7.2 is desirable under at least some circumstances, and that it can be realized by first implementing Combination B. That is, an instructional system can be designed to teach students that there are, in fact, cognitive strategies; and, furthermore, that if the students apply these strategies properly, their use will facilitate acquisition, retention, and retrieval. Although most

Explicitness of Cognitive Strategy	Control of Orienting Task	
	SA	ISA
Detached	A	B
Embedded	C	D

Figure 7.2 Alternative approaches to teaching and using cognitive strategies.

of this chapter is concerned with these possibilities rather than with subject matter variables, the content of the material to be taught cannot be ignored. In Figure 7.1, the term *content bridge* is used to signify a unit of subject matter incorporated into the instructional sequence and displayed to the student in combination with a *content-orienting task,* which, in this context, describes the specific processing operations that the student is to perform on this unit. The term *content bridge* is used instead of *content unit* because, despite its awkwardness, it signifies the idea that the perception of stimulus materials in the external world—particularly meaningful stimulus material—excites processes in long-term memory in the internal world (e.g., schema of Bobrow & Norman, 1975), and in that sense is a bridge between external-world events and internal-world events. According to this idea, learning is a matter of modifying already existing, highly organized, internal representational systems and processes. The term *content-orienting task* is essentially equivalent to the processing operations inherent in the content, which may also be most of what is to be learned about that subject matter, as in mathematics, or computer programming, or which may be already known processing operations, such as reading, used to extract meaning from a text.

Sometimes the content-orienting task is implicit in the way the content bridge is presented and sometimes it is not. For example, if the following problem is displayed

$$2 + 4 = \underline{\hspace{2cm}}?$$

students usually infer that they are to add the two numbers and supply the sum. This content bridge assumes that the students already know the meaning of "+" and "=" and know how to perform the operations. In other cases, there may be a separate description of the operations the student is to perform to produce the required outcome. For example, in statistics, if the task is to compute the inverse of a matrix, the content-orienting task could be a printed algorithm the student should use. Of course, this quite complicated task could be analyzed into a series of simpler tasks, each specified in this way. Cognitive strategies that helped the student to acquire and to retrieve the algorithm for inverting a matrix would be useful to that student for acquiring and retrieving other algorithms. It is likely, though, that cognitive strategies vary in generality and applicability. Mental imagery, for example, seems to be applicable in a variety of learning tasks (Bower, 1972). Converting the letters of consonant–vowel–consonant strings (CVCs) to words that form meaningful phrases clearly is a strategy of less generality (Prytulak, 1971).

According to this view of instruction, the instructional sequence is designed to help the student to develop and to organize internal mediational processes (Box 1 of Figure 7.1). In these terms, external facilitation is a set of techniques for inducing internal mediation. The subject matter must be organized into content bridges, including content-orienting tasks, to guide students' information processing operations until they can respond correctly.

Observe that students may be induced to respond in different ways to the same content bridges by giving them different cognitive/orienting tasks to perform. For example, a student who is told to memorize a text passage will process it differently than will a student who is told to learn the meaning of the passage. But in both cases, the student reads the passage. Thus, cognitive-orienting tasks can modify the execution of content-orienting tasks.

In the traditional approach to education and training, teaching content-specific mediation has been the primary goal. Learning to learn has been recognized in the literature of verbal learning only as a by-product of practice in rote memorization (Duncan, 1960; Postman, 1969), and learning to remember has been, until the late 1960s (Bower, 1970) left to the purveyors of commercial memory courses. According to the traditional approach, requiring students to solve lots of problems will increase their ability to solve other problems; requiring students to process lots of text will increase their general text-processing ability, etc. In short, the approach to teaching students cognitive strategies has been through content-based instruction. There is no question that this kind of transfer does occur at least some times for at least some students. It is not clear, however, how this development occurs, or what variables are related to its occurrence, which, at best, must be a haphazard phenomenon, and which must be strongly dependent upon individual student characteristics.

The possibility of going the other way, of using cognitive strategies to facilitate acquisition, retention, and retrieval of content-based mediation, has become the subject of an increasing number of investigations. Most of the recent work on doing this has been concerned with the use of mental imagery. There is, by now, a vast literature on the effects, usually positive, of student-generated mental imagery on the recall of CVCs, noun lists, and the like (Rigney & Lutz, 1974).

Atkinson (1975) and his associates demonstrated powerful effects of a two-stage, acoustic link, imagery link, keyword method for learning foreign vocabulary. Students were instructed in how to use this method, in which the keyword for the acoustic link was experimenter-supplied, whereas each student then supplied a mental image for an item.

Other cognitive strategies that have been investigated include several forms of inserted questions (R. C. Anderson & Biddle, 1975; Frase, 1968; Rothkopf & Bisbicos, 1967). These, if inserted immediately after a text passage, resulted in better later retrieval of the information in the passage to which the inserted questions pertained.

Rigney and Lutz (1976) investigated the effects of interactive graphic representations of abstract concepts on acquisition of the concept. Shimron (1975) investigated the relative effectiveness of several acquisition strategies on the learning of maps. Schallert (1975) varied orienting tasks to induce different levels of processing in prose passages and found that students remembered more information when induced to process at a semantic level. Dansereau et al. (1975) developed and evaluated a rather elaborate "effective learning strategy training program," for teaching more effective processing of text. They investigated the relative effectiveness of three techniques:—question–answer, paraphrase, and imagery—which they taught different groups of students to use on passages each student had identified as difficult to comprehend. Dansereau and his associates may be the first to try a combination of strategies in a systematic way on text processing. They gave their students instructions on four aspects of the learning process: (*a*) identifying important, unfamiliar, and difficult material, (*b*) applying techniques for comprehending and retaining this material; (*c*) retrieving this information; and (*d*) coping with internal and external distractions during learning. In the last case, however, no specific coping techniques or behaviors were taught. The students were merely exposed to auditory distractions while they were applying some of the other techniques. (See Chapter 1 of this volume for more detail.)

It is likely that techniques for coping with external distractions can be identified and taught. One that some dormitory students have discovered is the use of music, ocean shore sounds, or even white noise from an amplifier, to mask nearby conversations. Methods for coping with internal distractions may be even more important to facilitating learning processes. (See Chapter 3 of this volume for more detail.) The application of biofeedback techniques might lead to fruitful results in this case.

This growing research interest suggests the need for a more organized view of the field. Just how many cognitive strategies are there, how many different means exist for teaching students to use them, and how do these relate to what is known about learning and memory processes?

In this chapter we will explore the idea that it may be possible to teach students how to be more effective learners; that is, to be more effective in acquisition, retention, and retrieval of information and in performance. This is not to say that I suppose that self-directed learning would work for all students, all learning requirements, or all contexts, or that self-applied cognitive strategies are always alternatives to instructional systems with built-in instructional strategies of which the student is never aware. Teaching students how to learn and how to retrieve what has been learned, as the primary objective, might, in fact, be done best by an instructional system: and having been taught these skills, students might, in fact, profit more from an instructional system with the primary objective of teaching content. Beyond this, though, a time comes when a student finishes the course, graduates from school, and must then cope with requirements for further learning in an independent style. The material to be mastered may not be preprogrammed or prescheduled. It may, for example, be a technical manual accompanying a complex electronic equipment.

EXTERNAL FACILITATION AND INTERNAL
MEDIATION IN INSTRUCTIONAL SYSTEMS

An instructional system, as diagrammed in Figure 7.1, creates a special environment in which the student is supported while learning to be more-or-less self-sufficient with respect to performing in some future environment. The system is designed to assist the student in progressing at a suitably rapid rate from maximum dependence on external information and instruction to an appropriate degree of reliance on information in long term memory, self-generated instructions, and self-monitoring. External facilitation and internal mediation are not mutually exclusive: Some mixture of both is always required. The instructional system must determine the appropriate starting mixture for each student, the most effective ways to assist the student in achieving an optimal rate of progression, and an appropriate mixture for the termination of instruction. Some of these determinations involve considerations external to the instructional system, which itself is embedded in other systems.

The patterns of knowledge, skills, and abilities that the individual student brings to the learning situation obviously must be dealt with in some fashion by the instructional system; it must assess these in some way. Students will already possess capabilities that are useful to some extent in mediating the desired responses. In the matrix inversion case, an individual may know elementary matrix arithmetic, something about determinants, or even some algorithms for performing matrix inversion. If so, it would be inefficient to teach those topics again. The situation is diagrammed in Figure 7.3 for each objective of instruction.

Whatever is required to mediate the desired response(s) to some stimulus configuration in the subject matter, Student A knows more of it than Student B, who requires nearly full external facilitation by the instructional sequence. In an extreme case of **no** content known, the student would start at what can be called the fully instructed baseline for a population. Student C would be at that point. Student C might first have to learn all relevant elementary matrix algebra, whereas Student A might need only to review an algorithm for matrix inversion.

The concept of a content bridge is related to "step-size" in programmed instruction. The exact nature of both is difficult to specify. Programmed instruction dealt with the problem by using proportion of errors on a step, or frame, for a given population of students, as an operational definition of step-size. To reduce error rates, content was reduced to very small steps, or frames, which might be called a fully instructed baseline for that population. As students learned from a programmed instruction sequence, they would develop more internal processing from content bridges. Frames in later parts of a linear sequence could presume more

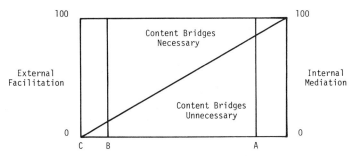

Figure 7.3 Relative amount of internal mediation and external facilitation required for different levels of entering skills and knowledge.

internal mediation, so that the student could be given processing tasks requiring more internal mediation between stimulus and response, and the frames could be less explicit about all the intervening operations.

Multiple strands alternating in the instructional sequence, used by Atkinson (1968) and others, is another way of serially organizing content bridges. In one example, material relating to the development of different skills was put in different strands. An instructional sequence optimizer controlled the progress of students along a turnpike path which includes both strands (Chant & Atkinson, 1975).

The semantic network provides the foundation for a third way of dealing with the organization of subject matter for instruction. Here, each topic or concept is ultimately related to every other topic or concept, and the student can progress either by asking or by answering questions, there not necessarily being one starting or one stopping point or any standard sequence through the material. Norman (1976) calls this approach *web learning*. He has characterized it as follows:

> Suppose we have a large body of knowledge to teach—what would be the best way of doing it? Presumably, we need to interconnect the new information with the existing structure. One way to do this is to construct a supporting web structure first, and then to fill in the details. To do the details first would not work, for without a supporting structure, the new material simply could not become integrated. In teaching, this means that an outline of the material to be learned should be acquired first, then a more detailed overview, and then progressively more and more detailed structures.
>
> The network representation of knowledge can guide the process of instruction in two different ways: (*1*) if we have a good representation of the knowledge we wish to teach, then we can organize it properly for efficient learning: (2) if we try to discover the network representation of the student, we can use this to guide our teaching. Knowing the knowledge structure of the student helps in devising the original level of organization of the material. In addition, as the lessons progress, we can use our understanding of the student's developing structures to guide us in teaching, telling us what old material has not been acquired and what new material might perhaps already be known. Thus, it is theoretically possible to tailor instruction to the knowledge base and competence of the student.
>
> Whether the network representation makes the goal easier to attain remains to be seen. The major drawbacks have resulted from the expense of using tutorial methods in mass education, and from the lack of sophistication in the implementation of most teaching machine programs and computer-assisted instructional systems to attempt these goals [p. 12]. . . . Nonetheless, the analysis is instructive even if the complete implementation remains in the future.
>
> We can characterize two different strategies of presenting material: two different strategies of teaching. One is to present a cohesive organized structure to the student, carefully adding one piece of information after another to the developing structure. This might be called *linear teaching*. It is the system that characterizes lectures, textbooks, and even the structure of this report. The other method is to present a coarse web of information, outlining the topics to be discussed, then giving a general overview followed by more detailed overviews, and finally the detailed substructure. This procedure might be called *web teaching*. Web teaching is often prescribed, seldom done. It is difficult to perform well. But we wish to suggest that for the learning of complex topic matters, web teaching may at times be more efficient [p. 13].

A number of theorists are investigating the semantic network representation of information for purposes related to instruction (Brown & Burton, 1975; Collins,

Warnock, Aiello, & Miller, 1975; Norman & Rumelhart, 1975). This network organization could be the basis for various ways of teaching students to add to their structure of knowledge. Collins (1976) is developing the Socratic method of tutoring for interacting with the student. He asserts that the central notion of this method is to force the student to reason for himself, derive general principles from special cases, and apply the general principles that have been learned to new cases. His objective is to develop a computational theory of the Socratic method, using production rules to represent specific strategies, to express the theory in a general procedural formalism. He has listed 23 specific strategies, identified in discourses from sample content domains, which forces students to develop different parts of a knowledge structure in order to answer the questions that are asked of them. These would be classified, in the terms of this chapter, as embedded cognitive strategies. All of these ways of dealing with content bridges require that the subject matter be specially structured or programmed for instructional purposes. (See Chapter 5 of this volume for more detail.)

To summarize, the elements of external facilitation in the instructional sequence are orienting tasks, content bridges, cognitive strategies, and knowledge of results. The stages of learning—acquisition, retention, and retrieval—are composed of processes operating on external content bridges and on the existing structure of knowledge in long-term memory (LTM). Content bridges are chunks of subject matter presented to the student during instruction. They include content-orienting tasks, which tell the student the kinds of operations to perform in relation to these chunks in order to respond appropriately. Cognitive orienting tasks may be used to tell the student what kinds of cognitive processes to use to facilitate the learning and retrieval of internal mediational representations from content bridges. Given the same instructional sequence, because of individual differences in world knowledge—acquisition, retention and retrieval skills, and processing capacity—each student in a population could start at a different place and progress at a different rate, from primary dependence on external facilitation of performance to primary dependence on internal mediation of performance. Because of the interrelationships and interactions of the elements in the instructional sequence, and because of individual differences among students, procedures for control over outcomes of instruction must be sensitive to these complexities. The scheduling of these elements, as illustrated in Box 4 of Figure 7.1, should be done by an adaptive controller. Under ideal conditions, scheduling would be guided by an optimizer, also indicated in Box 4 of Figure 7.1, although suitable techniques for optimization of instruction (Chant & Atkinson, 1975), are not yet widely available in instructional systems.

Types of Content

The preceding discussion sets forth a general concept of instruction as the development in the student of internal mediation from external content, without regard for the type of content, which clearly is an important consideration for the application of cognitive strategies, as well as for the design of instructional systems.

Although it is beyond the scope of this chapter to deal exhaustively with the enormous variety of subject matter included in education and training, the implications of major categories for cognitive strategies must be noted, in the context of the acquisition of internal mediational equivalents which are the basis for knowing about something and for knowing how to do something. For this purpose, the domains will be divided first into information and performance. What are proposed to be major, relevant categories in each of these will then be considered briefly.

Information

Knowledge of the world stored in memory is acquired from direct observation of and participation in events and through the medium of language and other external representational systems presented in the form of speech, textual, and graphic materials. Some major forms of information are narrative accounts of sequential events, or episodes; scientific explanation using abstract formalisms; representations of objects in the external world; and descriptions of operations or procedures. These will be labeled *narratives, explanations, representations,* and *prescriptions.* Each of these kinds of information has an intrinsic structure, or organization. Examples of these types are history (narrative), electronics (explanations using abstract concepts), descriptions of the structure and function of a machine (representations), and instructions for operating a vehicle or for computing a correlation coefficient (prescriptions).

A current view is that this information is transformed by internal representational systems:—perceptual, imaginal, and verbal—into propositional form stored in LTM. Acquisition of this information seems to involve interactions between imaginal and verbal systems, and inference based on existing world knowledge already in memory.

Performance

Performances to be learned can be classified in terms of the requirements for guidance by information stored in LTM, and in terms of the complexity, timing, and precision of contractions of muscles used for the performance. Some performances, such as typing or playing the piano, are guided by complex semantic codes, and also require great muscular precision. Other performances, such as skating or skiing, also require great precision of movement, but are less dependent on complex semantic codes. Requirements for learning and remembering these different kinds of performance are undoubtedly different, calling for different uses of the representational and motor systems, and, presumably, for different cognitive strategies. (See Chapter 4 of this volume for more detail.)

Cognitive Strategies and Individual Differences

It is unlikely that all students would find the same cognitive strategies equally effective. Information in the literature about cognitive styles (e.g., Pask & Scott, 1972) suggests this conclusion.

Although some students learn faster than others and some students retain material longer than others, or can retrieve more of it, not much is known about the causal differences in terms of internal processing and storage.

Can cognitive strategies compensate for low capacity? Since such strategies must enable the more effective utilization of capacity during acquisition, retention, and retrieval, the answer must be, yes, to some extent. Do bright students use different strategies for learning and remembering than dull students? We can reasonably assume that they do. Weinstein, in Chapter 2 of this volume, provides some empirical evidence for this point. Teaching low-capacity students cognitive strategies should improve their acquisition and retrieval efficiency, but they still would not be able to comprehend subject matter as complex as that comprehended by students with high capacity. We can reasonably assume, too, that detached strategies generally might be more appropriate for bright students, who probably would be more able to direct themselves; whereas embedded strategies might be more effective with dull students, who might need simpler orienting tasks, more support and encouragement, and who might be less venturesome and less motivated.

Cognitive capacity (Kahneman, 1973) is one of several general terms now current in cognitive science. The term is used here in the sense of some inherent, neurophysiologically determined intellectual power. The term *expended processing capacity* (EPC) used by Griffith (1976) and others, refers to the mobilization of processing resources for a particular information processing task, as described in the next section. The implication is that at any one moment, more or less of these resources will be occupied by the task. Thus, deep, or elaboration processing in semantic memory is thought to require the expenditure of more processing capacity than shallow, or maintenance processing, such as rehearsal in short-term memory. As described in what follows, secondary tasks often are superimposed on primary tasks to provide an estimate of expended processing capacity. This term has strong attentional implications. Norman and Bobrow (1975) used *resource limited* and *data limited* to denote cognitive processing that is degraded by limited processing resources of the subject, or that would not be facilitated by the mobilization of more of the subject's processing resources because there is nothing more in the input data to be processed to meet the requirements of the orienting task(s). They proposed that learning can shift processing from a resource-limited to a data-limited state. It seems, then, that Griffith's EPC depends upon how many of Norman and Bobrow's processing resources must be mobilized to meet the moment-by-moment processing load that may be inherent in the task or that may be varied by the student, depending upon intentional considerations, between Craik and Lockhart's Type I or Type II processing (Craik & Lockhart, 1972)! If students mobilize all the cognitive resources at their disposal and these still are not sufficient, the processing will be pushed into a gracefully degraded state. They will, for example, guess.

These are useful ideas that will lead to a better understanding of cognitive processing and processes. Cross-classifying the notion of cognitive capacity assumed to be built into the central nervous system and the notion of processing resources as having somehow accumulated through learning results in the Figure 7.4.

Processing	Cognitive Capacity	
Resources	High	Low
High	A	B
Low	C	D

Figure 7.4 Relationships between cognitive capacity and processing resources.

Of the possible combinations, B seems most unlikely, since an individual with low cognitive capacity would not be able to accumulate a rich "library" of cognitive resources. The individual with combination C might be most helped by the kinds of cognitive or learning strategies discussed in this volume.

Parameter estimation procedures have been used to estimate learning ability for instructional optimization techniques (Chant & Atkinson, 1975). Also, error information obtained from retrieval tasks performed during acquisition might be used to build up some kind of model of the individual student that could guide selection and scheduling of cognitive strategies in an instructional system, as noted earlier. The instructional models being investigated by Norman (1976), Brown (1975), and Westcourt (1975) seem to be moving in this direction, although their models are likely to be concerned primarily with embedded cognitive strategies rather than with detached strategies. These approaches have potential for dealing with individual differences at the individual and microinteraction levels.

Of course, the organization of instruction for different levels of intellectual capacities and other aptitudes has been and continues to be a primary concern of the educational and training world. There are courses in military training that tens of thousands of students take annually. Reduction of attrition rates in such courses is a matter of sufficient economic importance to encourage investigating the usefulness of cognitive strategies in this context.

LEARNING AND MEMORY PROCESSES

The terms *acquisition, retention,* and *retrieval,* signify processes that are poorly understood and that must be very complex at the functional level in the central nervous system (CNS). For the purposes of this discussion, acquisition is defined to include all processes from entrance into sensory registers (SR) to storage in long-term memory (LTM). Retrieval is defined to include the processes required to access and to recover information in short-term memory (STM) and in LTM. Retrieval is an unavoidable stage in testing for acquisition and for retention. The only way to know if a student has learned something, is to require recognition or recall of the items to be learned which obviously requires the student to engage in retrieval operations. The outcomes of retrieving also provide feedback, which is the basis for all forms of adaptive control of instruction.

The learning processes that constitute acquisition, retention, and retrieval could be divided into operations that have been, or could be described at a verbal level, and neurophysiólogical processes that are almost totally unknown and that are not under the learner's direct control. Some of these processes are responsible for well-known effects, for example, the sudden appearance of the solution to a problem, or a creative idea in consciousness. Still another example is the apparent shift of control over performance out of the focus of attention with practice to fluency. The focus of attention shifts from the details of the task itself to more general aspects of the situation and to the consequences of the performance (see Chapter 4 of this volume for more detail).

There are many current theories of memory systems. The multistore theory (Atkinson & Shiffrin, 1968) and the levels of processing theory (Craik & Lockhart, 1972) seek to account for processes and events during acquisition, retention, and retrieval in different ways, although both emphasize the central role of information processing guided by orienting tasks. These theories will be reviewed first.

In an outline of the multistore view (Atkinson & Shiffrin, 1968; Atkinson & Wickens, 1971) the sequence of events (see Figure 7.5) with respect to acquisition during learning was described more-or-less as follows: Information from external displays enters sensory registers via receptors, where it is available to CNS process-

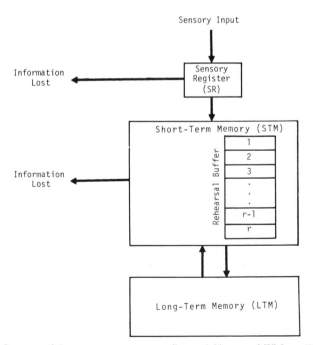

Figure 7.5 Structure of the memory system, according to Atkinson and Wickens (1971, p. 72).

ing. This information in sensory registers is sampled by selective attention and is transferred to LTM, where identification and other processing, for example, pertinence judging (Norman, 1969), occurs, and back to STM. There, it may be retrieved, by a serial scanning process, serve some immediate goal, and be forgotten when that goal is achieved. Otherwise, the information is stored in LTM.

In the development of the multistore theory of memory, Atkinson and his associates emphasized the importance of what they called *control processes:*

> The term control process refers to those processes that are not permanent features of memory, but are instead transient phenomena under the control of the subject; their appearance depends on such factors as instructional set, the experimental task and the past history of the subject.
>
> Since the subject-controlled memory processes include any schemes, coding techniques, or mnemonics used by the subject in his effort to remember, their variety is virtually unlimited and classification becomes difficult. Such classiciation as is possible arises because these processes, while under voluntary control of the subject, are nevertheless dependent upon the permanent memory structures described in the previous section [Atkinson & Shiffrin, 1968, p. 106].

Atkinson and Shiffron (1968) reviewed control processes in terms of the boxes in the multistore model: SR, STM, and LTM. Generally speaking, they discussed processes that select information from sensory registers to be transferred to STM: storage, search, and retrieval strategies in STM, noting the importance of rehearsal for maintenance of information in STM; coding processes and transfer between STM and LTM; and storage and long-term search processes in LTM.

Atkinson and Wickens (1971) analyzed the influence of reinforcement on these control processes, taking the view that reinforcement is the modulation of information flow in the memory system; that it is a means of controlling control processes. They viewed reinforcement as a compex process derived from other, more fundamental aspects of the learning situation, and their discussion of reinforcement in these terms illustrates possibilities for getting better control over cognitive strategies. Rather than reviewing these possibilities here, I will assume that these possibilities can be incorporated in combinations B and D in Figure 7.2, and that the term, "knowledge of results" in the instructional sequence box in Figure 7.1 can be expanded to include reinforcement as conceived by these authors.

Craik and Lockhart (1972) proposed a modification to the multistore model in which they focused on the encoding operations as determining relative permanence of storage. They conceived of a limited-capacity information processor that can be deployed over a series or hierarchy of processing stages such as analysis of physical or sensory features of the physical stimulus, matching the input against stored abstractions from past learning, and extraction of meaning. Greater depth of processing implies a greater degree of semantic or cognitive analysis. They suggested that the persistence of the memory trace is a function of depth of analysis, with the deeper levels of analysis resulting in more elaborate, longer-lasting, and stronger traces.

Thus, in this view, retention is a function of depth of processing, and memory is a continuum "from the transient products of sensory analyses to the highly durable products of semantic-associative operations [p. 676]." They noted, however, that a second way in which stimuli can be retained is by recirculating information at one level of processing. This they called *primary memory* (PM)—which is STM renamed—and equated PM retention with continued processing, which they called *Type I processing*. Type I processing is repetition of analyses that have already been carried out. The deeper levels of analysis of the stimulus they called *Type II processing*. Only Type II processing leads to improved memory performance; to the extent that the subject utilizes Type II processing, memory will improve with total study time (the total time hypothesis). When the subject does only Type I processing, the total time hypothesis does not hold.

According to the levels-of-processing model of acquisition; repetition, or practice, merely provides opportunities to learn, it does not necessarily, without the intervention of cognitive processing during the trials, result in storage in LTM. The burden of acquisition is placed on the kind of processing that is elicited by orienting tasks, either assigned to the learner or self-imposed by the learner. Craik and Lockhart reviewed several examples of the effects of different orienting tasks in the incidental learning paradigm, which illustrates these differential effects.

Craik and Tulving (1975) elaborated on the concept of depth of processing from the results of a series of 10 studies. They found that many of the ideas expressed by Craik and Lockhart are in need of considerable modification:

> Is spread of encoding a more satisfactory metaphor than depth? The implication of this second description is that while a verbal stimulus is usually identified as a particular word, this minimal core encoding can be elaborated by a context of further structural, phonemic, and semenatic encodings. Again, the memory trace can be conceptualized as a record of the various pattern-recognition and interpretive analyses carried out on the stimulus and its context; the difference between the depth and spread viewpoints lies only in the postulated organization of the cognitive structures responsible for pattern recognition and elaboration, with depth implying that encoding operations are carried out in a fixed (p. 290) sequence and spread leading to the more flexible notion that the basic perceptual core of the event can be elaborated in many different ways....However, while spread and elaboration may indeed be better descriptive terms for the results reported in this paper, it should be borne in mind that retention depends critically on the qualitative nature of the encoding operations performed—a minimal semantic analysis is more beneficial for memory than an elaborate structural analysis . . . [p. 291].
>
> It seems necessary to bring in the principle of integration or congruity for a complete description of encoding. That is, memory performance is enhanced to the extent that the encoding question or context forms an integrated unit with the target word . . . [p. 291].
>
> The question immediately arises as to why integration with the encoding context is so helpful. One possibility is that an encoded unit is unitized or integrated on the basis of past experience and, just as the target stimulus fits naturally into a compatible context at encoding, so to retrieval, representation of part of the encoded unit will lead easily to regeneration of the total unit. The suggestion is that at encoding the stimulus is interpreted in terms of the system's structured record of past learning, that is, knowledge of the world or "semantic memory" (Tulving, 1972); at retrieval, the information provided as a cue again utilizes the

structure of semantic memory to reconstruct the initial encoding. An integrated or congruous encoding thus yields better memory performance, first, because a more elaborate trace is laid down and, second, because [p. 291] richer encoding implies greater compatibility with the structure, rules, and organization of semantic memory. This structure, in turn, is drawn upon to facilitate retrieval processes . . . [p. 292].

It is abundantly clear that what determines the level of recall or recognition of a word event is not intention to learn, the amount of effort involved, the difficulty of the orienting task, the amount of rehearsal the items receive (Craik & Watkins, 1973); rather it is the qualitative nature of the task, the kind of operations carried out on the items, that determines retention. The problem now is to develop an adequate theoretical formulation which can take us beyond such vague statements as "meaningful things are well remembered . . ." [p. 290].

Finally, the major question generated by the present approach is what are the encoding operations underlying normal learning and remembering. The experiments reported in this article show that people do not necessarily learn best when they are merely given "learn" instructions. The present viewpoint suggests that when subjects are instructed to learn a list of items, they perform self-initiated encoding operations on the items. Thus, by comparing quantitative and qualitative aspects of performance under learn instructions with performance after various combinations of incidental orienting tasks, the nature of learning processes may be further elucidated. The possibility of analysis and control of learning through its constituent mental operations opens up exciting vistas for theory and application [p. 292. Copyright 1975 by the American Psychological Association. Reprinted by permission.]

A study by Griffith (1976) illustrates interrelationships among attention, intention, and student-supplied or experimenter-supplied mediators using the same subject matter in the context of a paired-associates paradigm modified to involve a measure of depth of processing. Griffith used a secondary task during acquisition and recall to estimate the processing demands of Type II and Type I processing, which he called *expended processing capacity* (EPC). This secondary task required subjects to press a "yes" button when they heard a digit from a designated set of four, and a "no" otherwise. This had to be done at the same time the subjects were doing verbal processing both during acquisition and during recall. The choice reaction time (CRT) was taken as a measure of EPC; the greater the processing demands of the primary task, the slower the reaction times on the secondary task, and the greater the inferred expended processing capacity. The primary task was to learn lists of pairs of high imagery nouns by either making a sentece of the form "article *noun 1* verb article *noun 2*" (Type II processing) or repeating sentences of this form supplied by the experimenter (Type I processing). The intentional condition was created by telling one group of subjects that they were going to be given a recall test after the acquisition session.

As expected, subject-generated mediators resulted in better recall accuracy under both intentional and incidental learning conditions. The EPC measure (CRT in milliseconds) did indicate that generating sentences used more processing capacity (1147 msec) than merely repeating experimenter-supplied sentences (917 msec). Conversely, during recall, CRTs were lower for the subject-generated sentence condition (1183 versus 1386 msec), implying that retrieval of the more deeply processed words required less processing capacity. The intentional variable did not affect depth of processing.

The significance of these two views of the memory system for this chapter is that both recognized the central role of cognitive strategies used by the learner for effective acquisition and retrieval. The STM they discussed will be viewed here as forming, with selective attention, a limited input channel, or window into LTM as well as serving as the buffer memory that has been so extensively investigated in the experimental laboratory (e.g., Sternberg, 1969).

It is likely that the paradigms using extremely simple stimulus material or digits and concentrating on storage and processing in STM have not revealed the whole story. The visual system clearly is designed to do parallel processing at certain levels, and visual pathways from retina to striate cortex contain millions of axons. It is not unreasonable to expect that visual pattern information could be input to LTM through a broader channel than the STM defined by short-term memory theorists. That nonsemantic, pattern information also is stored in LTM was reported by Kolers (1976), who demonstrated that practice in reading text composed of lines rotated about their own horizontal axes resulted in substantially faster reading of the passages, when compared with new passages 13 to 15 months later. Additionally, although Sternberg's classic studies revealed search and retrieval processes in STM, these are trivial in comparison to the processing that goes on in LTM, where the attention of theorists is currently focused.

Types of Long-Term Memory

Semantic Memory

Current theories of one kind of LTM (J. R. Anderson & Bower, 1973; Fiksel & Bower, 1976; Norman & Bobrow, 1975; Norman & Rumelhart, 1975; Tulving, 1972) maintain that it is a semantic network. There are differences of opinion as to the kinds of nodes, internode relations, information stored, and processing. Some theorists include operations and self-programs in the semantic network, others do not. Some theorists suggest that semantic networks in LTM develop from cognitive primitives, which are irreducible concepts and relations. Cognitive primitives are presumably common to a species. It is reasonable to assume that they are the products of genetic blueprints guiding early developmental experience during embryologically critical periods. It is assumed by some theorists that these primitives initially are the foundations of understanding.

Bobrow and Norman (1975) proposed a theory of memory that is an amalgamation of principles from the literature on semantic networks, on actors, and on frames:

> In conclusion, we proposed that memory structures be comprised of a set of active schemata, each capable of evaluating information passed to it and capable of passing information and requests to other schemata. We suggest that a memory schema refers to others by means of a description that is only precise enough to disambiguate the reference within the context in which the original situation occurred. This context-dependent description thereby

provides an automatic process for creating general memory references from specific events, allowing for automatic generation of analogical or metaphorical memory matches. The retrieval mechanism then operates upon the descriptions and context in a meaningful, useful manner, and it must be relatively insensitive to mismatches and underspecifications.

The processing structure of the memory system is one that has a limit on resources that are available. Any given process is either data-or resource-limited. Some scheduling device is necessary to keep things operating smoothly. We believe the system to be driven both by the data (in a bottom-up fashion) and conceptually (in a top-down fashion). The principle that ''all data must be accounted for'' guides the bottom-up processing. We believe that a single, conscious high-level mechanism guides the conceptual processing, taking into consideration the motivation and purposes of the organism.

Conscious processes are invoked whenever underlying schemata provide information for evaluation, whenever new processes must be invoked or old ones terminated, or whenever the output of one schema must be communicated to others not immediately invoked. Any time that there is a mismatch between data and process or expectations and occurrences, conscious processes are brought in. The automatic, active schemata of memory and perception provide a bottom-up, data driven set of parallel, subconscious processes. Conscious processes are guided by high-level hypotheses and plans. Thus consciousness drives the processing system from the top down, in a slow, serial fashion. Both the automatic and the conscious processes must go on together; each requires the other [p. 148].

Fiksel and Bower (1976) described semantic memory as a collection of finite automata at nodes, with labeled arcs connecting the nodes. They developed a theory of memory that utilizes parallel, local processing among automata to accomplish retrieval, without the requirement for an executive level of processing. The idea of finite automata linked together by relational paths is reminiscent of notions from physiological psychology (e.g., Pribram, 1971) that collections of neurons accomplish processing via local graded potentials in cell membranes and dendrites, sending the results on to other groups of cells via all-or-none spike potentials along longer axons. The Fiksel and Bower conception clearly assumes parallel processing. They point out that this is in distinction to artificial intelligence theories of memory, which tend to emphasize serial processing because they can be implemented on computers.

Meyer and Schvaneveldt (1976) used the reaction time method to help reveal how stored semantic information is retrieved. They used existential affirmatives such as ''some pines are trees'' and universal affirmatives such as ''all pines are trees'' to explore comprehension based on set relations. Their reaction time data could be explained in terms of a semantic network structure for LTM. However, the sentence-judging process (true or false) appeared to depend on comparison of defining attributes of the two items being compared rather than on checking labels of links between notes in a semantic network. These authors speculated that links may lack precise labels, whereas comparing attributes of the categories would provide a way to compute the exact relations from other information.

Gentner (1975) reported a study of the structure and recall of narrative prose in which he decomposed a short passage from a history book into smaller units, using Rumelhart's (1975) story grammer. This resulted in a semantic network of 143 ''facts'' corresponding to units described by the story grammer, interconnected by approximately 200 predicates or relations. Neighboring facts are connected by a single predicate or relation. There were clusters of neighbors varying from two to several. The 143 facts also could be arranged in serial order, as they occurred in the passage. A tape recording of the text was played four times. Verbal recalls were collected after each presentation. The serial structure at first influenced which facts were recalled, but as the subjects learned the passages they evidently organized the passage in LTM closer to its underlying meaning structure. As this happened, the story-grammer structure dominated recall of elements on subsequent trials.

Recall of knowledge may be strongly influenced by organization imposed by acquisition strategies. For example, Shimron (1975) found differences in recall of details of a map that were determined by three different kinds of strategies for acquisition: associating details with schemes, like rivers, highways, or mountains; learning details from one section of the map at a time; or integrating details from the map into two stories which had the map as the background of the events described.

These theoretical formulations and studies of semantic memory suggest certain tentative conclusions, which are listed as follows:

1. Semantic LTM also must be the site of much of the information processing required for acquisition, retention, and retrieval. This information processing is parallel processing (Bobrow & Norman, 1975; Fiksel & Bower, 1976).

2. The limited input channel of selective attention and STM is not so limited as experimental studies suggest. Although attention can span only a few chunks at a time, these activate a large amount of processing; they "turn on" portions of the semantic network, so that serial verbal input is not stored a word at a time, but rather influences complex, already existing internal representations and contexts, resulting in the acquisition of much more than just the words in the serial input string (Norman, 1976).

3. Cotton (1976) pointed out that these semantic network models raise a question about practice effects or tasks requiring extensive practice during acquisition as a central aspect of learning. He argued that one of the finest learning models available, that of Norman and Rumelhart (1975), discussed practice only peripherally as a side issue to treatment of memory storage.

4. Retention of knowledge, because of the web of relationships, is robust. Parts of knowledge forgotten or even never learned can be reconstructed by inferential processes (Norman, 1976; Tulving, 1972).

5. Retrievel of information from LTM is strongly influenced by the structure of knowledge in LTM. Retrieval of information from semantic memory may utilize pathways represented by interrelationships among nodes, resulting in searches of varying length and duration (Gentner, 1975; Meyer & Schvaneveldt, 1976).

6. Retrievel of information from LTM is influenced by acquisition strategies (Shimron, 1975).

Episodic Memory

Retrieval of some information may be strongly dependent on the temporal cues that were stored during acquisition. A good strategy for remembering where some lost object, such as car keys, checkbooks, or glasses might be, is to recall the sequence of events from the last time the object was known not to be lost. This is said to be dependent upon episodic memory, or memory for autobiography. Tulving (1972) distinguished between semantic memory and episodic memory, suggesting that semantic memory is not the kind of memory that psychologists have been studying in their laboratories since the time of Ebbinghaus.

Lateralization of Cerebral Functions

There is a general assumption among many semantic memory theorists that semantic networks in LTM represent propositional knowledge; that both imagery and language can be generated from this propositional base. These theorists (e.g., Pylyshyn, 1973) maintain that this view can be reconciled with experimental evidence for dual-coding systems (Paivio, 1975), and with evidence for dual-processing systems from studies of lateralization of function in the cerebral hemispheres (e.g., Nebes, 1974).

Evidence that some visual processing at the perceptual level may be propositionally guided was reported by Ross (1976). Using stereograms that change at random, he found that the visual perceptual system generates depth and motion information from combinations of visual input and some kind of preexisting visual record. Shapes constructed by the visual system from the combination of random-dot stimulus patterns are more idealized than real shapes. They are internal conceptions imposed on the external flow of visual information by processes within the visual system. On the other hand, Shepard and Judd (1976), in the most recent of a series of studies of mental rotation of geometric figures, found congruence between data for mental rotation and data for stimulus-induced apparent rotation. They maintain that this result cannot be accounted for by sequential, propositionally based processing. Cooper and Shepard (1975) presented evidence that subjects determine whether a visually presented image of a hand is a left or right hand by moving a mental "phantom" of one of their own hands into the portrayed position and then by comparing its imagined appearance against the appearance of the externally presented hand. This study suggested that the identification of "isomeric" objects is accomplished by a sequence of analog mental transformations and holistic matches.

The increasing evidence for lateralization of imagery and verbal processing in different hemispheres—with its implications for instructional theory—reviewed by Wittrock (1975) and by Rigney and Lutz (1975), suggests that although there can be a propositional form for both verbal and imagery processing that simplifies the cognitive scientist's task of constructing semantic memory models with computer programs, there nevertheless are interrelated dual-processing systems in the two sides of the cerebrum, which together comprise more processing capacity than either system alone. This duality plays an important role in determining the cognitive styles of learning and in increasing the different kinds of processing resources that could be brought to bear during learning. Research on lateralization of function using split-brain preparations or unilateral lesions (Cuénod, 1974; Milner, 1974; Sperry, 1974) has been focused primarily on identifying special functions of each hemisphere. Obviously, in the normal brain, the commissures are intact and there are no lesions. In the normal brain, does processing control alternate between hemispheres, depending on the task, or are the special functions of each somehow combined?

A study by Gordon and Bogen (1974) is an example of research on lateralization in the neurosciences. These two investigators studied hemispheric lateralization of singing after intracarotid sodium amylobarbitone. It was found that after right carotid injection, singing was markedly deficient, whereas speech remained relatively intact. Songs were sung in a monotone, devoid of correct pitch rendering; rhythm was much less affected. The observations indicated a double dissociation; the right hemisphere contributed more for singing, whereas the left demonstrated its usual dominance for speech.

Tulving's (1972) characterizations of episodic and semantic memories should not be fitted into characterizations of right and left hemisphere functions. It is not yet possible to relate theories of LTM from cognitive science to the evidence of lateralization of cerebral functions from the neurosciences. However, it is interesting that Tulving, and Gordon and Bogen, emphasized time-dependence as a primary difference, in one case between two kinds of LTM and in the other between functions of two cerebral hemispheres. Tulving proposed that episodic memory stores information about temporally dated episodes or events. Gordon and Bogen suggest that reliance upon time as a principle of organization may better distinguish the left from the right hemisphere.

Motor Memory

There is a third kind of LTM relating to control over the skeletal muscular system and the vocal chords for the control of speech and other motor performance that must be considered here. The variety of skilled performances that humans can learn must be controlled by some kind of stored information. Much of this skilled performance is probably initiated by information stored in semantic memory, and it is reasonable to presume that information about performance is included in the semantic memory. But there remains the requirement for something to control the patterns of muscle contractions that are required for speech and for other motor performances. The neuromuscular system is very complex and includes the cerebellum, a complex organ with a large and highly homogeneous cortex that sits astride the large ascending and descending columns of the upper spinal cord. The motor system in humans is divided into an upper and lower system. The upper system sends many different tracts to play upon the final common path, the spinal motoneurons of the lower system. There are many feedback and feedforward loops in the system. All this baffling complexity must require substantial control mechanisms which, in view of the remarkable capabilities of humans to learn skilled performances, must include some form of long-term storage. This storage will be called *motor storage* in this chapter.

In summary, then, acquisition, retention, and retrieval of information and performance are seen by theorists to depend strongly upon information processing under voluntary control of the learner or induced in the learner by externally imposed orienting tasks and operating within the wired-in framework of the memory system. The processing and storage characteristics of this memory system influence the kinds of cognitive strategies that can be effective during these three stages of learning. At least three different kinds of long-term stores have been described by theorists: semantic store (verbal and imaginal), episodic stores, and motor store. Different kinds of information are acquired by and are retrieved from these stores, and different kinds of cognitive strategies and likely to be effective for facilitating acquisition, retention, and retrieval in each.

Relationships between Strategies for Acquisition, Retention, and Retrieval and Long-Term Memory Structures and Processes

Discussing acquisition, retention, and retrieval as though they are separate and successive groups of processes is only a necessary consequence of the serial nature of language, since theorists maintain that these groups of processes go on simultaneously in parallel in LTM. Whereas some knowledge is being acquired, some is being retained and some is being retrieved. This point should be kept in mind.

Distinctions were drawn earlier in this section among three types of LTM. This might be taken to imply that there are *only* three kinds. Some theorists describe other kinds; for example, memory for spatial relationships and world-body distinctions has been called *spatial memory* (Miller & Johnson-Laird, 1976). Undoubtedly, spatial memory would be important in guiding performance. However, this kind of knowledge is considered here to be shared among semantic, episodic, and motor memories.

Of greater concern is the implication in discussing these three categories of cognitive processes individually that the course of learning is over with acquisition. Rumelhart and Norman (1976) have observed that complex human learning takes a very long time. They have identified three major kinds of complex learning: *accretion, restructuring,* and *tuning* of knowledge modules in LTM. Accretion in which additions are made to existing structures, is the first stage. Something new is learned, say, a foreign vocabulary, the multiplication tables, or the musical scales. Restructuring is the transformation of existing knowledge modules into new organizations. It represents additional learning beyond the accretion stage. Restructuring results in new ways of viewing knowledge. Insight and creative thinking could be results of restructuring processes. Tuning is the modification of existing knowledge modules in LTM to make them more efficient for controlling performance. As a consequence of tuning, performance of a series of activities or tasks becomes smoother, more economical of energy and time, and more automatized. That is, selective attention need not be fully engaged by the performance. Tuning is driven by practice, and also is a late stage of complex human learning.

These are extremely useful ideas that undoubtedly will stimulate much research and discussion. In the interests of space, they will be dealt with here in a highly oversimplified way.

Strategies for Acquisition

Strategies for acquisition are concerned with helping the student build internal knowledge structures that will mediate between stimulus conditions and appropriate responses. The coupling between stimulus conditions and desired responses may be clearly defined, as in training real-time driven operators to perform; or the coupling may be very vague, as in much of education, where acquired information may only be sampled by tests and subsequent behavior may only be weakly influenced by it, if at all.

Cognitive acquisition strategies would be concerned with locating and organizing subject matter, selecting from assembled material that information judged to be useful and ignoring the rest, and encoding it by processing operations that effectively transform it for storage in one or more forms of LTM. These strategies are, in effect, transfer operations between some nominal stimulus configurations, say, printed text and diagrams in a technical manual, and LTM. The map shown in Figure 7.6 illustrates these relationships.

The distinctions among different kinds of LTM made in the preceding section will be preserved here, with some additional distinctions and qualifications. Semantic LTM could be divided into imagery and verbal parts, even though both may have a propositional base, because there are occasions when mental imagery representations are more important as mediators than verbal representations. The functional and structural topography of mechanical and electronic devices, for example, are efficiently represented by mental images, even though these mental images may be encoded in propositional form. Although there is evidence for three different kinds of LTM, this does not mean that they are independent and isolated entities. In fact, Schank (1975) maintained that semantic and episodic LTM should be combined in what he called *conceptual episodic memory*. It seems most likely that all forms of LTM are involved to varying degrees in all learning processes. For the present, it may be useful to continue to distinguish among the three types of LTM. In those cases where acquisition processes must result in additions to or changes in an LTM if the mediational requirements of content-orienting tasks are to be met, an A for accretion processing is entered in the corresponding cell in the diagram in Figure 7.6. If we suppose that a type of LTM furnishes only processing resources to the acquisition processes, an M (for maintenance processing) is entered in the cell. Since processing resources are probably drawn from all the types of LTM by acquisition processes, it will be understood that this also occurs in those cells with A entries. The T in some cells signifies that LTM knowledge modules are

Types of Subject-Matter		Types of LTM		
		Semantic	Episodic	Motor
I N F O R M A T I O N	Narratives	A	A	M
	Explanations	A	M	M
	Representations	A	M	M
	Prescriptions	A	A	M
P E R F O R M A N C E	High Semantic/ High Skill	AT	AT	AT
	High Semantic/ Low Skill	A	M	M
	Low Semantic/ High Skill	T	T	T
	Low Semantic/ Low Skill	M	A	A

Figure 7.6 Tentative LTM transfer map for acquisition strategies.

modified by tuning processes driven by practice. This classification is highly speculative, but may serve useful in stimulating more thinking about these relationships.

The subject-matter headings require some explanation. Narratives, such as history, describe a stream of events or episodes with a time base. Chronological order is of some importance. Narratives transmitted by word of mouth probably are the oldest form for communicating information. Explanation refers to the concepts, symbols, and formalisms of science. Representations are descriptions of entities in the world, for example, a radar repeater. They describe structural and functional characteristics of such objects, often using some of the abstractions of science. Prescriptions are lists of action descriptions.

The categories of performance in Figure 7.6 also require some elaboration. The four categories refer to the guidance of performance. Some performances, such as troubleshooting, are guided by a large amount of semantic information but demand low motor skill. The acquisition of low semantic, high motor-skill performances may be done principally by practice, without substantial amounts of prior study; where high semantic guidance but low motor-skill is involved the converse might be true. In these terms, storage of information in motor LTM is assumed to occur as a consequence of repetition and feedback in the motor system.

Speech, writing, and singing are governed by highly complex rules and codes that have evolved over very long periods of time and that are heavily dependent on semantic LTM. Swimming and running are performances that place substantial demands on motor LTM but they are not governed by complex rules and codes, and thus may not depend so heavily on semantic memory. Motor LTM must be able to control vocal chords, trunk, limbs, and hands with great precision. Other performances are composed of simple motions that do not require much skill and that can be readily learned by anyone who can follow a simple list of instructions.

Strategies for Retention

Strategies for improving retention of storage in LTM would take into account what we know about the courses and causes of forgetting. For at least some kinds of material, the course of forgetting seems to be quite rapid for a short time after acquisition, and then the forgetting curve levels off. A major cause of forgetting under these circumstances is usually accepted to be retroactive inhibition. That is, subsequent experiences interfere in some way with the learned material, possibly disrupting response systems upon which retrieval processes depend more than interfering with storage processes, thus making information inaccessible rather than obliterating it. Proactive interference interferes with retention of subsequently learned material, insofar as this can be tested by retrieval tasks, by response competition. These two major kinds of interference have been thoroughly investigated in verbal learning laboratories. Other known causes and their different effects, such as traumas and aging, have been studied clinically (e.g., Williams, 1975). That other unknown causes also exist is a strong possibility.

Strategies for improving retention also should be sensitive to what is to be retained. Retention of semantic information may involve somewhat different processes than retention of episodic information, and each of these may involve different processes than retention of programs for motor skills. Retention is also influenced by the characteristics of prior acquisition episodes. The effectiveness of acquisition strategies is sometimes measured as a function of delay before retrieval.

These conditions suggest that different strategies for retention might be necessary, although the position could be taken that avoiding interfering and disrupting conditions and refreshing storage by appropriate reacquisition or review activities are the general strategies. Since there may be fundamental differences in storage processes in long-term memory for semantic information, episodic information, and information to guide motor performances, a tentative storage-maintenance map for retention strategies is given in Figure 7.7.

The I in the map refers to avoidance of interfering or distracting conditions over short retention intervals. The M refers to maintenance-level processing to refresh storage. Maintenance of information in LTM over long retention intervals could require some degree of reacquisition.

Strategies for Retrieval

Intuitively, a variety of retrieval strategies would be possible, depending on where retrieval occurs in the other two stages of learning and on the type of content involved. Retrieval of verbal material would call for different strategies than retrieval of motor performances, etc. An important fundamental distinction is between

Kinds of LTM	Retention	Interval
	Short	Long
Semantic	I	M
Episodic	I	M
Motor	I	M

Figure 7.7 Tentative storage maintenance map for retention strategies.

retrieval processes in recognition and retrieval processes in recall. Recognition clearly is a more sensitive measure of whether or not something is stored in LTM, as well as being particularly appropriate for testing for storage of nonverbal materials, which may be difficult to characterize by recall procedures. Another fundamental distinction is between verbatim and paraphrase, or inferential recall. The vast bulk of verbal learning research has been concerned with verbatim recall of isolated items, and thus, in Tulving's terms, have been studies of episodic memory; whereas semantic memory is of preeminent importance in human learning, and paraphrase recall requiring inferential processes is the most common form of retrieval. Finally, it is assumed here that retrieval drives restructuring learning.

Retrieval strategies have received less attention in the literature than acquisition strategies, probably because the primary emphasis in training and education is on inducing students to acquire information and skills, and because thorough learning seems to ensure good recall.

Retrieval is often required during acquisition. And in this sense it is part of acquisition. This retrieval goes on before any lengthy retention interval and is strongly supported by immediate cues in the acquisition situation and, on occasion, by knowledge of results.

What about retrieval separated from initial acquisition by a long retention interval? Here, effective retrieval may still depend on the circumstances of acquisition as well as on the other world knowledge in semantic memory. For example, if students reorganize information in a memorable way during acquisition, retrieval is likely to be more effective if they do not. Retrieving the height of Mt. Fujiyama, 12,365 feet, might be facilitated by remembering that there are 12 months and 365 days in a year.

Orienting tasks requiring retrieval from LTM must include information about what is to be retrieved to ensure that retrieval processes search for the right information. Recognition tasks can be designed with varying degrees of richness of cues from the acquisition situation. According to this view, richness of cues for retrieval is a function of the number and kinds of cues that were stored in LTM during acquisition that also are present in the specifications of the retrieval-orienting tasks or are generated as a consequence of performing the retrieval-orienting tasks. Gentner's study, reviewed earlier, indicates that in retrieval during acquisition cues for recall come at first from the episodic structure of the subject matter then later are generated by the learner from the semantic structure developing in LTM. The concept of cue richness relates to semantic network theories of LTM. There seem to be at least three parameters involved; number of effective entry points into semantic memory provided by cues in the retrieval orienting tasks, the nearness of these entry points to the knowledge structures that must be retrieved, and the scope of the information that the orienting task requires be retrieved. All are worthy matters for investigation.

Although cue richness could vary from extremely high for recognition tasks to extremely low for free-recall tasks, the characteristics of the subject matter and the job tasks the student is being taught sometimes influence the variations in cue richness that can be designed into retrieval-orienting tasks. The job tasks may contain retrieval cues; There always are environmental cues in job situations that facilitate retrieval, and in many jobs sources of detailed technical information are provided. These greatly reduce the overall requirements for storage in and retrieval of information from LTM.

Since retrieval may occur during acquisition or retention stages of learning, retrieval strategies may be tentatively mapped with these two stages, as shown in Figure 7.8. In the figure L signifies low expenditure of processing capacity; H indicates high expenditure; R signifies restructuring processes. The thought is that retrieval during acquisition is likely to require less processing capacity because the information is more readily available, having been freshly stored. After longer intervals between acquisition and retrieval, more processing capacity would be required, even to the extent of reconstructing the knowledge from other related knowledge or of restructuring its organization. The notion of expended processing capacity is used here because some theorists consider retrieval to be active reconstruction or reaquisition from schemata in LTM, and thus to use processing capacity.

Retrieval during acquisition is usually employed, as discussed earlier, to obtain feedback about the states of acquisition, so that subsequent instruction can be scheduled more effectively. This feedback information is used in feedback loops in the instructional system, as knowledge of results for the student, and as part of the

Types of LTM	Stages of Learning	
	Acquisition	Retention
Semantic	L	HR
Episodic	L	HR
Motor	L	HR

Figure 7.8 Retrieval mapped with stages of learning and types of LTM.

student's sufficient history to be used for adaptive control (Figure 7.1). In addition, the processes of retrieval can influence the processes of acquisition.

Responding also influences in another way the kind of information that is acquired. The distinction often made in technical training between "nice to know" and "need to know" is made on this basis. In this sense, the job task contains the retrieval-orienting task which, in turn, determines the information to be reacquired to enable performing the job task. It is fair to say that in most military technical training today, the attempt is made to determine content by proceeding backwards from training objectives based on observable performances.

Retrieval after long retention intervals may have the objectives of providing feedback about how much is retained of practicing earlier learned responses, or of accessing information stored in LTM now needed for some other reason. If a substantial amount of forgetting has occurred during the retention interval from the first retrieval episode, then an effective retrieval strategy must be different than if retrieval occurs during acquisition. Whereas some form of directed recall may be the basic retrieval strategy during acquisition, relearning may be the basic strategy for retrieval after substantial forgetting. That something is still stored in LTM is, of course, demonstrated by the fewer trials required to relearn than were required for original learning. What is still stored in LTM even after retrieval other than relearning fails is not clear. It seems, on the basis of everyday experience, that the finer details are forgotten first, leaving more general impressions. But it could be that the finer details just become inaccessible sooner.

The notion of cue richness might be invoked as a bridging concept between retrieval during acquisition and retrieval during retention. It could be assumed that higher cue richness, even to the point of supplying all the original material, would be required in retrieval strategies after greater amounts of forgetting have occurred. This may be some use as a variable in retrieval strategies, although the "tip-of-the-tongue" phenomenon, and repressive amnesias indicate that retrieval processes are sometimes only temporarily blocked. At these times, the richness of retrieval cues might be immaterial. Retrograde amnesia, produced by traumas, in which most events over some interval stretching backward in time from the time of the trauma are forgotten temporarily, illustrates this, although presumably episodic memory is affected more than is semantic memory (Williams, 1975).

THE STRUCTURE OF COGNITIVE STRATEGIES

The premise of this chapter is that it is possible to improve the effectiveness of students as learners by gaining better control over the kinds of information processing they do while acquiring, retaining, and retrieving information and performance during the three modes of learning. Ths control might be achieved either through teaching the students more effective processing strategies, or through real-time monitoring and control of their processing, although the feasibility of the latter remains to be demonstrated (Rigney, 1976). The teaching might be done by describing particularly effective processing operations to the students and instructing them in how to use these operations, or by so arranging conditions in the learning environment that students are driven to use the desired kinds of processing operations, without explicitly describing these operations to them. The latter is a standard way of teaching students content. In mathematics, for example, students are given problems so designed that in order to get the right answers, they are forced to perform the operations and use the concepts it is desired that they learn.

Figure 7.9 contains a summary of basic variables in the domains that must be interrelated in the design of instructional systems to teach students to use more effective cognitive-processing operations for acquiring, retaining, and retrieving the information that is characteristic of complex human learning. Of the three domains illustrated, content blocks were discussed in an earlier section. Processing resources and orienting tasks will be described in this section.

Orienting tasks are the principle means of controlling the student's processing operations, although they must be combined with subject matter that is to be processed, and the subject-matter often also contains embedded orienting tasks at lower semantic levels, which it is assumed the student already understands. This use of orienting tasks is clearly illustrated by innumerable studies of memory and cognition in the verbal-learning laboratory. For example, Mandler and Worden (1973) described examples of semantic processing without permanent storage: processing during shadowing, reading stories to children while not attending, and skilled typists copying manuscripts. They suggested the following explanation for this phenomenon:

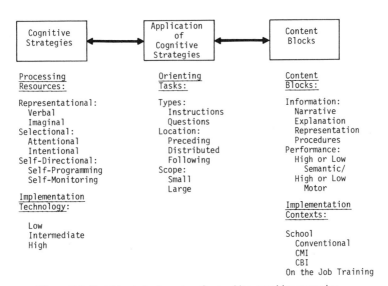

Figure 7.9 Variables in basic system for teaching cognitive strategies.

It is now possible to suggest the locus of the typist, parent, and shared-attention effects. The semantic organization of the primary task is apparently adequate at the time of input to produce a reasonable level of semantic processing. However, as time passes or intervening tasks intrude, the semantic organization is lost. As a result, recall drops to very low levels and synonym confusions appear. The semantic organization of the material, which is present to some degree immediately following presentation, disappears over time. The present data do not differentiate between 2 hypotheses, whether the organization is not stored permanently at input or whether the degree of semantic organization that is performed at the time of input is set at the (low) level required by the task. The latter case suggests the reasonable argument that task requirements set the degree of organization of material at the time of input. In any case, we conclude that shadowers, typists, and parents operate with the required semantic organization at the time of input, but fail to remember the contents at a later time because the organization was not adequately stored or only superficially performed [p. 282].

Categories of Orienting Tasks

Orienting tasks are familiar ingredients in the incidental learning paradigm of the verbal-learning laboratory, where they serve as an important means for implementing experimental variables. Thus, in Griffith's study, reviewed earlier in this chapter (see page 180), one experimental group was told to construct sentences in which the to-be-learned paired associates were embedded. The other experimental group was told to repeat sentences with embedded paired-associates supplied by the experimenter. These instructions were orienting tasks. Instructions to the student constitute one form of orienting task. Instructions are often given at the beginning of a session in which a number of items are to be processed in the same way. Thus, Griffith's students learned not one, but a series of paired associates by processing them according to the same instruction. This form of orienting task exerts fairly weak control over the desired cognitive processing operations. Students instructed to construct their own sentences in which to embed paired associates may or may not do that all the time. Students instructed to form mental images with embedded paired associates could use some other processing operations if they chose. Postsession questioning usually reveals that a fraction of the students admit they did not follow instructions any, some, or all the time. In these cases, students are following their own self-instructions. It seems likely that instructions calling for bizarre, complicated, or highly effortful processing operations would run a higher risk of being abandoned by students in favor of more familiar, simpler, or easier self-instructions. This is a serious weakness in the instruction form of orienting tasks. A remedy is to require the student to reproduce processing operations. Students instructed to form mental images can be instructed to draw these images. Students instructed to generate sentences with embedded paired-associates can be required to write the sentences. This adds time to the processing. Thinking is quicker than thinking plus drawing or writing. It also adds the motor response systems to the cognitive processing, and this changes the processing operations; drawing is not equivalent to imaging, writing is not equivalent to mentally generating sentences.

Questions are a second form of orienting tasks. Since questions do call for answers, they are the preeminent type of orienting task used in teaching content. In one form or another, they are used to teach everything from science and mathematics to history and English literature (Bloom, Hasting, & Madaus, 1971). As orienting tasks for cognitive strategies, they must be designed to require that desired kinds of processing resources be used in order to answer them. Questions are more readily used as the orienting task part of embedded cognitive strategies, where the processing that the question elicits is not identified by the student as a cognitive strategy. An example of this usage in the verbal-learning laboratory was reported by Craik and Tulving (1975) in their study of depth of processing and the retention of words in episodic memory:

> Subjects were induced to process words to different depths by answering various questions about the words. For example, shallow encodings were achieved by asking questions about type-script; intermediate levels of encoding were accomplished by asking questions about rhymes; deep levels were induced by asking whether the word would fit into a given category or sentence frame. After the encoding phase was completed, subjects were unexpectedly given a recall or recognition test for the words. In general, deeper encodings took longer to accomplish and were associated with higher levels of performance on the subsequent memory test. Also, questions leading to positive responses were associated with higher retention levels than questions leading to negative responses, at least at deeper levels of encoding [p. 268. Copyright 1975 by the American Psychological Association. Reprinted by permission.].

There is great current interest in question-answering instructional systems, in which students also can ask questions of the system. The thought is that this will allow students to pursue their curiosity about a topic, acquiring answers to questions they really want to have answered. When natural-language processing really becomes feasible, the instructional bandwidth of these systems might become sufficiently great to make them more powerful than simpler, cafeteria-style interactive systems.

Processing Resources for Cognitive Strategies

In learning content, a context of prior world knowledge into which the to-be-learned content can be embedded and which contains already-learned processing operations is the major resource. For learning to learn, retain, and retrieve information and performance, the emphasis is on effective utilization of more general representational, selectional, and self-directional processes.

Representational Processes

Representational processes represent important features of the external and internal worlds. They include sensors, intermediate-, and higher-level representational systems. Most of the processing that goes on in these systems is not available to consciousness or to voluntary control, and probably is parallel processing. In fact, in view of recent theories of semantic memory already noted, it could be said that parallel processing is characteristic both of the peripheral parts and of the higher centers of neural representational systems. The preeminent representational tools available to consciousness and to voluntary control are language and imagery. These two resources are almost inextricably intertwined. Language has the remarkable property that it can evoke rich imagery under certain circumstances, so that reading a novel can be a rich imaginal experience, full of scenes and characters and events that move through consciousness as dreamlike images. The fact that dreams are composed of images rather than text and that very few dreamers talk in their sleep probably has some implications for how language and imagery are related, leading to the speculation, encouraged by apparent developmental changes in sleep and in imaging capability, that imagery is the more primitive of the two great representational systems. In very young infants a very high proportion of sleep is rapid eye movement (REM) sleep. In adults, dreaming occurs predominantly during REM sleep (Berger, 1969).

Coupling these representational systems to learning and memory with orienting tasks depends, on the one hand, on common experience, and on the other, on increasing the knowledge of the roles of these representational processes in learning and memory that is beginning to be accumulated by cognitive scientists. Thus, it is not possible here to give definitive prescriptions for the most effective use of these processing resources for this purpose. Observations from learning assistance centers and studies of military recruit capabilities (Duffy, 1975) suggest that the capability to use language effectively for reading, writing, or speaking is less than universally distributed among people. One of the important requirements must be to increase this capability, and, thus, to increase the basic processing resources that are available for use in learning. It is interesting in this regard that there are remedial reading clinics but apparently not "remedial imaging" clinics. Both Bower (1972) and Wittrock (1975) remarked on the remarkable bias in education toward the language system, and suggested that the capability to image—relatively strong in children—is later neglected.

The ways in which language can be used for more effective learning and remembering seem to be primarily as follows: If acquisition is a problem of relating something new to something old, language can be used for the relational operations, which would include analogy and metaphor, as well as description, reorganization, and inference. The fundamental requirements for cognitive strategies is that the student actively use language as a learning tool rather than passively processing whatever lesson materials come along. The learner should be shown how to use these relational operations to facilitate acquisition. Retrieval, the search of LTM for information not immediately available, seems to involve using language to probe LTM in different ways, to reconstruct from fragments, or to construct by inference.

Although imagery is currently being very actively explored as a cognitive strategy, most of the investigators tend to use fairly simple subject matter, such as paired associates. In addition to providing an embedding and relational context during acquisition, mental imaging seems to be useful for reconstructing episodes during which material was acquired and for creating imaginary episodes in which performances can be reviewed as a way of checking on the level of acquisition as well as refreshing memory during retention. During this rehearsal of performance, language is a useful tool for self-instruction for example, for talking oneself through a series of movements a step at a time.

Selectional Processes: Attention

Selective attention is conceived as a conscious capability that can be focused on a broad range of internal and external events and processes. It is evidently a necessary constituent of deep or elaborative processing, and evidently has limited capacity. Its roles as a processing resource in cognitive strategies are not confined to deep processing; selecting material not to process may be an even more important function. It has been reported to me by the Stanford Learning Assistance Center that one of the most common deficiencies of students is an inability to select the important passages from textual material, such as a book or a scientific journal article, rather than plowing through the whole thing, word for word. Learning how to do this seems to be an important preprocessing use of selective attention. Indeed, a good part of a professional's expertise may consist of knowing where and how to access technical information quickly, rather than knowing the information itself.

Once the preprocessing selection of information has taken place, the attentional requirements of deep processing for acquisition must be met. Students must concentrate on what they are trying to learn, despite external and internal distractions. In this respect, attention is analogous to a priority interrupt system. Minimizing external distractions is a problem for cognitive strategies. However, it may be that self-generated distractions are the primary source of inefficient learning. The stream of consciousness may be less a stream than a bubbling cauldron where all sorts of odds and ends continually surface to interfere with the task of learning.

Methods that could be taught to the student for controlling internal distractions must have a high payoff in improved learning efficiency. Self-discipline and concentration are well-known words in the lexicon of education and training. Methods for accomplishing these are less well-known, but would seem to depend either on self-instructions or biocybernetic techniques. The latter require neurophysiological or electrophysiological indicators, which are at best crude. Pupillary dilation, first suggested by Hess and Polt (1964) as an indicator of mental effort, has been studied in many contexts, with positive results. There is a correspondence between cognitive load and pupillary dilation. Kahneman (1973) reviewed evidence for pupillary dilation both as a between and within-tasks indicator of changing cognitive loading. Pupillary dilation might be considered as an indicator to be monitored and transformed into some kind of signal to the subject in a biofeedback paradigm.

There also is the possible usefulness of cortical potentials as electrophysiological indicators that could be used to improve concentration. Theta activity has been associated with signal detection performance in a radar task (Beatty, Greenberg, Deibler, & O'Hanlon, 1974). This is a classic vigilance task, in distinction to cognitive information-processing tasks that are of interest here. Gopher (1976) and others have reported on plans to monitor ongoing electroencephalogram (EEG) of aviators to identify arousal states while flying, that might be undesirable and that might be avoided by providing feedback to the aviator. North and Gopher (1976) described a study of the multidimensional aspects of attention in flying. This is, of course, a real-time task that calls for flexibility in allocating among several requirements, rather than concentrating all attention on one kind of cognitive processing. The feasibility of using biocybernetic techniques to teach students to concentrate or to reduce internal distractions has not yet been demonstrated.

Selectional Processes: Intention

In most learning situations the individual student decides to a very large degree the amount of investment to make in a particular course. The fact that education and training take place in social contexts in which there is an implicit agreement with each student that the student will participate supports individual intentions with social pressures to achieve. Peer competition adds to these pressures. Fear of failure in this context may be a potent driving force that carries many students beyond the point where they would have quit had they been on their own. But the question here is how individual students can make a strong investment of their processing resources in learning. This seems to be an unploughed field. Indeed, the whole notion of self-discipline seems to be out of step in a manipulative and permissive society and in the climate of neo-Freudian, Skinnerian philosophy.

The bases of the intentional strategies that might be taught to students would be in knowledge about effective learning processes, learning as a contract with oneself, and self-generated goal structures. As the differences between effective and ineffective cognitive strategies for acquisition, retention, and retrieval become better differentiated this information should be transmitted to students so that they can deploy their processing resources more effectively on those things they want to learn. Learning anything takes time. Most of the learning with socially valuable outcomes requires years of commitment. These are well-known facts, but they still may not be clearly understood by students. A student who embarks on this kind of learning makes a self-contract to use a large block of time in an activity that presumably will have worthwhile payoffs. Such a student should be taught to relate the payoffs being sought with the payoffs society is likely to grant for completing this contract. What such a student really is looking for may or may not correspond to society's payoffs, and this may or may not make a difference.

The analysis of and generation of goal structures might also be taught to students to assist them in controlling their intentions to learn. The identification of intermediate goals and the paths from them to some top goal would allow organization of the learning task into modules that could be achieved in a stepwise fashion with intermediate successes to reinforce intentions and intermediate resting points before going on.

Goal-descriptive directions, that is, an embedded cognitive strategy, have been demonstrated to produce substantially higher recall performance on goal-relevant test items, in learning from textual material (Kaplan & Rothkopf, 1974; Rothkopf & Kaplan, 1972). Rothkopf and Billington (1975) have advanced a two-factor model to account for these effects, in which processing effort that has been applied to a particular text element is generally inversely related to a preexperiment experience factor associated with a particular text-element–test-item combination.

The question of interest here is whether students can be taught to develop their own goal-descriptive directions for guiding their learning of some subject matter that would yield similarly positive results. This might be done in response to externally imposed requirements or simply to answer self-generated questions efficiently.

Self-generated questions may be among the most potent orienting tasks, driving learners to search for answers they want to know. These questions presumably arise out of curiosity about the world and result in reducing uncertainty and increasing the possibilities for control over events. Since one question often leads to another, a great deal of what people learn probably results from this process. Critics of the current educational system (e.g., Holt, 1969) assert that it warps or destroys the child's native capacity for learning and creating. Nurturing this native capacity is a fundamental goal of question-answering instructional strategies in general and of the approach to instruction currently being developed by Papert (1973), Kay (1976), and others. Frase and Schwartz (1975) report positive effects on recall from prose of both question asking and answering.

The time spans over which these planning activities might be applied would be long for education and short for training. In both cases the student also makes a contract with the instructional institution delegating a certain proportion of this planning to the institution. In the case of military training the nature of this contract is, of course, quite different than it is with, say, a university. Bringing all this down to the point of allocation of processing resources on a real-time basis integrates intentional processes with attentional processes.

Self-Directional Processes

The effective use of representational and selectional processes ultimately depends on the individual's self-directional skills, even though instructional institutions provide highly organized curriculums and assume the responsibility for providing other forms of external facilitation of learning. And in early stages of learning, the student must rely heavily on this external facilitation. A reasonable view of the functions of the CNS in learning and memory is that they are divided into three levels: top level cognitive processes of which the learner can be made aware and can learn to control; intermediate-level neural substrate processes, which the cognitive processes activate but that cannot be brought under direct, voluntary control; and third-level neural machinery, which is assumed to be wired-in by the interaction of genetic and early developmental experiences, and is, apparently, far less plastic than the two higher levels, may be activated by the higher levels, but may be driven by its own internal pacemakers and is locally controlled by its own feedback and feedforward loops. Some of this lower-level neural machinery may be accessible to external modification by biofeedback techniques, but these are not as yet significant in education and training except, possibly, for physical therapy. We believe that the CNS contains both adaptive and self-organizing features that support the self-directional processes that will be discussed in what follows.

Self-Programming Skills

Cognitive scientists currently are developing interesting theories about different forms of self-programming in LTM. Some of these were reviewed briefly in an earlier section (see pages 182–183). A much simpler idea is involved here: that students can learn to organize their processing resources for performing a particular learning task. This organization would occur in anticipation of the task requirements and later, during the performance of the learning task, in response to local information. According to this idea, students can learn self-programming skills for matching their processing resources to learning task-requirements. Anticipatory self-programming, that is, planning, is common enough in other human affairs, although not necessarily in learning. It would require that the student be able to analyze the subject matter to be learned sufficiently well to do this. This skill might be acquired with some expert assistance, although the nearest thing to this assistance in current instructional institutions seems to be brief statements of prerequisites for intermediate and advanced courses. What would be needed in addition would be classification of subject matter by processing resources. Learning self-programming at this stage would be equivalent to learning self-assignment of different orienting tasks as subject-matter characteristics changed. Although this possibility seems scarcely to have been considered, there is evidence described by Kahneman (1973) that pupillary changes indicate overall level of effort, or allocation of general processing capacity, is adjusted to suit the perceived requirements of changes in information-processing tasks.

Self-Monitoring Skills

Most learning of any practical consequence extends over appreciable periods of time and involves sequences of interrelated actions. Self-monitoring skills are required to identify errors, to keep track of progress, to sense processing overload, and to monitor the performance of actions. In initial stages of learning many of these chores may be done for the student by the instructional system. But the attainment of proficiency both as a learner and as a performer, using what has been learned, includes the learning and use of self-monitoring skills that will free the learner and performer of dependence on external monitoring.

Some sort of self-monitoring must be done by most people most of the time. It is a requisite for survival. The concept of the self as an entity distinct from the rest of the perceived world is fundamental to protecting that self from the rest of the world. The awareness of students of what they are doing while they are learning possibly is another individual difference, although tests of self-monitoring skills do not come immediately to mind. The two points of application are in real time to be sure that planned actions are, in fact, now being performed and in looking back to review what has been done to check for errors. Self-monitoring skills obviously are of great importance where long sequences of operations must be performed in an exact pattern. Many everyday situations involve this: filling out an income tax return form, using a statistical algorithm, flying an airplane, finding a path through a freeway, etc. Self-monitoring requires allocation of attention to the detailed operations of cognitive processing and of performance and a concept, model, or guide, for how these operations should be done. In initial stages of learning this is supplied by the instructional system and in the final stages of learning it is retrieved from long-term memory, supplemented by extended memories characteristics of the task. It may be that episodic memory is the source of the warning feeling that something is wrong with a just-performed sequence of operations, while semantic memory supplies information about what is wrong. At least, the experience of sensing that an error has been made often seems to precede the identification of what that error was.

SOME THOUGHTS ON IMPLEMENTATION

However implementation of a learning strategies curriculum is managed in a particular context of limited resources and time, there are fundamental considerations for the design of the research.

Students might be taught about cognitive strategies first and then be required to apply them to content, or these activities could be combined. In either case, it is likely that an extra time cost would be involved. If the latter approach were taken the metainstructional and the instructional levels might be effectively implemented by a dual-display system under computer control. This would ensure close control over the instruction. But, so, to a lesser degree, would a programmed instruction package the student could do as homework. In all cases, teaching the detailed processing skills required to translate general desriptions of cognitive strategies into applications to particular content may require the most time. Some cognitive strategies may be content independent. Certainly much of the information category of content is conveyed by the printed word where text organizing and processing skills would apply.

Getting enough subjects to change their study habits for a long enough time do a formative evaluation, test for transfer, and test for gains in an implementation context is likely to be the biggest problem for this research.

The concept of a testbed facility, where the research and development community and the training community cooperate by combining their various talents and resources to work toward the common goal of improving the effectiveness of training would, if implemented, also significantly improve the effectiveness of research and development on learning strategies.

SUMMARY

The idea that students can be taught to be more effective learners as opposed to being taught subject matter has been explored in this chapter in relation to recent advances in cognitive psychology and other disciplines. The objective has been to integrate information from these sources into a unified viewpoint that can serve as a road map for research and as a context for discussion.

According to this viewpoint, cognitive strategies for facilitating acquisition, retention, and retrieval of information and of performance are composed of specifications, called *orienting tasks,* for how cognitive processes are to be used, and of cognitive processes drawn from representational, selectional, and self-directional resource. Representational resources include propositional and appositional processes of the left and right cerebral hemispheres, chiefly language and imagery. Selectional resources consist of attentional and intentional processes. Self-directional resources include self-programming and self-monitoring processes. Possibilities for teaching students better control over attentional and intentional processes by using neurophysiological indicators to reduce self-generated distractions during learning are noted.

Concepts of processing capacity, depth of processing, expended processing capacity, resource-limited and data-limited processing, top down-bottom up processing, and graceful degradation of output, advanced by several different theorists have been considered in terms of possible sources of individual differences, and implications for cognitive strategies. The importance of long-term memory in learning has been discussed. Three types of LTM—semantic, episodic, and motor—have been described. Semantic and episodic LTM are of great current theoretical interest. The implications, particularly of semantic LTM, for acquisition, retention, and retrieval have been discussed. The additional requirement for some kind of LTM for controlling skilled performances has been noted.

Several kinds of subject matter are described under information and performance and these have been tentatively cross-classified with types of LTM and strategies for acquisition, retention, and retrieval. Different approaches to teaching students cognitive strategies are described in terms of possible combinations of instructional control and explicitness of the strategy. Finally, techniques for implementation have been considered.

REFERENCES

Anderson, J. R., & Bower, G. H. *Human associate memory.* New York: Wiley, 1973.

Anderson, R. C., & Biddle, W. B. On asking people questions about what they are reading. In G. H. Bower (Ed.), *Psychology of learning and motivation* (Vol. 9). New York: Academic Press, 1975.

Atkinson, R. C. Computerized instruction and the learning process. *American Psychologist.* 1968, *23,* 225–239.

Atkinson, R. C. Mnemotechnics in second-language learning. *American Psychologist,* 175, *30,* 821–828.

Atkinson, R. C., & Shiffrin, R. M. Human memory: A proposed system and its control processes. In K. W. Spence & J. T. Spence (Eds.), *The psychology of learning and motivation: Advances in research and theory* (Vol. 2). New York: Academic Press, 1968.

Atkinson, R. C., & Wickens, T. D. Human memory and the concept of reinforcement. In R. Glaser (Ed.), *The nature of reinforcement.* New York: Academic Press, 1971.

Beatty, J., Greenberg, A., Deibler,W.P.,&O'Hanlon, J.F. Operant control of occipital theta rhythm affects performance in a radar monitoring task. *Science*, 1974, *183*, 871–873.

Berger, R. J. The sleep and dream cycle. In A. Kales (Ed.), *Sleep: Physiology and pathology.* Philadelphia: Lippincott, 1969. Pp. 1–32.

Bloom, B. S., Hastings, J. T., & Madaus, G. F. *Handbook on formative and summative evaluation of student learning.* New York: McGraw-Hill, 1971.

Bobrow, D. G., & Norman, D. A. Some principles of memory schemata. In D. G. Bobrow & A. Collins (Eds.), *Representation and understanding: Studies in cognitive science.* New York: Academic Press, 1975.

Bower, G. H. Analysis of a mnemonic device. *American Scientist,* 1970, *58,* 496–510.

Bower, G. H. Mental imagery and associative learning. In L. Gregg (Ed.), *Cognition of learning and memory.* New York: Wiley, 1972.

Brown, J. S. Paper presented at the meeting sponsored by the Office of Naval Research, Personnel and Training Research Programs, San Diego, November 1975.

Brown, J. S., & Burton, R. R. Multiple representations of knowledge for tutorial reasoning. In D. G. Bobrow & A. Collins (Eds.), *Representation and understanding: Studies in cognitive science.* New York: Academic Press, 1975.

Chant, V. G., & Atkinson, R. C. Application of learning models and optimization theory to problems of instruction (Tech. Rep. No. 264). Stanford: Stanford University, Institute for Mathematical Studies in the Social Sciences, October 1975.

Collins, A., Warnack, E. H., Aiello, N., & Miller, M. L. Reasoning from incomplete knowledge. In D. G. Bobrow & A. Collins (Eds.), *Representation and understanding: Studies in cognitive science.* New York: Academic Press, 1975.

Cooper, L. A., & Shepard, R. N. Mental transformations in the identification of left and right hands. *Journal of Experimental Psychology: Human Perception and Performance,* 1975, *104,* 48–56.

Cotton, J. W. Models of learning. *Annual Review of Psychology,* 1976, *87,* 155.

Craik, F. I. M., & Lockhart, R. S. Levels of processing: A framework for memory research. *Journal of Verbal Learning and Verbal Behavior,* 1972, *11,* 671–684.

Craik, F. I. M., & Tulving, E. Depth of processing and the retention of words in episodic memory. *Journal of Experimental Psychology: General,* 1975, *104,* 268–294.

Craik, F. I. M., & Watkins, M. J. The role of rehearsal in short-term memory. *Journal of Verbal Learning and Verbal Behavior,* 1973, *12,* 599–607.

Cuénod, M. Commissural pathways in interhemispheric transfer of visual information in the pigeon. In F. O. Schmitt & F. G. Worden (Eds.), *The neurosciences, third study program.* Cambridge, Mass.: MIT Press, 1974, Pp. 21–29.

Dansereau, D. G., Long, G. L., McDonald, B. A., Acktinson, T. R., Ellis, A. W., Collins, K., Williams, S., & Evans, S. H. *Learning strategy training program* (Tech. Rep. AFHRL-TR 75-41). Brooks Air Force Base, Tex.: Air Force Human Resources Laboratory, June 1975.

Duffy, T. M. *Literacy research in the Navy.* Paper presented at the Conference on Reading and Readability Research in the Armed Services, Monterey, California, October 1975.

Duncan, C. P. Descriptions of learning to learn in human subjects. *American Journal of Psychology,* 1960, *73,* 108–114.

Fiksel, J. R., & Bower, G. H. Question-answering by a semantic network of parallel automata. *Journal of Mathematical Psychology,* 1976, *13,* 1–45.

Frase, L. T. Effect of question location, pacing and mode upon retention of prose material. *Journal of Educational Psychology,* 1968, *59,* 244–249.

Frase, L. T. Structural analysis of the knowledge that results from thinking about text. *Journal of Educational Psychology Monograph,* 1969, *60.*

Frase, L. T., & Schwartz, B. J. Effect on question production and answering on prose recall. *Journal of Educational Psychology,* 1975, *67,* 628–635.

Gentner, D. R. *The structure and recall of narrative prose.* La Jolla: University of California, Center for Human Information Processing, October 1975.

Gopher, D. Paper presented at the annual ARPA Biocybernetics meeting, March 1976.

Gordon, H. W., & Bogen, J. E. Hemispheric lateralization of singing after intracarotid sodium amylobarbitone. *Journal of Neurology, Neurosurgery, and Psychiatry*, 1974, *37*, 727–738.

Griffith, D. The attentional demands of mnemonic control processes. *Memory & Cognition*, 1976, *4*, 103–108.

Hess, E. H., & Polt, J. M. Pupil size in relation to mental activity during simple problem-solving. *Science*, 1964, *143*, 1190–1192.

Holt, J. *How children learn*. New York: Pitman, 1969.

Kahneman, D. *Attention and effort*. Englewood Cliffs, N.J.: Prentice-Hall, 1973.

Kaplan, R., & Rothkopf, E. Z. Instructional objectives as directions to learners: Effect of passage length and amount of objective-relevant content. *Journal of Educational Psychology*, 1974, *66*, 448–560.

Kay, A. & The Learning Research Group. *Personal dynamic media*. Palo Alto, Calif.: Xerox Palo Alto Research Center, 1976.

Kolers, P. A. Pattern-analyzing memory. *Science*, 1976, *191*, 1280–1281.

Mandler, G., & Worden, P. E. Semantic processing without permanent storage. *Journal of Experimental Psychology*, 1973, *100*, 277–283.

Meyer, D. E., & Schvaneveldt, R. W. Meaning, memory, structure, and mental processes. *Science*, 1976, *192*, 27–32.

Miller, G. A., & Johnson-Laird, P. H. *Language And perception*. Cambridge, Mass.: Harvard University Press, 1976.

Milner, B. Introduction. In F. O. Schmitt & F. G. Worden (Eds.), *The neurosciences, third study program*. Cambridge, Mass.: MIT Press, 1974. Pp. 3–4.

Nebes, R. D. Hemispheric specialization in commissurotomized man. *Psychological Bulletin*, 1974, *81*, 1–14.

Norman, D. A. *Memory and attention. An introduction to human information processing*. New York: Wiley, 1969.

Norman, D. A. *Studies of learning and self-contained educational systems, 1973–1976* (Tech. Rep. No. 7601). San Diego: University of California, Center for Human Information Processing, March 1976.

Norman, D. A., & Bobrow, D. G. On data-limited and resource-limited processes. *Cognitive Psychology*, 1975, *7*, 44–64.

Norman, D. A., & Rumelhart, D. E. *Explorations in cognition*. San Francisco: Freeman, 1975.

North, R. A., & Gopher, D. Measures of attention as predictors of flight performance. *Human Factors*, 1976, *18*, 1–13.

Paivio, A. Perceptual comparisons through the mind's eye. *Memory & Cognition*, 1975, *3*, 635–647.

Papert, S. *Uses of technology to enhance education* (Memo No. 298). Cambridge, Mass.: Artificial Intelligence Laboratory, June 1973.

Pask, G., & Scott, B. C. E. Learning strategies and individual competence. *International Journal of Man-Machine Studies*, 1972, *4*, 217–254.

Postman, L. Experimental analysis of learning to learn. In G. H. Bower & T. Spence (Eds.), *The psychology of learning and motivation: Advances in research and theory* (Vol. 3). New York: Academic Press, 1969.

Pribram, K. H. Languages of the brain. *Experimental paradoxes and principles in neuropsychology*. Englewood Cliffs, N.J.: Prentice-Hall, 1971.

Prytulak, L. S. Natural language mediation. *Cognitive Psychology*, 1971, *2*, 1–56.

Pylyshyn, Z. W. What the mind's eye tells the mind's brain: A critique of mental imagery. *Psychological Bulletin*, 1973, *80*, 1–24.

Rigney, J. W. *On some possibilities for investigating changes in slow cortical potentials in learning tasks*. Paper presented at the annual ARPA Biocybernetics meeting. New Orleans, LA., March 1976.

Rigney, J. W., & Lutz, K. A. *CAI and imagery: Interactive computer graphics for teaching about invisible processes* (Tech. Rep. No. 74). Los Angeles: University of Southern California, Behavioral Technology Laboratories, January 1974.

Rigney, J. W., & Lutz, K. A. *The effects of interactive graphic analogies on recall of concepts in chemistry* (Tech. Rep. No. 75). Los Angeles: University of Southern California, Behavioral Technology Laboratories, May 1975.

Rigney, J. W., & Lutz, K. A. Effect of graphic analogies of concepts in chemistry on learning and attitude. *Journal of Educational Psychology,* 1976, *68*(3), 305–311.

Ross, J. The resources of binocular perception. *Scientific American,* 1976, *234,* 80–86.

Rothkopf, E. Z., & Billington, M. J. A two-factor model of the effect of goal-descriptive directions on learning from text. *Journal of Educational Psychology,* 1975, *67,* 692–704.

Rothkopf, E. Z., & Bisbicos, E. E. Selective facilitative effects of interspersed questions on learning from written prose. *Journal of Educational Psychology,* 1967, *58,* 56–61.

Rothkopf, E. Z., & Kaplan, R. An exploration of the effect of density and specificity of instructional objectives on learning from text. *Journal of Educational Psychology,* 1972, *63,* 295–302.

Rumelhart, D. E. Notes on a schema for stories. In D. G. Bobrow & A. Collins (Eds.), *Representation and understanding: Studies in cognitive science.* New York: Academic Press, 1975.

Rumelhart, D. E. & Norman, D. A. *Accretion, tuning, and restructuring; three modes of learning* (Tech. Rep. No. 7602). San Diego: University of California, August 1976.

Schallert, D. L. *Improving memory for prose: The relationship between depth of processing and context* (Tech. Rep. No. 5). Urbana: University of Illinois, Laboratory for Cognitive Studies in Education, November 1975.

Schank, R. C. The structure of episodes in memory. In D. G. Bobrow & A. Collins (Eds.), *Representation and understanding: Studies in cognitive science.* New York: Academic Press, 1975.

Shepard, R. N., & Judd, S. A. Perceptual illusion of rotation of three-dimensional objects. *Science,* 1976, *191,* 952–954.

Shimron, J. *On learning maps.* La Jolla, Calif.: University of San Diego, Center for Human Information Processing, September 1975.

Sperry, R. W. Lateral specialization in the surgically separated hemispheres. In F. O. Schmitt & F. G. Worden (Eds.), *The neurosciences, third study program.* Cambridge, Mass.: MIT Press, 1974. Pp. 5–19.

Sternberg, S. Memory-scanning: Mental processes revealed by reaction-time experiments. *American Scientist,* 1969, *57,* 421–457.

Tulving, E. Episodic memory. In E. Tulving & W. Donaldson (Eds.), *Organization of memory.* New York: Academic Press, 1972.

Wescourt, K. Paper presented at the meeting sponsored by the Office of Naval Research, Personnel and Training Research Programs, San Diego, November 1975.

Williams, M. Retrograde amnesia. In A. Kennedy & A. Wilkes, (Eds.), *Studies in long term memory.* New York: Wiley, 1975. Pp. 323–326.

Wittrock, M. C. The generative processes of memory. *UCLA Educator,* 1975, *17,* 33–43.

8

Program Evaluation[1]

HAROLD WAGNER and ROBERT J. SEIDEL

As noted in the previous chapters, the learning strategies projects currently supported by the Defense Advanced Research Projects Agency (DARPA) are in their formative stages. The theme of this chapter is the application of an evaluation model that focuses on the perceptions of a program's participants (transactional evaluation) to formative evaluation of the DARPA research program. First, we give an overview of models of evaluation extant in education and training. We distinguish among these approaches as they apply to the **formative** or developmental process of a project and as they are appropriate to **summative** or final evaluation of completed projects or programs. In the second section, we introduce transactional evaluation (TE) as a means for dealing with a significant, though neglected, area which should be taken into account during a formative evaluation. Transactional evaluation draws on the perceptions of the project participants as indices of clarity of goals and project status during the formative stages of the project. Its importance comes from its emphasis on making explicit the relationships, roles, problems, and possible solutions as perceived by developers and potential users of a project's products. Last, we discuss the specific application of transactional evaluation to the DARPA Learning Strategies Research Program.

EVALUATION CONCEPTS AND MODELS

Evaluation is the process of delineating, obtaining, and providing useful information for deciding among alternative actions (Stuffelbeam, Foley, Gephart, Guba, Hammond, Merriman, & Provus, 1971). It is an action-related process, the major

[1]Preparation of this chapter was supported in part by the Defense Advanced Research Projects Agency under contract number MDA903-76-C-0210. Views and conclusions contained in this document are those of the authors and should not be interpreted as necessarily representing the official policies, either expressed or implied, of the Defense Advanced Research Projects Agency or of the United States Government.

characteristic of which is the determination of value, worth, or merit. The evaluation process is conceived as continuing rather than as having a discrete beginning or ending. Evaluation should facilitate the continuous improvement of a program. It should stimulate program development, not stifle it.

Evaluation procedures when applied to instructional development have been categorized as formative or summative (Scriven, 1967). Formative evaluation is that process which validates instruction during the ongoing, *initial* development phase. The results of this evaluation are acted upon immediately by modification of the instructional materials. In other words, the practice of conducting tryouts of draft materials during development, followed by measures that provide an assessment of the materials that lead to their revision is referred to as *formative evaluation*. Formative evaluation is performed for the purpose of diagnosing and correcting the weaknesses of a training package or product. Broadly speaking, it is characterized by repeated try–measure–revise cycles.

Those involved in the revision of instruction may be engaged in formative evaluation (in the loosest sense of the term). The materials are presumably being revised because the existing course has been judged unsatisfactory. As the materials are created and revised they are constantly "evaluated" as better or worse than that which already exists. However, **formal** formative evaluation effort employing various systematically applied assessment techniques provides the link between the development of course content and course improvement. By explicitly stating objectives and criteria, one can properly determine if the instructional package is achieving its goals, or if its goals are to be modified.

Summative evaluation as applied to instruction is performed for the purpose of assessing a fully implemented training package with respect to its capability to produce graduates who can perform to minimum standards of performance. Also, the evaluation can determine whether or not efficient and effective use was made of educational resources. Summative evaluation should occur after instructional development, improvement, and stabilization of operational and administrative activities. This may vary from one training situation to another. In some cases, training objectives may not be measurable at the desired time of evaluation because they are either too costly to measure or are long-term objectives.

Results of a summative evaluation, while of interest to the developer, are of primary concern to those who will decide whether or not a course of instruction is to be continued or adopted. Summative evaluation, therefore, provides the basis for policy decisions that do not necessarily concern revision of the instructional product (Borich, 1974; Johnson, 1970).

The differences between formative and summative evaluations are mainly in their purposes and the timing of their application. Formative evaluation is continuous and serves to refine a given instructional product through an iterative feedback process; summative evaluation produces final judgments concerning the degree to which the objectives and goals set for that product have been attained. The information obtained from a summative evaluation allows users to judge whether the product meets their needs, whether it should be widely disseminated, and if alternative products exist, which are to be preferred.

Evaluation Models

The formal distinction between formative and summative evaluation is attributed to Scriven (1967). However, the purposes for which such evaluation data are used have been discussed for many years in the training and education literature. Cronbach (1963) stated that "the greatest service evaluation can perform is to identify aspects of the course where revision is desirable." Baker and Alkin (1973) point out that the evaluative process was an integral part of programmed instruction development, which antedated the surge of interest in formative evaluation during the past decade.

Early models of the systems approach to training development contained quality control components which emphasized the need for feedback for improvement in the training. Smith (1965) described the purpose of a quality control system as "a means for continuous monitoring of the quality of the graduates and for improving the training when it is deficient [p. 3]."

Quality control procedures are needed both at the training site and on the job. Information from both locations must be "fed back" so that the instruction can be appropriately adjusted. Training developers require two types of feedback information. The first type assesses the ability of a course graduate to perform acceptably those tasks the instruction claims to teach. This type of information assesses the ability of the instruction to teach well whatever it is that it claims to teach. In most instances, this assessment can be made at the training site.

A second type of feedback information deals with the discrepancies between the course graduate performance and job requirements. "Relevancy control" information assesses whether or not the instruction teaches the **appropriate** subjects or tasks, and whether or not the student can transfer these skills to the job. Also, this feedback should provide information dealing with changing job requirements and with more precise descriptions of job activities.

Models of the evaluative process include those of Stake (1967), Scriven (1972), Stufflebeam et al. (1971), Sanders and Cunningham (1973), and Rippey (1973). These models were developed for educational evaluation purposes but are general enough to be applied to a variety of program types. They will be discussed in what follows in the context of instructional program evaluation. Scriven (1972) feels that it is best if evaluation is performed by someone other than the developer. Scriven calls his approach *goal-free evaluation,* which calls for the summative evaluator to assess the actual effects of the program. The evaluator operates without knowledge of the purposes, goals, or objectives of the program developers. Another model is described by Stake (1967) as *responsive evaluation,* which calls for the summative evaluator to be external to the instructional development activity, and therefore to have a certain independence and objectivity presumed not to be present in an internal evaluator. The Stake model provides a process evaluation strategy that contains a two-stage procedure: The first determines congruence between what is intended and what is actually observed (that is, discrepancies from program specifications) and the second with making sure the program has the type and quality of components implied by its objectives.

Less dependence is placed on the external evaluator by Stufflebeam *et al.* (1971). Because this model emphasizes the need for evaluation data to serve decision-making purposes in a timely manner, it permits the formative evaluator to be part of the development team. The "process" evaluation component calls for provision of continuous feedback during program implementation. In a similar framework, Sanders and Cunningham (1973) identify four stages of the evaluation process. The first is called "the predevelopmental stage," which seeks to identify needs. The second stage is called, "evaluation of objectives," in which one develops, revises, and clarifies objectives. The third is called, "interim evaluation," and seeks to evaluate each piece of the instruction as it is developed. The fourth stage is called, "product evaluation," in which the instruction as a whole is summatively evaluated, after which it may be recycled for further development.

Churchman, Petrosko, and Spooner-Smith (1975) discuss the question of whether to use internal or external formative evaluators. They make the point (with which we agree) that, in practice, the evaluator will become so involved in the program during its formative stages that the independence expected from an external evaluator will be of little significance. It is only in the summative evaluation in which the independence of the external evaluator is important to the decision maker. Assurance of independence, although necessary, does not guarantee the validity of the evaluator's findings nor his or her competence, but it does enhance the credibility with which the findings are perceived.

Our view of evaluation is that evaluator involvement can be useful during the formative stages of a project. In this sense, our position is similar to that of Churchman *et al.* (1975). However, none of the above-noted models explicitly addresses the importance of perceptions of project participants in the formative process. Transactional evaluation (Rippey, 1973; Seidel, 1975) fills that need.

Transactional evaluation differs from other evaluation models in that it focuses on the effects of perceptions of project team members and the user population. Its usefulness in evaluation comes from its emphasis on making explicit the relationships, roles, problems, and possible solutions as perceived by developers and potential users of the instruction. The formal involvement of these people in clarifying the goals and objectives of a given program contributes to its improvement during the early formative stages. (The applicability of this model to research program evaluation will be discussed in the following section.)

TRANSACTIONAL EVALUATION AS A TECHNIQUE FOR ASSESSING RESEARCH PROGRAMS

To be effective, evaluation must be a cooperative effort. For valid and useful conclusions to be reached, it is essential to achieve agreement between the evaluator and research program administrator (decision maker) with regard to the goals of a given activity. If evaluation is a process that furnishes information useful in guiding decision making, the first operational step is identification of the most useful information. This can be obtained by the evaluator only in interaction with the decision-maker. An evaluation cannot be conducted sensibly in the absence of a detailed statement of the purposes of those persons to be served by the evaluation.

In assessing research programs, it is critical to establish a congruence of interests between the overall program goals and those of each research project. An evaluation model and methodology uniquely suited for this purpose is transactional evaluation. The implementation of transactional evaluation methods to research programs involves the participation of project managers and users of the research products, as well as the research program managers and evaluators. A description of these techniques is presented in what follows to provide the reader with an understanding of the procedures for applying transactional evaluation to any given program.

All the other evaluation models discussed earlier, though differing in their conceptual and methodological framework, have one attribute in common. They all focus on the **object** of the innovation—a change in the process of learning by the student, attaining mastery of new objectives, affective change, etc. What seems to be missing from these approaches to program evaluation, and what transactional evaluation seems to provide is a focus on the effects of **perceptions**—of the program managers, project team members, users of the products or systems, and the people in the surrounding environment where the implementation or experimentation is taking place.

Transactional evaluation gives a snapshot of what has happened in a project to date, in that it shows the state of the human system at a point in time. A collection of these "snapshots" provides an overview related to human issues in implementing a program. As transactional evaluation obtains its data from opinions of participants having potentially high biases, it is essential that the technique be applied by an independent evaluation team. Since opinions are solicited through active discussion, it is not generally feasible to use in groups of more than 20–30 participants. However, on occasion, modifications to the procedures are made, which permit it to be used with larger groups.

Transactional evaluation has its formal origins in education (Rippey, 1973), but is not restricted to educational evaluation. It can be applied to any program development. Although the bulk of the illustrative detail in this section will come from the field of education, examples will be described from other settings as well. Applying transactional evaluation to a specific situation will accomplish the following ends:

1. Provide information about where the program is at that point in time,
2. Define in what direction the participants want it to move in the future,
3. Identify present and potential problems in the program,
4. Clarify participants' understanding of goals and possible solutions to perceived problems.

Procedures

The steps to take in a complete and comprehensive transactional evaluation are as follows:

1. A meeting of program participants is convened. One of the program participants volunteers to present a brief (3–5 min) description of the program to the other
members of the group.

2. The remaining group members play roles of different user populations (e.g.,
administrators, trainees, or instructors) for the designated program. In so doing,
they provide feedback in the way of comments, reactions, and questions to the
presenter so that issues and ambiguities are made explicit for the different user
groups. Depending upon how heated the discussion or how defensive the volunteer
presenter becomes, an evaluation consultant or facilitator points out that all the
opinions are legitimate data for analysis by transactional evaluation.

3. A facilitator, usually a member of the evaluation team, has all members of the
participating group prepare a list of the **purposes** or **goals** of the program under
consideration. (It is helpful to have the participants place priorities on the objectives
or purposes as they list them.) These lists are then collected after a designated period
of time (5–10 min).

4. The "listing" procedure outlined in Step 3 is repeated with respect to the **obstacles** to reaching the goals of the program as perceived by the individual. Then these
items are collected by the evaluators.

5. The same "listing" procedure is repeated once more with respect to the **solutions** that each individual thinks would be necesary to overcome the previously designated obstacles to enable satisfactory attainment of the project goals.

6. The listed items (i.e., goals, obstacles, and solutions) are then collated by the
evaluation team. Duplication is eliminated, and the three sets of items are organized
into an attitude questionnaire with a scale of either four or five points ranging from
"strongly agree" to "strongly disagree." A five-point scale is often selected to
provide an entry for those raters who (a) feel neutral about the statement, (b) do not
understand the item, or (c) do not think it is relevant to the program being evaluated.
Discussion then enables clarification of the raters' positions. Limitations to five-
point scales are as follows:

1. Most persons have some opinion no matter how slight.

2. The attitude literature shows no consistent reliable advantage to the five-point
scale.

3. Raters take longer to decide.

4. Subsequent clarifying discussion is an intrinsic part of the transactional evaluation procedure anyway (see Steps 8 and 9). With these deficiencies in mind, we
used a four-point scale in our administration.

The items are written to maintain, as much as possible, the "affective tone"
intended by the originator. If possible, the statements are presented verbatim. The
resulting questionnaire then becomes an instrument developed by the participants,
not by the evaluator or any single subgroup of the participants. The questionnaire
represents, to the maximum degree feasible, contributions from all of the participating members. This latter characteristic is extremely important in that at least a subset

of the items is familiar and plausible to each participant—thereby enhancing the credibility of the entire instrument.

7. After the items are organized and copies of the questionnaire are prepared (this can be done immediately or over a 24-hour period), the questionnaire is administered to the participant group. This approach, using verbatim statements as items and ensuring their universal representation, motivates the participants to respond, and highlights areas of poor communication.

8. The data are analyzed as soon as possible by the evaluation team with respect to potential areas of ambiguity, consensus, and polarization. These categories are defined as:

(*a*). *Consensus:* This is demonstrated when the ratings are clustered at either end of the rating scale.

(*b*). *Polarization:* This is evidenced by ratings grouped at *both* ends of the rating scale.

(*c*). *Ambiguity:* When the distribution is flat, there are approximately equal entries over the entire scale, and/or the ratings are clustered around the neutral category. This indicates ambiguity in the perceptions of the participants about either the content, or the wording of the item.

Each of the classifications are important for determining subsequent action. For example, rating distributions that indicate ambiguity in the group's perceptions show a need for clarification about the statement. The first question to be asked is whether the wording of the item makes responding difficult. This is often the case with compound items, where more than one thought is presented in a single statement. The problems with instances of poorly worded items are solved by discussions to clarify the item and then rerating the statement(s). Another potential source of ambiguity occurs if the responders do not understand the content of the item and are not willing to commit themselves about it. In this instance, there is a need for increased communication of information to the group to enable them to make an informed decision. These findings are then provided as feedback to the participants. During the collation of the data, it may be useful to categorize the various items which indicate specific difficulties or agreements into broad perceptual areas (e.g., program management or support requirements).

9. Feedback is then provided to the group members in the form of summarized data analyses. The data may suggest the need for discussions among the participants of such issues as disagreements about values or ambiguities in communication. Recommendations for these discussions may be made either by the evaluation team or by the group members themselves. This feedback session provides the groundwork for making modifications to the overall program thrust or to specific future activities so that the program can proceed more smoothly in reaching desired goals.

10. A series of meetings are scheduled in order to act upon new strategies for achieving the desired purposes of the program and its components.

(a). To take action on those statements upon which there is a consensus among groups of participants. This includes the elimination of preceived obstacles via the implementation of agreed upon solutions, as well as modifications to policies which are in conflict with stated goals.

(b). To resolve issues which have polarized responses and clarify those which are ambiguously rated. This usually requires increased communication among participants, and a commitment on the part of authorities to make required changes.

11. Repeated applications of the transactional evaluation approach are made at timely intervals in order to provide continuous monitoring of the program and to enhance decision making.

Applications

Transactional evaluation can be applied whenever any group of program participants seeks to accomplish common purposes. Stated in this way, the application areas appear virtually limitless. There are some limiting considerations, however, and these are related to the structure of the group, team, or organization concerned. Transactional evaluation will not be effective in any organization in which the structure is hierarchical and separates authority from responsibility for the accomplishment of its purposes. It is not a cure for morale problems among personnel in different levels within an organization. It can be most helpful, however, in delineating, clarifying, and ameliorating ambiguities and difficulties that may exist in cooperative group ventures. Where input from each of the group's members is given serious consideration and will be acted upon as real data, then transactional evaluation can be extremely useful as a means for performing a formative evaluation and changing the dynamics of interaction. The results of this evaluation can be used to facilitate the administration of traditional or innovative programs, techniques, etc. Transactional evaluation, therefore, seems particularly well suited to help clarify goals and directions of the DARPA Program in Learning Strategies Research. We will describe that application in the following section.

We have obtained evidence of the effectiveness of transactional evaluation applications in a number of areas: workshops at the American Educational Research Association, at Civil Service Training Seminars, and at a Veteran's Administration hospital; a project concerned with the problems in disseminating computer-based learning materials through higher education (CONDUIT); a project concerned with the adoption of computer-based learning materials in a league of high schools (DC SSPACE Program); a project concerned with the adoption of job-relevant, higher-education programs for school librarians (School Library Manpower Project). Each of these applications used transactional evaluation in a different environment with slight variations in the procedures.

We have found that this technique is particularly applicable to the educational or training uses of computers. We have found repeatedly that the problems in successful implementation of computer-based learning depend on the human elements involved in the project rather than the technical problems of coding of instructional materials, providing sophisticated hardware, etc. Transactional evaluation is particularly useful as an evaluative aid when the decision-making environment within which a program is introduced may require radical alterations. This can happen when individualized instruction using the computer has an impact upon school or departmental structures by affecting the scheduling of students on the terminals, housing of the terminals, etc. Examples of transactional evaluation as applied to a number of Human Resources Research Organization projects are provided in what follows. The application of transactional evaluation to computer use for education in the Washington, D.C. school system is discussed first because it is most representative of a complete and comprehensive application.

HUMAN RESOURCES RESEARCH ORGANIZATION PROGRAM EVALUATIONS

The DC SSPACE Program

The DC SSPACE program (Secondary Schools Project for Adopting Computer-Aided Education) was sponsored by a grant[2] awarded to the Human Resources Research Organization (HumRRO) from the National Science Foundation (Office of Technological Innovation in Education). The purposes of the 2-year program were (a) to introduce computers and already developed computer-based curricular materials into the secondary schools of the District of Columbia, and (b) to study and make explicit the process of adopting the computer-based materials.

The evaluation effort was designed to satisfy the need for a systematic, yet flexible, method of gathering, analyzing, and presenting information bearing on a very wide range of complex and interrelated factors. The researchers concluded from previous studies that to focus on purely technical or cost factors would be to ignore the most critical factors in the adoption of educational innovations. Attitudes, values, roles, and interpersonal relationships needed to be addressed if the study was to reflect the **real** process of change. Such "objective" measures as student grades, attendance, computer usage, or cost breakdowns would be meaningful only if interpreted in context. Therefore, participating student, teacher, and principal attitude data were gathered periodically during the school year. These attitude measures helped to locate potential obstacles to smooth operation of the project in the relationships between administrative, technical, and educational areas. Periodic meetings were held with teachers and principals to implement strategies for solving problems revealed by transactional evaluation.

[2] "A Coherent Strategy for Computer-Based Instructional Innovation: The Adoption and Change Process in a League of Secondary Schools," NSF Grant No. EC-44000. Robert J. Seidel, Principal Investigator.

Analysis of the adoption process per se started with the application of transactional evaluation at teacher training sessions. It included role-playing (e.g., administrators, parents, teachers, and students) by the participants. We obtained statements from each person concerning their perceived goals, potential problems in meeting these goals, and suggested solutions for overcoming the problems. With the aid of a questionnaire based on these statements we were able to focus on anticipated difficulties in the adoption process.

Transactional evaluation was used with the participating principals as well. Initial concerns of the principals related to their need to become familiar with both the equipment and with the position of the project within the schools. Over time, repeated administration of transactional evaluation questionnaires helped to form workable solutions to anticipated difficulties. Apparently, the organizational arrangements took hold and the relationships between persons involved in the project became favorable.

Subsequent transactional evaluation data from all participants reflected a shift away from original concerns about implementation to other concerns of post project planning. Plans were made and subsequently implemented for integration of the project within the school system following withdrawal of external funding and HumRRO staff support.

The School Library Manpower Project

In 1970–1973, HumRRO served as program evaluator for the American Library Association's School Library Manpower Project (SLMP). This project supported six experimental educational programs for those persons who operate, manage and provide district-level supervision for school library media centers (Case, Lowrey, Fink, & Wagner, 1975). As part of our job, we performed a transactional evaluation in meetings with the SLMP staff and advisory committee, and the directors of the six experimental programs. This approach proved extremely useful in assisting them to clarify their objectives and to develop formative evaluation plans. This formative evaluation provided a basis for action whereby continuous program assessment could lead to constructive program development, could facilitate self-correction and modification, and could permit accountability for program quality. It was not the intent of this formative evaluation to establish any arbitrary comparisons among programs, but rather to discover what was appropriate for the attainment of specific goals based on clearly stated objectives within an individual institution. Each experimental program conducted its own formative evaluation using the indices, measuring devices, and data gathering activities that appeared to be most applicable to each program's goals. Much of the data gathering was standardized for all six programs, whereas other findings related specifically to a unique aspect of a singular program. No attempt was made to compare the six experimental programs. Rather, a uniform structure was applied to evaluate the success of each program in meeting its own objectives. The success of the overall project, then, was summatively evaluated by judging the degree to which the School Library Manpower Project fostered the establishment of successful component programs.

The Civil Service Instructional Technology Conference

This application took place in one, 3-hour workshop. The objectives of the workshop (Seidel, 1975) were (a) to conduct a transactional evaluation of another previously attended workshop at the conference; (b) to identify other areas relevant to the participant's field where transactional evaluation would be appropriate; and (c) to design a plan to incoporate transactional evaluation into the monitoring and modification of a projected training program.

All the participants were in some way involved either in managing a training program or supervising training managers of programs in various federal agencies. The content that provided the vehicle for the transactional evaluation application was a previously attended workshop at the same conference. That workshop, conducted by a colleague (Hillelsohn, 1975) dealt with the application of a systems approach to the development of instructional materials. A significant number of the participants in the transactional evaluation workshop had attended that earlier workshop and were therefore able to provide a volunteer "expert" for the presentation step in the transactional evaluation procedures. The remaining members played the roles of users of the materials to be produced by the systems approach (trainees, training managers, and instructional developers).

Five minutes were permitted for the presentation by the volunteer "expert" of the previously attended workshop's goals. Five minutes were allowed for questioning the expert, and five minutes each were provided for writing down goals, obstacles, and solutions. This approach was designed to reveal the most important goals, obstacles, and solutions for using the systems approach to develop modular course materials as perceived by the attendees. The remainder of the time was used for discussion of the results and a discussion of possible applications of transactional evaluation in the various organizations represented by the participants.

This transactional evaluation application was perceived by the participants as effective in only a single session. Many of the participants saw transactional evaluation as an extremely useful instructional management tool, and some proposed using it following the workshop to modify their own courses. That is, they plan to apply transactional evaluation at the beginning of a course once objectives have been stated, and then at various times during the instruction in order to use trainee feedback for modification of the materials.

Implications for Research Programs

To perform a research program evaluation, evaluators must become aware of the impact and effects of each component project. The data collected for each project must be consonant with program evaluation needs, and thereby reflect the overall research program's goals and objectives. To facilitate such an evaluation, efforts need to be directed toward ensuring that each project director has an accurate perception of the overall program's goals, information needs, etc. Transactional evaluation can provide the methodology to accomplish these tasks.

The usefulness of transactional evaluation to a variety of instructional, educational, and other contexts has already been shown. In our work as program evaluators for DARPA, this methodology is being applied to research program development and evaluation. A description of how transactional evaluation techniques have been used as part of the Learning Strategies Research program evaluation will be presented in the next section.

Application of Transactional Evaluation to DARPA Research Program Evaluation

A conference dealing with the Learning Strategies Research Program of the Defense Advanced Research Projects Agency was held August 2–5, 1976. The conference had several purposes. First, information was provided to the various service representatives (Army, Navy, Air Force) who serve as technical and contractual monitors for some of the projects within the Learning Strategies Research Program. This information was presented to help assure a congruence of interest and understanding regarding program goals between them and the program sponsor, the DARPA Cybernetics Technology Office. Second, DARPA contractors who were involved in existing learning strategies projects were brought together in order to exchange information regarding the nature and status of their projects. Third, other attendees who were research scientists in the field were informed about the nature of the Learning Strategies Research Program. They were able to exchange information with the program manager that helped to clarify certain issues and determine which problems could be potentially solved as part of the DARPA research program.

Procedures

Transactional evaluation procedures were used with a slight variation in the procedures described in the previous section. Instead of having a volunteer "expert" make the initial presentation to the participants, the DARPA program manager presented his goals and an outline of the program. (See Table 8.1 for a list of the program goals as perceived by the participants and agreed to by the DARPA program manager.) In addition, a description of an ongoing learning strategies project was presented. This served as an example of the kind of effort in which the sponsor was interested. Thus, the purpose of applying transactional evaluation following these presentations was to generate veridical congruence between the goals and interests of service representatives, DARPA contractors, and other research scientists with the stated goals of the sponsor.

The collating of information generated through the *goals, obstacles,* and *solutions* listing exercises of the transactional evaluation procedure was accomplished

TABLE 8.1
Goals of the DARPA Learning Strategies Research Program

1. To design and field test a synthesized instructional program that will improve basic ability learning skills.
2. To examine learning strategies in order to compensate for ability deficiencies of incoming recruits by adjusting training, redesigning training, or attempting totally new technologies.
3. To develop techniques for facilitating the acquisition and application of knowledge that is relatively domain independent.
4. To improve the types of learning strategies that individuals can apply in learning material.
5. To develop a curriculum, and materials for those components of the curriculum, that allows students to be efficiently self-instructive.
6. To instruct students in a number of study procedures that can facilitate learning, retention, and application of knowledge and information.
7. To aim these study procedures at military training applications, especially skill training.
8. To produce increased efficiency of training (decrease time, reduce costs).
9. To reduce the requirement for administrative and support personnel in training.
10. To provide strategies that can be placed at the "front end" of any module, unit, or course.
11. To develop a training package or packages, preferably adaptable for use on Department of Defense, Computer-Managed Instruction systems.
12. To make the primary focus instructional programs of the various military schools.
13. To disseminate the results elsewhere.
14. To encourage input from many disciplines (social science, humanities, etc.) so that the learning strategies will be less aversive and more consistent with life style and high payoff learning.

following the two presentations. The questionnaires derived from these lists were administered the following evening. The feedback session was held the following day. An analysis of the results was presented, and a general discussion ensued concerning areas of consensus, ambiguity, or disagreement.

Results

The results of the analysis are reported separately for Service representatives and the contractor and other scientist participants. We will present the data for the Service representatives ($N = 10$) first.

Generally speaking, there was extremely good communication of program goals from the DARPA sponsor to the service representatives. There was consensus[3] obtained regarding the following goals:

1. To lower training costs.
2. To develop instructional materials to teach basic learning strategy skills.
3. To focus on military training.
4. To apply the basic skills instruction at schools rather than to on-the-job training.

[3]The criterion adopted for consensus was 7 of 10 in agreement.

All were in agreement with those of the DARPA sponsor. One disagreement between the sponsor and service representatives was revealed. The service representatives, for the most part, did not perceive a need for learning strategy packages that would reduce the requirement for administrative and training support personnel. This was a goal intended by the sponsor, that is, the learning strategy packages **are** intended to reduce overall training support personnel requirements. These packages are to be somewhat self-contained and, thereby, require less overall support in an operational training environment.

Another point requiring clarification concerned the DARPA goal of modularizing the learning strategies training packages. The purpose of modularizing these packages and adding them to the front-end of existing courses is to lower the cost of instruction normally expended for the administration and support of students who eventually dropped out, or were washbacks. (The latter students eventually complete a course but only after an inordinate and costly amount of time.) By reducing the numbers of dropouts and washbacks, the learning strategy packages would lower total training costs.

Sorting out the items submitted by the service representatives as potential difficulties in reaching the goals of the DARPA Learning Strategies program revealed a total of 13 *obstacles* (see Table 8.2). The problem areas could be grouped into three large categories:

TABLE 8.2
Problems Perceived by Service Representatives in Attaining DARPA Goals

1. State-of-the art in psychology and instructional technology very primitive. This does not preclude gains but does create problems in interpreting success and failures and applying lessons learned to new situations.
2. It is nice to be heuristic but we are going to need more solid foundations in research of cognitive and affective processes before a model can be meaningfully implemented.
3. Paucity of good innovative ideas.
4. The unnecessary conflict being created by the presenters between learning strategies and behavioral objectives.
5. In military application, the problem of additional overhead learning which may increase initial learning time.
6. Difficulties in generalizing the techniques to a range of types of training.
7. Resistance by potential users to any reorganization of the training programs to enhance the effectiveness of any developed program.
8. Limitations in resources.
9. Determining which of the processes account for how much of the variance in increasing learning effectiveness.
10. No hope of evaluating the long-term effect of implementing such a program.
11. The accusation that the program is a multi-million dollar project to develop a 'study skills' curriculum.
12. Little account of individual differences.
13. A basic assumption of the linearity of generalizing from a restricted study to a more open, less controlled situation, is rarely achieved.

1. Items concerned with the questionable nature of the principles from psychology and instructional technology that are being applied. (Items 1, 2, and 3 of Table 8.2.)
2. Items concerned with interpreting the practical significance of any research finding for military training applications. (Items 5–8.)
3. Items concerning experimental design and difficulties in analyzing and interpreting findings. (Items 9, 10, and 12.)

In the first category, the service representatives felt that there would be difficulty in obtaining enough solidly based, applicable research principles to provide a worthwhile program. In the second category, there was a good deal of concern about increased overhead in learning time because of the additional learning strategy packages, as well as resistance by users to self-pace or reorganize their training programs. Experimental questions concerned the following problems:

1. Long-term evaluation of effects involved in implementing the learning strategies program. (Item 10 of Table 8.2.)
2. Isolating the effects of individual differences. (Item 12.)
3. Combining appropriate learning processes to maximize their effects on learning in the applied military environment. (Item 5.)

The *solutions* offered by the service representatives were grouped in a manner analogous to the problem areas (see Table 8.3). Possible solutions included the following:

1. Suggestions to concentrate on a few major high-payoff areas of research that would yield a significant amount of information regarding the learning processes as might apply to the military training situation. (Items 1, 2, 3, 6, and 10.)

2. A long-term research effort would overcome the additional difficulty concerning user resistance. Such a project, which includes user organization participation during the initial stages of the study, would enhance the probability that the learning strategy packages will be used appropriately. (Items 12 and 13.)

3. The results of such a study could then be acted on by reorganizing training programs so as to take full advantage of the benefits provided by the self-contained learning strategy instruction. (Items 1, 9, and 14.)

Such an approach should provide for an opportunity to do follow-up studies using on-the-job performance measures. This could allow us to determine the relevance of formal school-based military training to on-the-job training.

Not as much understanding of DARPA program goals was revealed in the results of the contractors and other researchers ($N = 27$) as compared to those of the service representatives. Of the goals intended by the DARPA sponsor, half were communicated ambiguously or were disagreed with by the contractors and other research scientists. This necessitated a good deal of discussion to clarify the position of the

TABLE 8.3

Solutions to Problems Perceived by Service Representatives in Attaining DARPA Goals

1. More emphasis on fundamental research after phenomena or techniques have been demonstrated to have practically significant effects.
2. Have broad based problem but concentrate major share of resources in a few high payoff areas and a few high calibre investigations.
3. Identify different styles of learning so that instruction can be geared accordingly.
4. Define goals of learning in quantitative, reliable, and valid terms.
5. Differentiate between learning and creative processes and goals.
6. Relate aptitudes to learning rates, styles of learning, and transfer of learning to real life situations.
7. Confront the issues of the linkage of student behaviors to the assessment system earlier than as planned.
8. Distinguish earlier 'study skills' programs from the present effort.
9. Show how a behavioral objective can be a demonstrated capability to optimally select and use a strategy.
10. Concentrate on a smaller set of processes.
11. Derive techniques in relevant military training situations with follow-on to on-the job performance and training.
12. A longer term effort which includes the user organizations at the initial stages.
13. Longer term effort which includes considerably more emphasis on the interaction of individual differences with strategies.
14. Initial effort should be under fairly well defined boundaries; analyzed for their information value, and then assessed for how well they may generalize.

sponsor. Goals for which there was consensus[4] and were perceived in congruence with those intended by the program manager were the following:

1. Have the learning strategy modules constitute front-end additions to existing courses.
2. Decrease the costs of training.
3. Concentrate on applied developmental efforts in order to make the results practical for military application.
4. Develop curricula that are relatively domain independent or, in other words, that teach basic learning skills.
5. Package the results of the learning strategy research projects and put them into useable form for Department of Defense computer-managed instruction systems.

The remaining perceived goals seemed to reflect the participants' own research interests rather than the intended goals of the sponsor (e.g., "Emphasize learning/ teaching processes in a key conceptual framework referred to as 'networking' "). One of the stated goals by the sponsor was to provide for dissemination of the results of the learning strategies program to the civilian sector, as well as to the defense community. However, there was a polarization of opinion with respect to whether or not this purpose was part of the overall program. Also, there was some misunderstanding concerning Dansereau's presentation (see Chapter 1). As presented,

[4]The criterion adopted for consensus was 20 of 27 in agreement.

Dansereau's project was to be seen as an example of the kind of effort that would be considered relevant for the learning strategies research program. Unfortunately, nine of the contractor or participants saw that example as the sponsor's total interest.

Unlike the relative optimism expressed by the government representatives, the contractor and other scientist participants perceived many problems in attempting to implement the learning strategies program. Some 41 different problems were cited by these individuals. However, when we sifted through the many suggested difficulties, we found 11 items for which we had consensus (see Table 8.4). We found a great degree of similarity in these items with the obstacles raised by the government representatives. For example, the practical significance of obstacles such as overcoming user resistance and convincing operational users of the value of the learning strategies materials for cost-effective training were very similar to the concerns of the service representatives (Items 1 and 2 of Table 8.4). Also, there was concern about the soundness of the theoretical basis underlying learning strategy concepts (Item 3).

The general problem of implementation in a practical environment was raised by these scientists. They were concerned with the problem of dealing with an established bureaucracy that may be committed to a traditional approach to training (Items 6 and 8).

Last, concerns were raised regarding the program's experimental and interpretation problems. These were similar to the concerns stated by the service representatives. The problems pertained to difficulties in measurement and evaluation which would not allow for generalizability of findings to other programs (Items 9 and 11).

The 15 suggested solutions (see Table 8.5) to the obstacles described in Table 8.4 were grouped similarly to those given by the service representatives with some contrasts. For example, there was a good deal of similarity in the need for early coordination, both internally, in DOD, and with the end user in order to facilitate

TABLE 8.4
Problems Perceived by Scientist Participants in Attaining DARPA Goals

1. To convince the operational people that the program will result in cost-effective materials and materials developments.
2. To overcome the resistance to innovation, particularly in Department of Defense and military commands, that this program will generate.
3. The gap between speculative, theoretical conceptions of learning strategies and practical useful training programs that can validly operationalize those conceptions.
4. The need to deal with interactions among a multitude of variables.
5. Lack of adequate resources (money, time, talent).
6. Some results and techniques will be hard to apply—time and effort.
7. Some research questions will be unanswered at the end of the time frame.
8. Dealing with ponderous military bureaucracy that has a commitment to the traditional.
9. Difficulties in measurement.
10. Gaining acceptance of change indicated by any results of such a short-term program.
11. Reasonable evaluation—can the proposed Department of Defense field tests be given enough resources to fairly replicate programs developed on a small scale by researchers?

TABLE 8.5
Solutions to Problems as Perceived by Scientists

1. Adequate funding of small pilot projects to attempt various approaches to trainee deficiencies; refunding if merit shown.
2. Somehow you will need to coordinate *long before* your "cut and paste" phase begins, in order to have something useful by 1982.
3. Lobby internally to gain maximal authority for controlling the implementation of useful results in DOD.
4. Do not confine program to computer-managed instruction systems—include other kinds of training, especially on-the-job training where the student is confronted with nonprogrammed information.
5. The expectations for this project must be realistic. A lot of interesting and probably productive work will occur.
6. Possibly try more of a marriage between artificial intelligence and learning strategies (more from systems theory).
7. Increase communications among various groups working on various aspects of necessary research.
8. It would be useful for there to be a more structured picture of the application areas for this project—not that these projects must be narrow but the application of their findings should be clearly and unambiguously defined.
9. Regional follow-up conferences and/or institutional visits.
10. Stimulate interest on part of various ultimate users in training environments.
11. Find out how to make learning the cognitive strategies really enticing.
12. Support empirical research developing diagnostic measures of individual differences in cognitive processes, such as verbal and imaginal ones.
13. Research and models of useful cognitive processes and their implications for learning strategies.
14. Encourage interdisciplinary approaches to investigative techniques, social sciences, communications sciences and humanities on research teams.
15. Specification (more precisely) not only of cognitive styles but of knowledge structures, of processes, etc.

acceptance and implementation of the program on a DOD-wide basis (Items 2 and 3). In addition, the scientists suggested that empirical research be supported to develop strong diagnostic indices of individual differences in the various cognitive processes, and to determine the implications of these differences for training in learning strategies (Items 12, 13 and 15). They also felt the need for more communication among the individuals or groups who were sponsored by DARPA to perform the various research studies—to exchange information that would continually upgrade the quality of the products (Items 7 and 14).

CONCLUSIONS

A degree of understanding of current DARPA and service program interests was established in the Learning Strategies Research Conference through the use of transactional evaluation. Transactional evaluation was used with (*a*) service representatives to help clarify DARPA and service congruence of interest; and (*b*) the developers of learning strategies packages, who generated their own interpretations of learning strategies program goals. In the Learning Strategy Research Conference, the use of transactional evaluation resulted in (*a*) clarifying DARPA program goals for service representatives and project directors; (*b*) identifying issues for potential solution by research scientists in the field; (*c*) aiding the implementation of a reasonable reporting system; and (*d*) providing suggestions for follow-up evaluation activities, as noted below.

Plans for the Near Future

We plan to proceed with our evaluation of the Learning Strategies Research program by

1. Providing information to project directors of methods to acquire and report evaluation data to the sponsor in a uniform manner.
2. Assuring that data collected in each project are congruent with program evaluation requirements.
3. Holding additional Learning Strategies Research Conferences to facilitate information exchange and provide the context for program review.

In a few years we plan to package effective training procedures and field test them in operational military training settings. In this way, a summative evaluation will be performed that will validate each component project's claims and assess the attainment of overall program goals.

REFERENCES

Baker, E. L., & Alkin, M. C. Formative evaluation of instructional development. *AV Communication Review,* Winter 1973, pp. 389–418.

Borich, G. D. (Ed.). *Evaluating educational programs and products.* Englewood Cliffs, N.J.: Educational Technology Publications, 1974.

Case, R. N., Lowrey, A. M., Fink, C. D., & Wagner H. *Evaluation of alternative curricula, approaches to school library media education.* Chicago, Ill.: American Library Association, 1975.

Churchman, D., Petrosko, J., & Spooner-Smith, L. *The theoretical basis for formative evaluation.* Paper presented at the annual meeting of the American Educational Research Association, Washington, D.C., 1975.

Cronbach, L. Evaluating for course improvement. *Teacher's College Record,* 1963, *44*(8), 672–683.

Hillelsohn, M. J. Instructional modules: Using the systems approach. In *Proceedings of the Conference on Instructional Technology for Government Trainers.* Washington, D.C.: Interagency Advisory Group (Committee on Development and Training) and the U.S. Civil Service Commission, 1975.

Johnson, G. H. The purpose of evaluation and the role of the evaluator. *Evaluation Research: Strategies and Methods,* November 1970, American Institutes for Research.

Rippey, R. (Ed.), *Studies in transactional evaluation.* Berkeley, Calif.: McCutchan, 1973.

Sanders, J. R., & Cunningham, D. J. A structure for formative evaluation in product development. *Review of Educational Research,* 1973, *43*, 217–236.

Scriven, M. The methodology of evaluation. In R. Ryler, M. Gagné, & M. Scriven (Eds.), *Perspectives of curriculum evaluation.* Chicago: Rand McNally, 1967.

Scriven, M. Pros and cons about goal-free evaluation. *Evaluation Comment,* 1972, *3*(4), 1–4.

Seidel, R. J. Transactional evaluation: A technique for coping with human problems. In *Proceedings of the Conference on Instructional Technology for Government Planners.* Washington, D.C.: Interagency Advisory Group (Committee on Development and Training) and the U.S. Civil Service Commission, 1975.

Smith, R. G. *Controlling the quality of training* (Tech. Rep. No. 65–6). Alexandria, Va.: Human Resources Research Organization, 1965.

Stake, R. E. The countenance of educational evaluation. *Teacher's College Record,* 1967, *68,* 523–540.

Stufflebeam, D. L., Foley, W. J., Gephart, W. J., Guba, E. G., Hammond, R. I., Merriman, H. O., & Provus, M. M. *Educational evaluation and decision making.* Itaska, Ill.: Peacock, 1971.

Index